The

of
His Blood
and the
New Covenant

David Olander

The Greatness of His Blood and the New Covenant
©2015 Tyndale Seminary Press

by David Olander, Ph.D, Th.D

Published by Tyndale Seminary Press
Ft. Worth, TX

ISBN-13:978-1519357212

ISBN-10:1519357214

All Scripture quotations, except those noted otherwise are from the New American Standard Bible, ©1960,1962,1963,1968,1971,1972,1973,1975, and 1977 by the Lockman Foundation.

My hope is built on nothing less than
Jesus' blood and righteousness

This book is dedicated
*To those who appreciate His literal
precious blood*

What can wash away my sin?
Nothing but the blood of Jesus
What can make me whole again?
Nothing but the blood of Jesus

Table of Contents

Introduction

"And according to the Law, *one may* almost
say, all things are cleansed with blood, and
without shedding of blood there is no
forgiveness" (Heb. 9:22)

God established literal blood atonement for man's sin almost from the very beginning. When Adam sinned God provided animal skins for covering. "And the LORD God made garments of skin for Adam and his wife, and clothed them" (Gen. 3:21). As this did not take away sin, there was a temporary covering by the death of an animal for the skins which only covered the sinners. There was in essence a shedding of blood by God Himself for sinful man.

Because of Adam's sin, man was confirmed as a condemned sinner (Rom. 5:12-21).[1] Men's sins kept piling up until the entire human race was engrossed in sin. God chose a man named Noah for deliverance of the human race. "Then God said to Noah, "The end of all flesh has come before Me; for the earth is filled with violence because of them; and behold, I am about to destroy them with the earth" (Gen. 6:13). God delivered eight persons and from them the human race was re-established, but sin continued unabated.

God chose a Gentile from Ur of the Chaldees named Abram. "Thou art the LORD God, Who chose Abram And brought him out from Ur of the Chaldees, and gave him the name Abraham" (Neh. 9:7). God made an unconditional covenant with Abram literally spelling out God's entire

---

[1]"So then as **through one transgression there resulted condemnation to all men,** even so through one act of righteousness there resulted justification of life to all men" (Rom 5:18 NAS). Man became a condemned sinner in Adam.

program with all men and how the whole earth is to be blessed through him and in his seed.

"It is you who are the sons of the prophets, and of the covenant which God made with your fathers, saying to Abraham, 'And in your seed all the families of the earth shall be blessed" (Acts 3:25). There was a literal Seed who was coming and this literal Seed can be traced back to Adam and Eve.[2] "And I will put enmity between you and the woman, and between your seed and her seed; He shall bruise you on the head, and you shall bruise him on the heel" (Gen. 3:15).

When Israel was brought out of bondage from Egypt, literal blood was required as a sign of deliverance from Egyptian bondage. "And the blood shall be a sign for you on the houses where you live; and when I see the blood I will pass over you, and no plague will befall you to destroy *you* when I strike the land of Egypt" (Exodus 12:13). The first 'passover' was instituted as the Passover for national Israel. 'These are the appointed times of the LORD, holy convocations which you shall proclaim at the times appointed for them. In the first month, on the fourteenth day of the month at twilight is the LORD's Passover" (Lev. 23:4-5). The LORD literally passed over His people when He saw the literal blood. There was a great truth of deliverance through *literal blood* which the Lord established, not man.

When Israel was given God's law known as the Mosaic Law or covenant, God based the entire system on blood atonement. Forgiveness of sins was exclusively and only through literal blood. "For the life of the flesh is in the blood, and I have given it to you on the altar to make atonement for your souls; for it is the blood by reason of the life that makes atonement" (Lev. 17:11). The entire Mosaic Law was rooted in literal blood atonement for forgiveness of sins. The approach to

[2] It must be noted that the promised Seed would come by Eve not Adam. It is the seed of the woman that would crush the serpent's head.

God for national Israel was by means of literal blood. Blood was not a figure of speech in any sense. God required by covenant design *literal* blood for Israel's approach to God. There could be and would be no approach to God without literal blood atonement. There would be no redemption without blood atonement.

God established His law exclusively with Israel, and this law was based on blood atonement. Blood atonement was the basis of the Mosaic Law and man's approach to God. There must be cleansing from sin, and God required literal blood for a literal blood atonement and cleansing. It must be continually kept in focus that without the shedding of blood there is absolutely no forgiveness of sin.

God's entire program with man and the world is based on His literal covenanted program which started with Abram. Israel is defined by these eternal covenants[3] but not the church. This covenanted program was to be carried out with Abraham, Isaac, Jacob, David, Israel, and Christ. These are literal covenants which spell out God's literal program with man which only He can carry out and fulfill. These covenants can only be fulfilled by God with Abraham, Isaac, Jacob, David, the nation Israel, and Christ. The church and certainly no gentile can fulfill one jot or tittle of these covenants or contracts. The Lord has literally put Himself under contract, and He will carry these contracts out literally.

---

[3]These covenants (which are actually contracts) are the Abrahamic, the land, the Davidic, and the new covenants. These covenants are eternal, unilateral, and unconditional, being dependent on God alone to carry out all the promises spelled out in them. Only God can fulfill these covenants with the direct recipients of these covenants. These direct recipients are Abraham, Isaac, Jacob, Israel, David, and Christ. No other persons can fulfill these covenants or contracts, not even the church as there is no covenant or contract/s made with the church. For further information on these eternal covenants see the articles in the appendix: *The Biblical Covenants with Israel* (This article is from CTJ 9:28 December 2005) and *The Heart of Dispensationalism* (This article is from CTJ 8:25, December 2004).

God truly defined His people Israel when they were brought out of Egyptian bondage[4] and given His law. Israel's approach to God was by literal blood atonement, for they could not approach or come to God without forgiveness or cleansing. But under law, everything was temporal that is nothing was eternal. "For the Law, since it has *only* a shadow of the good things to come *and* not the very form of things, can never by the same sacrifices year by year, which they offer continually, make perfect those who draw near" (Heb. 10:1). "And according to the Law, *one may* almost *say*, all things are cleansed with blood, and without shedding of blood there is no forgiveness" (Heb. 9:22).

It must be kept in focus that God established literal blood atonement for His people, the nation Israel. It must also be noted that very rarely is the term *blood* a figure of speech[5] in the Scriptures. The following verses and many more refer to Jesus literal blood and the atonement purchased by His precious blood.

- "Whom God displayed publicly as a **propitiation in His blood** through faith. *This was* to demonstrate His righteousness, because in the forbearance of God He passed over the sins previously committed" (Rom 3:25).

- "In Him **we have redemption through His blood**, the forgiveness of our trespasses, according to the riches of His grace" (Eph 1:7).

---

[4] The blood of the lamb on the doorpost would become a great and constant reminder of the blood He would require for His provided atonement.

[5] "For our struggle is not against **flesh and blood,** but against the rulers, against the powers, against the world forces of this darkness, against the spiritual *forces* of wickedness in the heavenly *places*" (Eph 6:12). Blood may be a figure of speech such as we have in English or any language. [UBS] αἷμα, τος n blood; death; murder; σαρξ καὶ αἷμα man, human nature; ἐξ αἱμάτων through human procreation (Jn 1.13). But when referring to Christ and His work on the cross, blood refers to His precious blood atonement, and that of the new covenant.

- "But now in Christ Jesus you who formerly were far off have been brought near **by the blood of Christ**" (Eph 2:13)

- "And through Him to reconcile all things to Himself, having made peace **through the blood of His cross**; through Him, *I say*, whether things on earth or things in heaven" (Col. 1:20).

- "For this is **My blood of the covenant,** which is poured out for many for forgiveness of sins" (Mat 26:28).

- "Knowing that you were not redeemed with perishable things like silver or gold from your futile way of life inherited from your forefathers, **but with precious blood**, as of a lamb unblemished and spotless, *the blood* of Christ" (1Pet. 1:18-19).

This book stresses the essential nature of God's eternal, unconditional, unilateral covenants. These covenants are the Abrahamic, the land, the Davidic, and the new covenants. These literal covenants, God graciously made by promise and oath, define His entire program with man and His creation.[6] What is so important to understand is His provided *eternal* blood atonement. This eternal blood atonement can only be attained through the blood of the new covenant for the forgiveness of sins.

Up to the time of the establishment of the new covenant by His precious blood, atonement was temporal and conditional through the Mosaic Law. Christ made it very clear that His

---

[6] Sin entered the world by one man, the first Adam (Rom. 5:12). The last Adam bought redemption by His blood. "For as through the one man's disobedience the many were made sinners, even so through the obedience of the One the many will be made righteous" (Rom 5:19). "And not through the blood of goats and calves, but through His own blood, He entered the holy place once *for all*, having obtained eternal redemption" (Heb 9:12).

blood was that of the new covenant.[7] Eternal redemption is now through His *literal* precious blood of His cross. This is the greatness of His blood of the new covenant for the eternal forgiveness of sin. "For this is My blood of the covenant, which is poured out for many for forgiveness of sins" (Mat. 26:28).

---

[7] "For this is My blood of the covenant, which is poured out for many for forgiveness of sins" (Mat. 26:28). "And in the same way *He took* the cup after they had eaten, saying, "This cup which is poured out for you is the new covenant in My blood" (Luke 22:20).

Chapter I

Life is in the Blood
Leviticus 17:11

Blood atonement

"For the life of the flesh is in the blood, and I have
given it to you on the altar to make atonement for
your souls; for it is the blood by reason of the life
that makes atonement" (Lev. 17:11).[8] כִּי נֶפֶשׁ הַבָּשָׂר
בַּדָּם הוּא וַאֲנִי נְתַתִּיו לָכֶם עַל־הַמִּזְבֵּחַ [9]לְכַפֵּר עַל־נַפְשֹׁתֵיכֶם כִּי־
הַדָּם הוּא בַּנֶּפֶשׁ יְכַפֵּר:

[8] The reason for the command in v. 11, "For the soul of the flesh (the soul which
gives life to the flesh) is in the blood, and I have given it to you upon the altar, to
make an atonement for your souls," is not a double one, viz., (1) because the blood
contained the soul of the animal, and (2) because God had set apart the blood, as the
medium of expiation for the human soul, for the altar, i.e., to be sprinkled upon the
altar. The first reason simply forms the foundation for the second: God appointed the
blood for the altar, as containing the soul of the animal, to be the medium of
expiation for the souls of men, and therefore prohibited its being used as food. "For
the blood it expiates *by virtue of* the soul," not "the soul" itself. בְּ with כִּפֵּר has only a
local or instrumental signification (Lev. 6:23; 16:17, 27; also 7:7; Ex. 29:33; Num.
5:8). Accordingly, it was not the blood as such, but the blood as the vehicle of the
soul, which possessed expiatory virtue; because the animal soul was offered to God
upon the altar as a substitute for the human soul. Hence every bleeding sacrifice had
an expiatory force, though without being an expiatory sacrifice in the strict sense of
the word.
[9] The concept of sacrificial atonement was not limited to the sin and guilt offerings,
for the burnt offering is clearly designated to make atonement (*kipper*, intensive form
of *kāpar*) for the worshiper. There are two major views on the etymology of the verb
kipper. It is (a) an Arabic verb *kafara*, meaning "to cover," or (b) one of two
Akkadian homonyms—*kapāru*—meaning alternately "to wipe off" or "to smear" (cf.
Harold R. Cohen, *Biblical Hapax Legomena in the Light of Akkadian and Ugaritic*.
Missoula, Mont.: Scholars Press, 1978, pp. 53–4, n. 8). Numerous evidences,
including the poetic parallelism in Jeremiah 18:23 between *kipper* and another

The book of Leviticus is called by some the book of atonement.[10] God required of His people Israel a holy or separate walk. This was a walk or life separated from the world and a life separated from sin. "Leviticus is the book of *holiness*. (This keynote idea occurs 87 times.) God says to the redeemed, 'Be holy, because I am holy' (11:44–45; 19:2; 20:7, 26), and this book stresses the necessity of keeping the body holy as well as the soul. The redeemed must be holy, for their Redeemer is holy. A walk with God is on the basis of holiness which is by *sacrifice* and *separation*."[11]

The origin of the sacrificial system was most likely connected with Adam when he sinned.[12] "God's preparation of

Hebrew verb (*māḥâh*, "to wipe out, blot out"), support the second view"… Thus the actual usage in ritual passages allows for either nuance of the Akkadian *kapāru*, either "to wipe off" or "to smear" (e.g., the blood was sometimes smeared on the horns of the altar, as in Lev. 16:18, or the offense was regarded as "wiped off," i.e., cleansed and removed; cf. 16:10, 19). Lindsey, F. D. (1985). Leviticus. In J. F. Walvoord & R. B. Zuck (Eds.), *The Bible Knowledge Commentary: An Exposition of the Scriptures* (J. F. Walvoord & R. B. Zuck, Ed.) (Le 1:4). Wheaton, IL: Victor Books.

[10] Leviticus, The book of atonement, Nature of the book. Genesis is the book of beginnings, Exodus the book of redemption, and **Leviticus the book of atonement and a holy walk.** In Genesis we see man ruined; in Exodus, man redeemed; in Leviticus, man cleansed, worshiping and serving. Leviticus says, *'Get right with God'* (the message of the five offerings: burnt offering, meal offering, peace offering, sin offering, trespass offering, ch. 1–7). Leviticus also says, *'Keep right with God'* (the message of the seven feasts: Passover, Unleavened Bread, First Fruits, Pentecost, Trumpets, Atonement, Tabernacles, ch. 23). Leviticus is the book of *holiness*. (This keynote idea occurs 87 times.) God says to the redeemed, 'Be holy, because I am holy' (11:44–45; 19:2; 20:7, 26), and this book stresses the necessity of keeping the body holy as well as the soul. The redeemed must be holy, for their Redeemer is holy. A walk with God is on the basis of holiness which is by *sacrifice* and *separation*. As an illustration to NT believers, Leviticus pictures the holiness that comes not through the rituals of the law but through faith in Christ who fulfills the law. Unger, M. F. (2005). *The new Unger's Bible handbook* (Rev. and updated ed.) (89). Chicago: Moody Publishers.

[11] Unger, M. F. (2005). *The new Unger's Bible handbook* (Rev. and updated ed.) (89). Chicago: Moody Publishers.

[12] The sacrificial system, Origin of the sacrifices. Although the divine origin of sacrifices is not explicitly declared, the fact is everywhere implicit in the Bible. The way sinful man was to approach God was revealed to Adam and Eve immediately

garments of skin for Adam and Eve may intimate His revelation that the guilt of sin must be paid for with the blood of an innocent victim (Gen. 3:21)."[13] The very nature of blood atonement was put in place by God for His creatures from the beginning. Blood atonement carries over to His people national Israel when they sinned. Blood atonement was required by Levitical law for the life that went astray from the Law Giver. When the nation or anyone strayed from the life God required by law, the means of restoration for that life was blood atonement. Blood atonement for life was required by God for the nation Israel under Levitical law. God made this very clear to national Israel.

The context of mandatory literal blood atonement was given in the law under the section for the prohibition of eating or drinking blood. There are other issues which may be noted, yet the key issue within the prohibition of the consuming of literal blood[14] by Israel is blood atonement for one's soul or life.

---

after the Fall. God's preparation of garments of skin for Adam and Eve may intimate His revelation that the guilt of sin must be paid for with the blood of an innocent victim (Gen 3:21). Accordingly, divinely revealed and divinely ordered sacrifice is recorded in the case of Cain and Abel. Cain repudiated God's way of approach in worship. Abel accepted it and was received into God's presence on the basis of God's stipulated means of access to Himself (Gen 4:1–7; Heb 11:4). Likewise Noah (Gen 8:20), Jacob (Gen 31:54), Job (Job 1:5; 42:8) and God's people down to the eve of the Exodus knew the way of access to God and practiced it (Ex 10:25). When Moses led Israel out of Egypt, the sacrificial system that had at least in part existed from the beginning of the race was now expanded, given fresh meaning in the light of experienced redemption, organized, codified and written down by inspiration in the sacrificial codes of Exodus and Leviticus. Unger, M. F. (2005). *The new Unger's Bible handbook* (Rev. and updated ed.) (89). Chicago: Moody Publishers.

[13] Unger, M. F. (2005). *The new Unger's Bible handbook* (Rev. and updated ed.) (89). Chicago: Moody Publishers.

[14] "God also prohibited the ingesting of blood (v. 11; cf. 3:17; 7:26-27; 19:26; Gen. 9:4; Deut. 12:15-16, 23-24; 15:23). From this law the Jews developed methods of draining or washing the blood out of meat that resulted in kosher (meaning fit or proper) meat.333 The incidence of blood disease among livestock was much higher in ancient times than it is today.334 Careful observance of this law would have resulted in healthier Israelites as well as obedient Israelites. Blood is the life-sustaining fluid of the body (vv. 11, 14). It is inherently necessary to maintain animal life, thus the close connection between blood and life. Life poured out in bloodshed

"Then the LORD spoke to Moses, saying, [2] "Speak to Aaron and to his sons, and to all the sons of Israel, and say to them, 'This is what the LORD has commanded, saying, [3] "Any man from the house of Israel who slaughters an ox, or a lamb, or a goat in the camp, or who slaughters it outside the camp, [4] and has not brought it to the doorway of the tent of meeting to present *it* as an offering to the LORD before the tabernacle of the LORD, bloodguiltiness is to be reckoned to that man. He has shed blood and that man shall be cut off from among his people. [5] "The reason is so that the sons of Israel may bring their sacrifices which they were sacrificing in the open field, that they may bring them in to the LORD, at the doorway of the tent of meeting to the priest, and sacrifice them as sacrifices of peace offerings to the LORD. [6] "And the priest shall sprinkle the blood on the altar of the LORD at the doorway of the tent of meeting, and offer up the fat in smoke as a soothing aroma to the LORD. [7] "And they shall no longer sacrifice their sacrifices to the goat demons with which they play the harlot. This shall be a permanent statute to them throughout their generations.'" [8] "Then you shall say to them, 'Any man from the house of Israel, or from the aliens who sojourn among them,

made atonement for sin. Consequently the eating or drinking of blood was inappropriate since blood had expiatory value and represented life. "By refraining from eating flesh with blood in it, man is honoring life. To eat blood is to despise life. This idea emerges most clearly in Gen. 9:4ff., where the sanctity of human life is associated with not eating blood. Thus one purpose of this law is the inculcation of respect for all life."335 332Sailhamer, p. 343. 333Harrison, p. 181. 334Fawver and Overstreet, p. 275. 335Wenham, The Book . . ., p. 245. Cf. Hertz, p. 168. 88 Dr. Constable's Notes on Leviticus 2015 Edition The animals in view here seem to be those slain in hunting; they were not sacrificial animals (v. 13; cf. Deut. 12:15). However the restriction about eating blood applied to all animals that the Israelites ate. Since God forbade eating blood before the Mosaic Law (Gen. 9:4), which Christ terminated, people today should also refrain from eating it, especially when it is associated with pagan worship (cf. Acts 15:29). What is in view is not simply eating "rare" meat (pink or red meat with a little blood in it) but larger quantities of blood either separately or as a kind of side dish. Eating raw, uncooked meat was also inappropriate." Constable's notes, Sonic Light, Leviticus 17:8-9, pages 87 & 88.

who offers a burnt offering or sacrifice, [9] and does not bring it to the doorway of the tent of meeting to offer it to the LORD, that man also shall be cut off from his people. [10] 'And any man from the house of Israel, or from the aliens who sojourn among them, who eats any blood, I will set My face against that person who eats blood, and will cut him off from among his people. [11] 'For the life of the flesh is in the blood, and I have given it to you on the altar to make atonement for your souls; for it is the blood by reason of the life that makes atonement" (Lev. 17:1-11).

In context all the blood referred to can only mean literal blood. There is no such thing in this context as a figure of speech used here for anything but literal blood and literal blood atonement. This is one main reason why the eating of the blood was absolutely forbidden. "Two reasons are given for the command not to eat blood; the life of the body is derived from it, and it is the means by which atonement for sins is made."[15]

"Of the seven prohibitions in the Pentateuch against eating blood (Gen. 9:4; Lev. 3:17; 7:26–27; 17:10–14; 19:26; Deut. 12:15–16, 23–24; 15:23), this one (Lev. 17:10–14) is the clearest and provides the underlying rationale. Verse 11 gives two reasons for the prohibition against eating blood: (1) **The life of a creature is in the blood** (blood is inherently necessary to maintain animal life, so its blood is virtually identified with its life); therefore to refrain from eating blood is to show respect for the sanctity of life. (2) **The blood … makes atonement for one's life** (God has chosen sacrificial blood as the ransom price for a person's life, so the life of a substitute is given up in death); therefore to refrain from eating blood is to show respect for its sacredness as a vehicle of atonement. The fact that God said, **I have given it to you to make atonement for yourselves on**

[15] The Ryrie Study Bible, Mood Press, Chicago: 1978, Lev. 17:11, page 186.

the altar, rules out the view that blood was inherently efficacious. Its atoning value was only because God had "given it" for this purpose; He had chosen it as a fitting symbol of the reality of atonement and forgiveness. Again, the penalty for violating this prohibition was being **cut ... off from his people**".[16]

The word atonement is from the Hebrew root verb כפר and the meaning may take various forms. Some commentators believe that the basic meaning might be 'cover.' Others hold that its significance is that of wiping away[17], or smearing.[18] Langenscheidt embraces several features of the word i.e. to cover, to forgive, to expiate and to atone for.

[16] Lindsey, F. D. (1985). Leviticus. In J. F. Walvoord & R. B. Zuck (Eds.), *The Bible Knowledge Commentary: An Exposition of the Scriptures* (J. F. Walvoord & R. B. Zuck, Ed.) (Le 17:10–12). Wheaton, IL: Victor Books.

[17] כפר (of foll.; orig. mng. dub., but most prob. *cover*, cf. Ar. *kafara cover, hide;* > RS who thinks of Aram. כָּפַר, *kpar* Pa. *wash away, rub off* whence כַּפֵּר, כֹּפֶר, of *washing away, obliteration* of sin : NH כַּפֵּר, Aram. כַּפַּר and derive.; Ar. *kaffaÁraaʰun an expiation* (see RS:OTJC 438; 2. 381 Kn on Lv 4:20 Ri:Begr. Der Sühne We:Comp. 335 f. Sm:AT Rel. Gesch. 321 Now:Arch. ii, 192 Dr:Dt 425 Schmoller:St,Kr. 1891, 205 ff. Lag:BN 230 ff.)).

[18] The concept of sacrificial atonement was not limited to the sin and guilt offerings, for the burnt offering is clearly designated to make atonement (*kipper*, intensive form of *kāpar*) for the worshiper. There are two major views on the etymology of the verb *kipper*. It is (a) an Arabic verb *kafara*, meaning "to cover," or (b) one of two Akkadian homonyms—*kapāru*—meaning alternately "to wipe off" or "to smear" (cf. Harold R. Cohen, *Biblical Hapax Legomena in the Light of Akkadian and Ugaritic*. Missoula, Mont.: Scholars Press, 1978, pp. 53–4, n. 8). Numerous evidences, including the poetic parallelism in Jeremiah 18:23 between *kipper* and another Hebrew verb (*māḥâh*, "to wipe out, blot out"), support the second view. A third option suggested by a number of authors (cf. Leon Morris, *The Apostolic Preaching of the Cross*. Grand Rapids: Wm. B. Eerdmans Publishing Co., 1955, pp. 142–52) traces the significance of *kipper* to the Hebrew noun *kōper*, "ransom." But since the etymology of *kōper* is apparently an Akkadian word related to *kapāru*, this should not be regarded as a third possible *etymology* but a significant word in determining the *usage* of *kipper*—"to make atonement." Thus the actual usage in ritual passages allows for either nuance of the Akkadian *kapāru*, either "to wipe off" or "to smear" (e.g., the blood was sometimes smeared on the horns of the altar, as in Lev. 16:18, or the offense was regarded as "wiped off," i.e., cleansed and removed; cf. 16:10, 19). Lindsey, F. D. (1985). Leviticus. In J. F. Walvoord & R. B. Zuck (Eds.), *The Bible Knowledge Commentary: An Exposition of the Scriptures* (J. F. Walvoord & R. B. Zuck, Ed.) (Le 1:4). Wheaton, IL: Victor Books.

There are two major views on the etymology of the verb *kipper*. It is (a) an Arabic verb *kafara*, meaning "to cover," or (b) one of two Akkadian homonyms—*kapāru*—meaning alternately "to wipe off" or "to smear" (cf. Harold R. Cohen, *Biblical Hapax Legomena in the Light of Akkadian and Ugaritic*. Missoula, Mont.: Scholars Press, 1978, pp. 53–4, note 8). Numerous evidences, including the poetic parallelism in Jeremiah 18:23 between *kipper* and another Hebrew verb (*māḥâh*, "to wipe out, blot out"), support the second view"... Thus the actual usage in ritual passages allows for either nuance of the Akkadian *kapāru*, either "to wipe off" or "to smear" (e.g., the blood was sometimes smeared on the horns of the altar, as in Lev. 16:18, or the offense was regarded as "wiped off," i.e., cleansed and removed; cf. 16:10, 19)."[19]

The word atone has also the design of making amends or reparation. This carries the weight of making restitution. There is the implication of bringing offended parties back together 'at one.' There may be two or more parties offended, yet they can be together as one i.e. 'at one.' No matter which direction one may take the basic meaning atone or atonement has the overall idea in context of diverting His wrath by means of the sacrifice's life blood for the life of the sinner. The sacrifice's body does not make this possible. Only the sacrifice's blood has made this possible.

The blood atonement in Levitical law may refer to atonement as ceremonial, cleansing, or sacrificial. What is most significant in Leviticus 17:11 is the literal sacrificial blood

[19] Lindsey, F. D. (1985). Leviticus. In J. F. Walvoord & R. B. Zuck (Eds.), *The Bible Knowledge Commentary: An Exposition of the Scriptures* (J. F. Walvoord & R. B. Zuck, Ed.) (Le 1:4–5). Wheaton, IL: Victor Books.

required for atonement for one's life. The sacrifice's life blood was 'poured out' for the required atonement being made. Only literal blood of the sacrifice could be poured out for 'the life' under Levitical law. God has given this blood its power, for it stands for the life of the sacrifice. Blood atonement for life was God's decree, for this was God's law for the nation Israel.

"For the life of the flesh is in the blood, and I have given it to you on the altar to make atonement for your souls; for it is the blood by reason of the life that makes atonement" Leviticus 17:11. "This verse explains the basis of blood atonement. The life of animals and humans is in the blood. If a creature loses its blood, it loses its life. **I have given** emphasizes that blood has no intrinsic power to atone for sin. God appointed blood to have this power because it represents the life of the creature. A life may receive atonement only by the sacrifice of a life. The author of Hebrews emphasized the temporary nature of animal blood sacrifices. They required constant renewal. However, Jesus' one-time sacrifice of Himself is effective eternally (Heb. 9:12-14; 25-28)." [20]

God sovereignly required literal blood atonement for man's sin

God had sovereignly assigned literal blood as the atoning sacrifice of sin for Israel. Atonement for the life or soul of the sinner or the life of the nation for sin was not simply the death of the sacrifice. Blood atonement was accomplished not by the death of the sacrifice, but by the death of the sacrifice and then the proper application of the sacrifice's blood. The lawful application of the sacrificial blood was specifically given by law for each type of offence, ordinance, ceremony, etc. It

---

[20] The Nelson Study Bible, Nelson Ministry Services Bible, 1997, page 204.

must be continually repeated that it is only the sacrifice's literal blood that makes the atonement.[21]

The death of the sacrifice made the blood efficacious for atonement. Yet under Levitical or Mosaic law, the officiating priest was to make proper assigned application of the sacrifice's literal blood. Even though the death of the sacrifice established the efficacy of the sacrificial blood, there was the necessity by law for the exact literal application of this literal blood. If the Levitical priest did not carry out every detail of the law for the application of the sacrifice's literal blood, there would be absolutely no literal atonement. For lawful blood atonement there must be:

- Death of the sacrifice
- Blood of the sacrifice becomes efficacious
- Lawful and proper application of the sacrificial blood by the priest
- Then there would be proper blood atonement

While other nations may have had a form of blood sacrifice/s, God demanded the death of the sinner for sin. Sacrificial blood atonement could take the place of the sinner for sin required by God. Note the exact construction of Lev.17:11 from the Hebrew Text. Literally and emphatically 'it (the blood not the victim) I have given to/for you upon the altar.' What was literally placed or sprinkled on Israel's altar was literal blood. Only this could and would make the required atonement.

---

[21] Leviticus 17:11 'For the life of the flesh is in the blood, and I have given it (it refers to the blood.. literally it I have given to/for you to make atonement for your soul/life) to you on the altar to make atonement for your souls; for **it is the blood** by reason of the life that makes atonement.' note well: it is the literal blood which makes the atonement not the death. There must be the death of the victim, but it it's blood that makes the atonement.. nothing else!! And this is emphatic in this verse. Note again the Hebrew Text.   כִּי נֶפֶשׁ הַבָּשָׂר בַּדָּם הוא וַאֲנִי נְתַתִּיו לָכֶם עַל־הַמִּזְבֵּחַ לְכַפֵּר עַל־נַפְשֹׁתֵיכֶם כִּי־הַדָּם הוא בַּנֶּפֶשׁ יְכַפֵּר:

"In spite of the fact that circulation of the blood as the current through which all vitality moves and waste is eliminated was not established by science until 1615 A.D., the body's blood has in all human history been recognized, though it involved mystery, as the container of life and the symbol of relationships. The shedding of blood has always been accompanied by some degree of fear and daring. Bloodshed spells the taking of life. None who consider the Scriptures can doubt the truth that God relates blood to the life. Early in Genesis (9:4–6) He declared: "But flesh with the life thereof, which is the blood thereof, shall ye not eat. And surely your blood of your lives will I require; at the hand of every beast will I require it, and at the hand of man; at the hand of every man's brother will I require the life of man. Whoso sheddeth man's blood, by man shall his blood be shed: for in the image of God made he man." Blood had to be eliminated from Jewish foods, nor could it be mingled with sacrifice other than in shedding it. The direct statement of Leviticus 17:11 gives a clear and final declaration from God, "For the life of the flesh is in the blood: and I have given it to you upon the altar to make an atonement for your souls: for it is the blood that maketh an atonement for the soul." The Biblical doctrine accordingly is subject to a threefold division—(1) sacrificial blood, (2) cleansing blood, and (3) blood as the seal of a covenant. "[22]

Conclusion
    God required and still requires literal blood for atonement for a human. The atoning blood God required had no value in itself. The death of the sacrifice made the blood of that sacrifice valuable and precious for the life of the sinner. That life of the sacrifice was poured out for another life. There is great value and power in atoning blood, for God gave it this importance. "The sanctity of the blood was clearly in view.

[22] Chafer, L. S. (1993). *Vol. 7: Systematic theology* (52). Grand Rapids, MI: Kregel Publications.

The commandment against eating blood was renewed. First given to Noah (Gen. 9:4), it was repeated in Leviticus 3:17 and 7:26. The reason was stated: The life of the flesh is in the blood. When poured out, it shows atonement, for it expresses the life taken. But why is life taken? Why is death required? Because, in essence, sin is an attack on God's holy throne and His very existence. It is, therefore, repelled by God by crushing the sinner's life. Jesus bore even this for man. "You killed the Prince of life" (Acts 3:15). However when our Lord fulfilled the type, He abrogated that law (John 6:53). We live by blood now, as we drink the poured-out life of the Son of Man."[23]

Peter spoke of the precious blood of Jesus. "Knowing that you were not redeemed with perishable things like silver or gold from your futile way of life inherited from your forefathers, but with precious blood, as of a lamb unblemished and spotless, *the blood* of Christ" (1 Peter 1:18-19). Believers have been purchased by the precious atoning blood of Jesus. This is His literal blood. There is no such thing here as a figure of speech. His blood is what is efficacious for eternal life. The apostles understood this and taught this. For this is His blood of the new covenant.

---

[23] Unger, Merrill F, (2002), Unger's Commentary On The Old Testament. Chattanooga, TN: AMG Publishers, p.167.

Chapter II

The Last Supper
His Body and His Blood

The last supper and the bread=His body

At the last supper Christ Jesus was very explicit about presenting His body and His blood as the Lamb of God for the sin/s of the world.[24] This begins with His twelve disciples. The twelve are the audience at this time (for proper exegesis and context) and the topic is His body and blood given for them, which are the twelve disciples. It can be easily proven that Judas was at this supper especially at this time.[25] If Judas were there this would give great support for unlimited atonement.

"And while they were eating, Jesus took *some* bread, and after a blessing, He broke *it* and gave *it* to the disciples, and said, "Take, eat; this is My body" (Matthew 26:26). "And while they were eating, He took *some* bread, and after a blessing He broke *it*; and gave *it* to them, and said, "Take *it*; this is My body" (Mark 14:22). "And when He had taken *some* bread *and* given thanks, He broke *it*, and gave *it* to them, saying, "This is

---

[24] "The next day he saw Jesus coming to him, and said, "Behold, the Lamb of God who takes away the sin of the world!" John 1:29 Τῇ ἐπαύριον βλέπει τὸν Ἰησοῦν ἐρχόμενον πρὸς αὐτὸν καὶ λέγει· ἴδε ὁ ἀμνὸς τοῦ θεοῦ ὁ αἴρων τὴν ἁμαρτίαν τοῦ κόσμου.

[25] Matthew 26:20 Now when evening had come, He was reclining *at the table* with the twelve disciples. [21] And as they were eating, He said, "Truly I say to you that one of you will betray Me." [22] And being deeply grieved, they each one began to say to Him, "Surely not I, Lord?" [23] And He answered and said, "He who dipped his hand with Me in the bowl is the one who will betray Me. [24] "The Son of Man *is to* go, just as it is written of Him; but woe to that man by whom the Son of Man is betrayed! It would have been good for that man if he had not been born." [25] And Judas, who was betraying Him, answered and said, "Surely it is not I, Rabbi?" He said to him, "You have said *it* yourself."

My body which is given **for you**; do this in remembrance of Me" (Luke 22:19).[26] Note the Lukan passage which specially marked His body *for them*. The bread was representing His body for them all, the twelve, yet each one individually. This was why He broke the bread to give to each one individually. He broke the bread to give them each a piece, but His body was *never* broken![27] He broke the bread to give them each a piece which is extremely obvious. His body which was given in substitution for them i.e. the twelve at this time (substitutionary atonement) was represented by the bread. It must be emphasized that both His body and His blood were essential for a complete atonement.[28] This will become very clear.

The last supper and His blood
   "And when He had taken a cup and given thanks, He gave *it* to them, saying, "Drink from it, all of you; for this is My blood of the covenant, which is poured out **for many** for

---

[26] Matthew 26:26 Ἐσθιόντων δὲ αὐτῶν λαβὼν ὁ Ἰησοῦς ἄρτον καὶ εὐλογήσας ἔκλασεν καὶ δοὺς τοῖς μαθηταῖς εἶπεν·λάβετε φάγετε, **τοῦτό**= ἐστιν **τὸ σῶμά μου**. Mark 14:22 Καὶ ἐσθιόντων αὐτῶν λαβὼν ἄρτον εὐλογήσας ἔκλασεν καὶ ἔδωκεν αὐτοῖς καὶ εἶπεν· λάβετε, **τοῦτό**= ἐστιν **τὸ σῶμά μου**. Luke 22:19 καὶ λαβὼν ἄρτον εὐχαριστήσας ἔκλασεν καὶ ἔδωκεν αὐτοῖς λέγων· **τοῦτό** ἐστιν **τὸ σῶμά μου** τὸ **ὑπὲρ ὑμῶν** διδόμενον· **τοῦτο**← ποιεῖτε εἰς τὴν ἐμὴν ἀνάμνησιν.
[27] "And while they were eating, Jesus took *some* bread, and after a blessing, **He broke it** and gave *it* to the disciples, and said, "Take, eat; this is My body" (Matthew 26:26). "And while they were eating, He took *some* bread, and after a blessing **He broke it**; and gave *it* to them, and said, "Take *it*; this is My body" (Mark 14:22). "And when He had taken *some* bread *and* given thanks, **He broke *it*,** and gave *it* to them, saying, "This is My body which is given **for you**; do this in remembrance of Me" (Luke 22:19). "For these things came to pass, that the Scripture might be fulfilled, **"Not a bone of Him shall be broken".** And again another Scripture says, "They shall look on Him whom they pierced" (John 19:36-37).
[28] A complete/d atonement is what is being presented by Christ. This is not some futuristic atonement, but a completed atonement that will replace the Mosaic or Levitical law. Christ did this by His body and blood. The new covenant promised eternal atonement. This went into effect at the death of Christ by His blood. "And in the same way He *took* the cup after they had eaten, saying, "This cup which is poured out for you is the new covenant in My blood" (Luke 22:20); literally by means of My blood.

forgiveness of sins" (Matthew 26:27-28). "And when He had taken a cup, *and* given thanks, He gave *it* to them; and **they all drank from it.** And He said to them, "This is My blood of the covenant, which is poured out **for many**" (Mark 14:23-24). "And in the same way *He took* the cup after they had eaten, saying, "This cup which is poured out **for you** is **the new covenant** in My blood" (Luke 22:20). There are many observations to be made with these verses. Jesus made it quite clear that this cup was representative of the new covenant. Jesus emphasized the soteriological aspect of the forgiveness of sins. The forgiveness of sins was repeated twice for the many and for them i.e. the twelve disciples. It must be kept in focus that there was a coming new covenant which was not like the old or Mosaic covenant (the law). This covenant would replace the old by presenting a completed atonement.

Jesus' emphasis was not an eschatological truth for these disciples.[29] There was the immediate truth that His body and blood, being represented by the bread and the cup, had some principle and application to these disciples. They did not fully understand this at that moment but they would understand very shortly. The body and the blood of the new covenant was for them and definitely has application. This can be shown very easily.

It is quite evident that they 'all' drank. Note well Luke 22:20 'This cup which is poured out **for you** is the new covenant in My blood.'[30] As there is no copulative in this

---

[29] Jesus' emphasis was not an eschatological truth for these disciples and the many. The emphasis was focusing on the disciples and not some futuristic beginning of His new covenant. There was going to be an application immediately to these disciples at the death of Christ and this was literally new covenant blood atonement.

[30] Mat. 26:27καὶ λαβὼν ποτήριον καὶ εὐχαριστήσας ἔδωκεν αὐτοῖς λέγων· πίετε ἐξ αὐτοῦ πάντες,[28] **τοῦτο γάρ ἐστιν τὸ αἷμά μου τῆς διαθήκης τὸ περὶ πολλῶν** ἐκχυννόμενον εἰς ἄφεσιν ἁμαρτιῶν. Mark 14:23 καὶ λαβὼν ποτήριον εὐχαριστήσας ἔδωκεν αὐτοῖς, καὶ ἔπιον ἐξ αὐτοῦ πάντες. Mk. 14:24 καὶ εἶπεν αὐτοῖς· **τοῦτό ἐστιν τὸ αἷμά μου τῆς διαθήκης τὸ ἐκχυννόμενον ὑπὲρ πολλῶν.**Lu22:20 καὶ

verse, the cup itself becomes representative of the new covenant.[31] The cup which was being poured out was for them=these disciples. "And when He had taken a cup and given thanks, He gave *it* to them, saying, "**Drink from it, all of you**; for this is **My blood of the covenant**, which is poured out for many for forgiveness of sins" (Matthew 26:27-28). "And when He had taken a cup, *and* given thanks, He gave *it* to them; and **they all drank from it**. And He said to them, "**This is My blood of the covenant**, which is poured out **for many**" (Mark 14:23-24). "And in the same way *He took* the cup after they had eaten, saying, "This cup which is poured out **for you** is **the new covenant in My blood**" (Luke 22:20).

It should not be overlooked in the context, Christ makes application of His new covenant blood to the apostles. It is clearly for them i.e. the apostles and the 'many'. This term 'many' appears to be a true Hebraism. The many can easily refer to more than the whole or totality by the Semitic mind.[32] The application/s of the new covenant would encompass much more or many more than the twelve. Christ made this very obvious. The one thing Christ was truly stressing was the forgiveness that would be very much given to them. The concern here is for the twelve, and understanding very specific application of His body and His blood of the new covenant to these men. These men had only the Hebrew Text, but now they also had Christ's very words.

τὸ ποτήριον ὡσαύτως μετὰ τὸ δειπνῆσαι, λέγων· **τοῦτο τὸ ποτήριον** = **ἡ καινὴ διαθήκη ἐν τῷ αἵματί μου τὸ ὑπὲρ ὑμῶν ἐκχυννόμενον.**

[31] Luke 22:20 καὶ τὸ ποτήριον ὡσαύτως μετὰ τὸ δειπνῆσαι, λέγων· **τοῦτο τὸ ποτήριον = ἡ καινὴ διαθήκη** ἐν τῷ αἵματί μου τὸ ὑπὲρ ὑμῶν ἐκχυννόμενον. Note well that there is no verb in the first part making a very possible and logical appositional construction for the cup=the new covenant. The ἐν τῷ αἵματί μου can easily mean 'by means of my blood'. **Note also the emphasis on 'for you'.. There is application of the new covenant to these disciples.**

[32] **πολλῷ μᾶλλον** v.9. **οἱ πολλοί** not "many" but *all* (who are many), the fact of a great number being more prominent to the Sem. mind than the fact of totality, cf Mt 20:28.(ref. Rom. 5:15); Zerwick, A Grammatical Analysis of the Greek New Testament, Pontifica Press, 1993, p. 470.

At the last supper, they knew two very specific things which were applicable to them. These were Christ's body and His blood of the new covenant. To say that none of this is directly applicable to them is just a gloss and a distortion of Christ's words at His last supper with them. He is making things very clear to His disciples. They will understand He is making a completed atonement for them and others (them and the many).

His emphasis on His blood of the new covenant

Christ's only concern was His blood, and this was His blood of the new covenant for forgiveness of sin. There was never a probability or possibility of separating His blood from the new covenant. He emphasized His blood clearly and accurately as 'My blood' but He *never* separated His/My blood from the new covenant. His blood and the new covenant are inseparable and the Text clearly shows this by 'My blood' and the articulated modifiers 'the covenant' in both Matthew and Mark. Luke was much more emphatic:[33]

- Matthew 26:28: for this is My blood of the covenant
- Mark 14:24: This is My blood of the covenant
- Luke 22:20: This cup which is poured out for you = the new covenant in My blood (there is no verb here probably stressing the emphasis as appositional)

---

[33] Mat. 26:28: for this is My blood of **the** covenant τοῦτο γάρ ἐστιν →τὸ αἷμά μου ῆς διαθήκης   Mark 14:24: This is My blood of **the** covenant τοῦτό ἐστιν→ τὸ αἷμά μου τῆς διαθήκης   Luke 22:20: This cup which is poured out for you is the new covenant in My blood τοῦτο τὸ ποτήριον = ἡ καινὴ διαθήκη ἐν τῷ αἵματί μου Note well Mat and Mark where the blood is modified by the covenant which is articulated. It is not just blood of itself or His blood apart from the new covenant. Luke is even more emphatic where the cup represents the new covenant and this (covenant) by means of His blood. Christ was actually cutting the new covenant at the cross. And this was for them. Not just a futuristic truth. They will find this out very clearly.

There seems to be a tendency by some to bifurcate the blood into two aspects i.e. His blood for the forgiveness of sins and His blood of the new covenant. Christ and His disciples would never have understood this. This is not taught in this context, nor in any other context when referring to the new covenant. As the apostles understood His body given *for them*, they would also have understood the forgiveness of sins through Christ's blood of the new covenant *for them* also. Christ and the apostles only knew of one unified blood, His blood of the new covenant for forgiveness of sins. This is what Christ taught them at the last supper. Why not just take the simple reading and meaning of the Text in its very context? To separate His blood from the new covenant is to do violence to the Text by contradicting Christ's very words. This would be violating the very jots and tittles which were so inspired by God the Holy Spirit and so emphasized by Messiah Himself.

To insinuate there is no application of the blood of the new covenant i.e. forgiveness of sins to these disciples, really misses the entire biblical teaching of Christ Himself at the last supper. He made it very clear that His body represented by the broken bread was given *for them*. He made it very clear that His blood of the new covenant was also *for them*. Both His body and His blood are very different aspects of the atonement but equally applicable. The bread represented His body given in substitution for them, a necessary component of the atonement. His blood was the blood of the forgiveness of sins for them covenanted in and by the new covenant exclusively. This was the promise of complete forgiveness of sins by the new covenant which Christ put into effect by His blood.[34] To say this covenant is simply inaugurated, ratified, etc. but not yet operable by way of application to the twelve (at the death of Christ) is simply to void the Text in lieu of some rather inconsistent method of interpretation. There is a rather grave tendency not to study the last supper in Matthew, Mark, and Luke and exactly what is

[34] It must be noted that this is His literal blood. This is not a figure of speech. His literal blood was necessary to make the completed atonement.

being said. There is just a warehouse of great gleanings from His last supper.

Judas and the last supper

While this may not seem very important, it actually has some great theological bearing. Luke records very accurately that Judas was there presently participating in both the bread and the cup. "But behold, the hand of the one betraying Me is with Me on the table. 'For indeed, the Son of Man is going as it has been determined; but woe to that man by whom He is betrayed!' And they began to discuss among themselves which one of them it might be who was going to do this thing" (Luke 22:21-23).[35] Christ was literally extending grace to all but especially those who He even knew would betray Him, literally His enemies. This is quite significant for if His body and blood is for 'all' i.e. the many (more than the whole),[36] then Christ is teaching unlimited atonement.

This would be in full agreement with *all* the verses supporting the biblical truth of unlimited atonement. **"The next day he saw Jesus coming to him, and said, Behold, the Lamb of God who takes away the sin of the world!"** (John 1:29). This is not just the sin of the elect, for all men are condemned in Adam. There is no such thing as separating the elect and non-elect from Adamic sin. This is the same sin which condemned both

---

[35] Note the context of what is being said about Judas in context. The paragraph begins with 22:14. "And in the same way *He took* the cup after they had eaten, saying, "This cup which is poured out for you is the new covenant in My blood. [21] "But behold, the hand of the one betraying Me is with Me on the table. [22] "For indeed, the Son of Man is going as it has been determined; but woe to that man by whom He is betrayed!" [23] And they began to discuss among themselves which one of them it might be who was going to do this thing. (Luke 22:20-23).

[36] πολλοί a Semitism, not opposing "all" but denotes "all" (who are many), the fact of a great number being more prominent in the Semitic mind than the fact of totality, cf Is 53:11f. (Hebr. and LXX) where "many" occurs twice. Zerwick, M., & Grosvenor, M. (1974). *A grammatical analysis of the Greek New Testament* (66). Rome: Biblical Institute Press.

literally all men (Rom 5:12-21). Christ the last Adam paid for this sin.[37] There is everything in the Text to support unlimited atonement, and Judas' presence makes this abundantly clear. For Christ gave His body and poured out His blood even for Judas. This establishes direct principle and application of the body and the blood of the new covenant even to Judas. This makes Judas fully accountable for the body and blood of the new covenant. There is nothing in the Text to support limited atonement even by Christ's own words. His sacrifice of His body and His blood were for the sins of the world. Here we have great application of the new covenant to the twelve disciples.[38] Remember they all 'drank' even Judas. "And when He had taken a cup, *and* given thanks, He gave *it* to them; and **they all drank from it**. And He said to them, "This is My blood of the covenant, which is poured out for many" (Mar 14:23-24). His blood of the covenant has direct application to each one of them and to the many more.

Does the new covenant being operational by way of application mean that the kingdom in some sense has arrived?

[37] "For if by the transgression of the one, death reigned through the one, much more those who receive the abundance of grace and of the gift of righteousness will reign in life through the One, Jesus Christ. [18] So then as through one transgression there resulted condemnation to all men, even so through one act of righteousness there resulted justification of life to all men. [19] For as through the one man's disobedience the many were made sinners, even so through the obedience of the One the many will be made righteous" Rom. 5:17-19. εἰ γὰρ τῷ τοῦ ἑνὸς παραπτώματι ὁ θάνατος ἐβασίλευσεν διὰ τοῦ ἑνός, πολλῷ μᾶλλον οἱ τὴν περισσείαν τῆς χάριτος καὶ τῆς δωρεᾶς τῆς δικαιοσύνης λαμβάνοντες ἐν ζωῇ βασιλεύσουσιν διὰ τοῦ ἑνὸς Ἰησοῦ Χριστοῦ. [18] Ἄρα οὖν ὡς δι᾽ ἑνὸς παραπτώματος εἰς πάντας ἀνθρώπους εἰς κατάκριμα, οὕτως καὶ δι᾽ ἑνὸς δικαιώματος εἰς πάντας ἀνθρώπους εἰς δικαίωσιν ζωῆς· [19] ὥσπερ γὰρ διὰ τῆς παρακοῆς τοῦ ἑνὸς ἀνθρώπου ἁμαρτωλοὶ κατεστάθησαν οἱ πολλοί, οὕτως καὶ διὰ τῆς ὑπακοῆς τοῦ ἑνὸς δίκαιοι κατασταθήσονται οἱ πολλοί.
[38] Those who believe nothing has happened i.e the new covenant is not operational in any sense by way of application are missing some great truth. Eternal redemption was a major promise of the new covenant.

Christ affirmed there was no kingdom yet in any sense.
He made it very clear this was not possible. "But I say to you, I
will not drink of this fruit of the vine from now on until that day
when I drink it new **with you** in My Father's kingdom"
(Matthew 26:29). "Truly I say to you, I shall never again drink
of the fruit of the vine until that day when I drink it **new** in the
kingdom of God" (Mark 14:25) "for I say to you, I will not
drink of the fruit of the vine from now on **until the kingdom of
God comes**" (Luke 22:18).[39] The term 'I will not drink of the
fruit of the vine' is the strongest of negations in Greek. The
coming kingdom is addressed here as Jesus attached the coming
kingdom to the last supper. This is very important to
understand as many believe we are in the kingdom now or there
is some form of the kingdom now. Christ taught against this.
Only at Christ's second coming will there be His covenanted
kingdom.

After Christ was raised from the dead, He taught for
about 50 days on one particular issue: "To these He also
presented Himself alive, after His suffering, by many
convincing proofs, appearing to them over *a period of* forty
days, and speaking of the things concerning the kingdom of
God" (Acts 1:3). Even Paul toward the end of his life was
preaching the coming kingdom. "And he stayed two full years
in his own rented quarters, and was welcoming all who came to
him, preaching the kingdom of God, and teaching concerning
the Lord Jesus Christ with all openness, unhindered" (Acts
28:30-31). The continued sufferings of the apostles and Christ's
followers were absolute proof that the kingdom was and is not

---

[39] Matthew 26:29 λέγω δὲ ὑμῖν, **οὐ μὴ πίω** ἀπ᾽ ἄρτι ἐκ τούτου τοῦ γενήματος τῆς
ἀμπέλου ἕως τῆς ἡμέρας ἐκείνης ὅταν αὐτὸ πίνω μεθ᾽ ὑμῶν καινὸν ἐν τῇ βασιλείᾳ
τοῦ πατρός μου. Mark 14:25 ἀμὴν λέγω ὑμῖν ὅτι οὐκέτι **οὐ μὴ πίω** ἐκ τοῦ
γενήματος τῆς ἀμπέλου ἕως τῆς ἡμέρας ἐκείνης ὅταν αὐτὸ πίνω καινὸν ἐν τῇ
βασιλείᾳ τοῦ θεοῦ. Luke 22:18 λέγω γὰρ ὑμῖν, [ὅτι] **οὐ μὴ πίω** ἀπὸ τοῦ νῦν ἀπὸ
τοῦ γενήματος τῆς ἀμπέλου ἕως οὗ ἡ βασιλεία τοῦ θεοῦ ἔλθη. As there is no
fulfillment of any of the covenants as yet, there is no kingdom. Thank God the
church is not a taste of the kingdom. If this is a taste of the kingdom, which church
are you in Ephesus (left their first love?).. Sardis which is dead.. Was it Laodicea
which was rather like vomit… PD has left the truth of the Text…

here in any sense. Those who hold to a now kingdom, an already type kingdom, a building of His kingdom or any such thing are really not listening to the words of the Text. For almost 2,000 years He has been building His church[40] and He is not the King of the church. Christ is the Head of the church, and the church is the bride. The church is the bride and He is the Groom. He is not King of the church for the church does not have a king in this relationship. He will come back to set up His kingdom as the covenanted Davidic King. He will be King for the 1,000 year kingdom or millennium. Satan must be bound for these 1,000 years. The church is not in any sense the covenanted kingdom. There are no unilateral, eternal, unconditional covenants with the church, but the church receives many blessings from the covenants. Again, the church is not the covenanted kingdom nor in the covenanted kingdom. The church will reign with Him for the literal 1,000 years or millennium as will all who are His going back to Adam.

All this is even more important than one might realize. Jesus is claiming there is no kingdom at the time He spoke or even now. The kingdom will not come and cannot come until He comes.[41] He took the disciples into the future without their

---

[40] "And I also say to you that you are Peter, and upon this rock I will build My church; and the gates of Hades shall not overpower it (Mat. 16:18) κἀγὼ δέ σοι λέγω ὅτι σὺ εἶ Πέτρος, καὶ ἐπὶ ταύτῃ τῇ πέτρᾳ οἰκοδομήσω μου τὴν ἐκκλησίαν καὶ πύλαι ᾅδου οὐ κατισχύσουσιν αὐτῆς. "Building His church was a yet-future work of Jesus Christ, for He had not yet started the process. He said, **I will build** (future tense) **My church**, but His program for the nation Israel had to be concluded before another program could be set in motion. This is probably why Jesus said not even **the gates of hades** would **overcome** this program. Jews would understand hades' gates to refer to physical death. Jesus was thus telling the disciples His death would not prevent His work of building the church. Later (Matt. 16:21) He spoke of His imminent death. He was therefore anticipating His death and His victory over death through the Resurrection." Barbieri, L. A., & Jr. (1985). Matthew. In J. F. Walvoord & R. B. Zuck (Eds.), *The Bible Knowledge Commentary: An Exposition of the Scriptures* (J. F. Walvoord & R. B. Zuck, Ed.) (Mt 16:17–20). Wheaton, IL: Victor Books.

[41] Matthew 25:31 "But when the Son of Man comes in His glory, and all the angels with Him, then He will sit on His glorious throne. (Mat 25:31). Only when He comes will He take the Davidic throne. Then the kingdom will truly begin. The kingdom will not and cannot come until He comes.

understanding or His fully explaining this truth at that time. There was no real explanation of the church or the church age and how this might last for thousands of years. If any application of the new covenant were delayed until the coming kingdom or even a later date it seems He would have told them. Also if there were nothing for them by way of application with reference to the new covenant for a few years or many years, then He would basically be deceiving them. This He would not and did not do. Again, they were drinking the cup of the new covenant. Luke 22:20: This cup which is poured out for you = the new covenant in My blood. They understood this was for them. If there were a 2,000 year delay or any delay of the application of the new covenant for them this would be deceit.

As there are those who hold there is no application of the forgiveness of sin promised in the new covenant until the kingdom or just prior to the kingdom, it seems He would have made this very clear especially to His disciples. There is a vast difference in His drinking of the fruit of the vine which won't happen until the kingdom (the lesser), and His shed blood for forgiveness and a completed atonement for the forgiveness of sin (the greater).[42]   If there were no direct application of the new covenant for His disciples until the kingdom, He certainly would have made this very clear. He did not do this. There is no confusion here in any sense; in fact there is great clarification. Again, the fact is Jesus would not drink of the fruit of the vine until His future kingdom (the lesser). He would apply the blood of the covenant to His disciples at that time (the greater).[43]   If this were not true, He would have made this very clear.

---

[42] He did apply to His disciples His shed blood for forgiveness of sins of the new covenant i.e. a completed atonement for the forgiveness of sin (the greater). If He taught on His not drinking with them until the kingdom, then there is no kingdom until then and there is no Davidic throne until then.

[43] Christ would have it clear concerning a delay of new covenant application for His disciples (the greater). He did not do this in any sense. To read back into these verses is to change the meaning of the Text as written and inspired.

The last supper and the forgiveness of sins

"And when He had taken a cup and given thanks, He gave *it* to them, saying, "Drink from it, all of you; for this is My blood of the covenant, which is poured out **for many for forgiveness of sins**" (Matthew 26:27-28). "And when He had taken a cup, *and* given thanks, He gave *it* to them; and **they all drank** from it. And He said to them, "**This is My blood of the covenant,** which is poured out for many" (Mar 14:23-24). "And in the same way *He took* the cup after they had eaten, saying, "This cup which is poured out for you is the new covenant in My blood" (Luke 22:20).[44]

Christ the Eternal Son of God was establishing His new covenant. It must be remembered the church will not exist for at least another fifty days so we are not concerned with the church in any sense at this time. The Text is very clear what the disciples heard and understood. The Text says that His blood was not only establishing the new covenant but the emphasis was on the forgiveness of sins provided by the new covenant and this by means of His literal blood. Just as His body represented by the bread had application to them, so would the blood of the new covenant have application to them. This would have full application for them very shortly at the death of Christ when He died on the cross. Other Text cannot be read back into these verses to change the meaning and application.

---

[44] Mat. 26:27καὶ λαβὼν ποτήριον καὶ εὐχαριστήσας ἔδωκεν αὐτοῖς λέγων· πίετε ἐξ αὐτοῦ πάντες,28 τοῦτο γάρ ἐστιν τὸ αἷμά μου τῆς διαθήκης **τὸ περὶ πολλῶν ἐκχυννόμενον εἰς ἄφεσιν ἁμαρτιῶν**. Mark 14:23 καὶ λαβὼν ποτήριον εὐχαριστήσας ἔδωκεν αὐτοῖς, καὶ **ἔπιον ἐξ αὐτοῦ πάντες.** Mk. 14:24 καὶ εἶπεν αὐτοῖς· τοῦτό ἐστιν τὸ αἷμά μου τῆς διαθήκης τὸ ἐκχυνόμενον **ὑπὲρ πολλῶν.**Lu22:20 καὶ τὸ ποτήριον ὡσαύτως μετὰ τὸ δειπνῆσαι, λέγων· τοῦτο τὸ ποτήριον = ἡ καινὴ διαθήκη ἐν τῷ αἵματί μου τὸ ὑπὲρ ὑμῶν ἐκχυννόμενον. Note well they understood no other truth than this cup represented the new covenant by mean of His blood and this was for the forgiveness of sins. This forgiveness was not only for them but for the many. Christ is stressing the forgiveness of sin provided in the new covenant. His is literally taking on this covenant as His very own. He is the Testator of His very own covenant and last will. As the Son of God, the Creator of the ages, He alone can do this especially with His own blood. The new covenant is a blood covenant set in full motion by Christ's very own literal blood.

The literal blood flowing through the veins of Christ while He lived had no efficacy. The moment He died, that blood became a veritable substance of infinite value especially for atonement. Just one millimicron and less or one picogram or infinitely less of His precious blood would and could cleanse any galaxy or trillions of galaxies eternally. The power in Christ's precious blood for eternal and continual cleansing is beyond any human comprehension.

The great truth emphasized at the last supper by Christ Himself was His precious sinless body and His precious and sinless blood being given for these twelve disciples and the many. He was in effect establishing the great truth of the new covenant and taking this covenant on as His very own. Being the Son of God and the Son of man He alone is the only One capable of doing this. As the Son of God He is the Creator of the ages and He alone can take this covenant on as His own for it is His own.[45] The essence of the new covenant is the forgiveness of sins. "Forgiveness of sins is one of the major benefits of the death of Jesus. It is the essence of the New Covenant (cf. Matt. 26:28; Jer. 31:31–34). Proclaiming the forgiveness of sins was the prominent feature of the apostolic preaching in the Book of Acts. Jesus was giving the apostles (and by extension, the church) the privilege of announcing heaven's terms on how a person can receive forgiveness. If one believes in Jesus, then a Christian has the right to announce his

---

[45]"By faith we understand that the worlds were prepared by the word of God, so that what is seen was not made out of things which are visible" (Heb. 11:3). Πίστει νοοῦμεν κατηρτίσθαι τοὺς αἰῶνας ῥήματι θεοῦ, εἰς τὸ μὴ ἐκ φαινομένων τὸ βλεπόμενον γεγονέναι.. Note the emphasis on the ages. The actual creation of the physical or material universe was really no big matter to God i.e. just the work of His fingers "When I consider Thy heavens, the work of Thy fingers, The moon and the stars, which Thou hast ordained; (Ps. 8:3). The ages are the bigger issue and redemption would be even greater as emphasized here "The LORD has bared His holy arm In the sight of all the nations, That all the ends of the earth may see The salvation of our God. (Isa 52:10). When it came to deliverance or redemption esp. for Israel He rolled up His sleeves and truly got to work.

forgiveness. If a person rejects Jesus' sacrifice, then a Christian can announce that person is not forgiven."[46]

The blood of Christ is literal blood

The blood of Christ is literal and His literal blood is what truly brings eternal redemption. His literal blood and His literal blood alone is what put the new covenant promised redemption into full operation. God demanded and required literal blood for atonement.[47] This literal blood is not a figure of speech, not a symbol, not a type spoken of here at the last supper. It is His literal blood that cleanses eternally. Christ is making this very clear to the twelve that it is His literal blood alone which brings the eternal redemption promised by the new covenant. No other covenant can do this. The new covenant promised eternal redemption. This eternal redemption was purchased with Christ's precious blood.

Christ is taking this new covenant on as His very own last will and testament while He is still living. No one is able to carry out His own will as the executor. The fact is they are dead, yet this immediately puts their will into full operation. Nobody except Christ was raised from the dead to execute or be the executor of His own will. He is at this present time mediating His very own will and covenant in the true tabernacle. It will be shown and proven this new covenant is from heaven, unilateral, eternal and is mediated only from heaven by the eternal High Priest that is Christ Himself.

At His death, the new covenant was immediately ratified and operational by way of application replacing the old Mosaic or Levitical law. The new covenant by means of Christ's literal blood was put into full operation. This is one reason the veil

---

[46] Blum, E. A. (1985). John. In J. F. Walvoord & R. B. Zuck (Eds.), *The Bible Knowledge Commentary: An Exposition of the Scriptures* (J. F. Walvoord & R. B. Zuck, Ed.) (Jn 20:21–23). Wheaton, IL: Victor Books.

[47] **Leviticus 17:11** 'For the life of the flesh is in the blood, and I have given it to you on the altar to make atonement for your souls; for **it is the blood by reason of the life that makes atonement.'**

was torn in two.[48] All Israel now had access to God as the Law ended and in its place was put the new covenant[49] with Israel is fully operative such as a will at the death of the testator.[50] This in no way suggests this covenant was or is being fulfilled even by Israel in any manner. It must be noted that this eternal covenant as well as the other eternal covenants are actually contracts made by God alone. These are contracts and not prophecy.[51]

Salvation is through the Eternal Son of God
Final redemption was available to the twelve immediately and to the many (all may come).[52] Access was

[48] **Matthew 27:51** And behold, **the veil of the temple was torn in two from top to bottom**, and the earth shook; and the rocks were split, Καὶ ἰδοὺ τὸ καταπέτασμα τοῦ ναοῦ ἐσχίσθη ἀπ᾽ ἄνωθεν ἕως κάτω εἰς δύο καὶ ἡ γῆ ἐσείσθη καὶ αἱ πέτραι ἐσχίσθησαν, **Mark 15:38 And the veil of the temple was torn in two from top to bottom.** Καὶ τὸ καταπέτασμα τοῦ ναοῦ ἐσχίσθη εἰς δύο ἀπ᾽ ἄνωθεν ἕως κάτω. **Luke 23:45** the sun being obscured; and **the veil of the temple was torn in two.**τοῦ ἡλίου ἐκλιπόντος, ἐσχίσθη δὲ τὸ καταπέτασμα τοῦ ναοῦ μέσον. Note all may now enter the earthly temple without fear. There was now full access by the blood of the new covenant. This literal blood of Christ set in motion the forgiveness of sin available to all. This proves the new covenant is fully operational at this time. This is not a future event, it is operational now and there was direct application for the many i.e. all.
[49] There was a change of law and there was definitely a change in priesthood. See the section dealing with this with the Hebrew passages. Hebrews 7:12 For when the priesthood is **changed**, of necessity there takes place a **change** of law also. μετατιθεμένης γὰρ τῆς ἱερωσύνης ἐξ ἀνάγκης καὶ νόμου **μετάθεσις** γίνεται.
[50] Pls see the section titled 'The Testator and His Will' (Heb. 9:16-17).
[51] The Abrahamic, Davidic, land, and new covenants are eternal, unilateral, and unconditional. They are actually eternal contracts made by God with very specific recipients or persons named in these eternal covenants or contracts. These contracts are not prophecy; they are eternal contracts with very specific persons or recipients. These persons are Abraham, Isaac, Jacob, Israel, David, and Christ Jesus. These contracts can only be fulfilled by God with Abraham, Isaac, Jacob, Israel, David, and Christ Jesus Himself.
[52] KJV Luke 23:45 And the sun was darkened, and the veil of the temple was rent in the midst.NAS Luke 23:45 the sun being obscured; and the veil of the temple was torn in two.NKJ Luke 23:45 Then the sun was darkened, and the veil of the temple was torn in two. τοῦ ἡλίου ἐκλιπόντος, ἐσχίσθη δὲ τὸ καταπέτασμα τοῦ ναοῦ μέσον.. At that very moment, at death of Christ there was now true access to God by the blood of the new covenant. While there was limited access before, now by His blood of the new covenant, access is open for all!! All must come by faith trusting in the One

now available to all (Israel especially at this time) who come by
faith believing in Who He is and what He did. Salvation is
completely in and by the Son of God. He is the eternal Son of
God, and this is biblical fact. Scripture is very, very clear and
specific on this issue. One has to know and believe this for
eternal redemption. There are those who deny the Eternal
Sonship of Christ. This means they do not know Him. They
may speak great things about Him, or even preach Him, but
they do not know Him unless they teach and preach Him as the
Eternal Son. "For the Son of God, Christ Jesus, who was
preached among you by us-- by me and Silvanus and Timothy--
was not yes and no, but is yes in Him" (2 Cor. 1:19).[53] The
construction is very powerful in this verse concerning His
eternal Sonship (2 Corinthians 1:19) ὁ τοῦ θεοῦ γὰρ υἱὸς
Ἰησοῦς Χριστὸς. Note the construction of the passage. The
articulation of the Son is brought forward for emphasis on
Christ being the Son of the God. He was always the eternal
Son; to deny this is to deny the Text and to deny the Text is to
deny Him. "But these have been written that you may believe
that Jesus is the Christ, the Son of God; and that believing you
may have life in His name" (John 20:31).[54] "These things I

Who died for them: "¹Now I make known to you, brethren, the gospel which I
preached to you, which also you received, in which also you stand, ² by which also
you are saved, if you hold fast the word which I preached to you, unless you believed
in vain. ³ For I delivered to you as of first importance what I also received, that Christ
died for our sins according to the Scriptures, ⁴ and that He was buried, and that He
was raised on the third day according to the Scriptures" (1Co 15:1-4).
[53] 2 Corinthians 1:19 ὁ τοῦ θεοῦ γὰρ υἱὸς Ἰησοῦς Χριστὸς ὁ ἐν ὑμῖν δι' ἡμῶν
κηρυχθείς, δι' ἐμοῦ καὶ Σιλουανοῦ καὶ Τιμοθέου, οὐκ ἐγένετο ναὶ καὶ οὒ ἀλλὰ ναὶ ἐν
αὐτῷ γέγονεν. Note the construction of the passage. The articulation of the Son is
brought forward for emphasis on Christ being the Son of the God. He was always the
eternal Son to deny this is to deny the Text. The emphasis on the Son is so clearly
shown in this Text, and Paul is addressing the substance of true heralding or
preaching. He preached the Eternal Sonship anything less is a false gospel of Who
He is by definition.
[54] John 20:31 ταῦτα δὲ γέγραπται ἵνα πιστεύ[σ]ητε ὅτι Ἰησοῦς ἐστιν ὁ χριστὸς= ὁ
υἱὸς τοῦ θεοῦ, καὶ ἵνα πιστεύοντες ζωὴν ἔχητε ἐν τῷ ὀνόματι αὐτοῦ. Note the
construction of the words. The verb or copulative is preceding the ὁ χριστὸς= ὁ υἱὸς
τοῦ θεοῦ. Very powerful as these things were written in order you might believe
Who He is. Jesus is Ἰησοῦς ἐστιν and only defined one way. Jesus is ὁ χριστὸς= ὁ

have written to you who believe in the name of the Son of God, in order that you may know that you have eternal life" (1 John 5:13).[55]   Even Satan and demons understand He is the eternal Son. He never became the Son. The Scriptures are perfectly clear about the Person of the Eternal Son. "And the tempter came and said to Him, "If You are the Son of God, command that these stones become bread" (Mat. 4:3).[56] "And whenever the unclean spirits beheld Him, they would fall down before Him and cry out, saying, "You are the Son of God!" (Mark 3:11).[57]

Salvation is exclusively of Him, the Eternal Son of God=Jehovah. "And Simon Peter answered and said, "Thou art the Christ, the Son of the living God. And Jesus answered and said to him, "Blessed are you, Simon Barjona, because flesh and blood did not reveal *this* to you, but My Father who is in heaven" (Mat. 16:16-17). No human can reveal this but God alone. What did He do? He died for our sins according to the Scriptures and was raised on the third day according to the Scriptures.[58] What Scriptures? They (the disciples and

υἱὸς τοῦ θεοῦ. To miss this is to miss Who He is by definition, biblical inerrant definition.

[55] 1 John 5:13 Ταῦτα ἔγραψα ὑμῖν ἵνα εἰδῆτε ὅτι ζωὴν ἔχετε αἰώνιον, **τοῖς πιστεύουσιν εἰς τὸ ὄνομα τοῦ υἱοῦ τοῦ θεοῦ**. All this was written that they may know they have eternal life. It was written especially about Him. This has nothing to do with what we do. This totally negates any form of lordship salvation, for by believing this you are saying and believing He is LORD=Jehovah. Note the construction τοῖς πιστεύουσιν εἰς τὸ ὄνομα τοῦ υἱοῦ τοῦ θεοῦ. Note what one is to truly trust/believe in. He is to believe in the name/Person of the Son of the God. Note the double articulation. This is definitely noting the identity of the very Son of God=Jehovah. He is LORD that is the confession of the true believer. One does not make Him LORD of anything for salvation i.e. eternal redemption.

[56] Matthew 4:3 καὶ προσελθὼν ὁ πειράζων εἶπεν αὐτῷ· εἰ υἱὸς εἶ τοῦ θεοῦ, εἰπὲ ἵνα οἱ λίθοι οὗτοι ἄρτοι γένωνται. Note this is a first class conditional statement. Since you are the Son of the God.

[57] Mark 3:11 καὶ τὰ πνεύματα τὰ ἀκάθαρτα, ὅταν αὐτὸν ἐθεώρουν, προσέπιπτον αὐτῷ καὶ ἔκραζον λέγοντες ὅτι σὺ εἶ ὁ υἱὸς τοῦ θεοῦ. You are the Son of the God.

[58] "Now I make known to you, brethren, the gospel which I preached to you, which also you received, in which also you stand, 2 by which also you are saved, if you hold fast the word which I preached to you, unless you believed in vain. 3 For I delivered

apostles) had the Old Testament Text[59] only. The disciples also had Christ's very last words at the last supper. He was making it very clear that it was His literal body and His literal blood that was being given for them. His literal body and blood was being connected fully to the new covenant. [60]

By taking and eating the bread they were participating in His body being given for them. In the same way when they drank from the cup, they were participating in His blood of the new covenant.[61] When they all drank at that moment, they were acknowledging this was for them. Christ made it clear this was for them. The Text obviously indicates they were not all believers. The elements (bread and wine) of His body and blood were not salvific in themselves. The bread (His body) being given for them was understood as substitution. His blood (the wine) was also for them and was directly connected to the forgiveness of sin/s of the new covenant. All these connections in the context are explicitly undeniable and inseparable.[62] This is virtually impossible by Christ's very words to and with His disciples.

There was nothing to contradict their normative understanding of the elements or to separate them from the forgiveness of sins in the new covenant. The only way this can be altered is by contradicting inerrant Text. Again, there was nothing to contradict this or to separate any of this. His blood, the new covenant, and forgiveness of sins are inseparably linked. There were no other writings at this time which would refute any of this in any sense. The new covenant was established or cut by Christ Himself at the cross. There was no

---

to you as of first importance what I also received, that Christ died for our sins according to the Scriptures, 4 and that He was buried, and that He was raised on the third day according to the Scriptures" (1Co 15:1-4).

[59] The Old Testament Text here refers to the Hebrew Scriptures and most likely the LXX. There were no other writings as yet to add to God's inerrant word.

[60] There were no other Scriptual writings as yet which could modify anything. The disciples had the inerrant Hebrew Text and the very words of Christ Jesus.

[61] It must be remembered nothing was in effect as yet, but it would be shortly.

[62] All these direct connections i.e. His blood, the new covenant, the forgiveness of sin in context are irrefutable, they cannot be separated.

becoming operative for His disciples especially completed and *eternal* forgiveness of sins by means od of the new covenant. His disciples would shortly unde. d this as they would not go back to the temple for cleansing or atonement.

There is no such teaching as inaugurating or ratifying the new covenant by Christ's death and blood and not being put into full operation at the very moment of Christ's last breath. His body, His blood, new covenant forgiveness of sin became fully efficacious for them and the many at His death. The new covenant fully replaces Levitical or Mosaic law (the Mosaic covenant). The new covenant was put into full operation at the death of the Testator, the Lord Jesus Christ (Heb. 9:15-17).

The disciples understood very simply His literal body was applied and given for/to them. Christ's very literal blood was applied and given for/to them. The new covenant forgiveness was applied and given for/to them. There is absolutely nothing which can violate what Christ had taught them at the last supper. As the disciples may not have fully understood this especially at the last supper, they would understand very shortly after His resurrection.

Is there any fulfillment of the new covenant by the twelve?

Christ as the Son of God and the Son of man was cutting the new covenant with the house of Israel and no one else. At the last supper there was only the twelve; the whole house of Israel did not need to be there. In fact, the twelve were not even needed. It must be remembered the original covenant was made with Abraham when he was still in Ur of the Chaldeans (Gen 11:31). "It is you who are the sons of the prophets, and of the covenant which God made with your fathers, saying to Abraham, 'And in your seed all the families of the earth shall be blessed" (Acts 3:25). When God made this a blood covenant with Abraham, He made sure Abraham was a non-responsive recipient. When Christ made or cut the new covenant with Israel, they were truly a non-responsive recipient. They are the ones who rejected Him, and they had no idea what was happening. "But Jesus was saying, "Father, forgive them; for they do not know what they are doing" (Luke 34:34). Very few understood what they were doing or what He was doing. Even the apostles did not realize immediately the magnitude of all that was transacted at the cross. Only God could make this unilateral, unconditional, eternal covenant, and He did this by the Eternal Son and by means of His precious blood. The entire Text boldly confirms this.

The new covenant can only be fulfilled or completed by God Himself. "For finding fault with them, He says, "Behold, days are coming, says the Lord, When I will effect[63] a new covenant with the house of Israel and with the house of Judah" (Heb 8:8). The word 'effect' in this verse is to finish, accomplish, or complete. Again, the Lord did not need the house of Israel present or responsive when He made this covenant with them, for this covenant is truly unilateral which means it depends exclusively on God not Israel. Only God can fulfill eternal, unconditional, unilateral covenants. This covenant can only be fulfilled by God with the house of Israel and the house of Judah. The church is neither of these.

The Eternal Son was claiming this covenant as quite literally His last will and testament. This is a blood covenant and only the perfect sinless blood of the Son of man could do this. These are Christ's very words to His disciples; it is His blood of the new covenant. As they did not understand all that was happening at that time, they understood that His blood was with reference to the new covenant and the forgiveness of sin

---

[63] "For finding fault with them, He says, "Behold, days are coming, says the Lord, When I will **effect** a new covenant With the house of Israel and with the house of Judah" (Heb. 8:8). εμφόμενος γὰρ αὐτοὺς λέγει· ἰδοὺ ἡμέραι ἔρχονται, λέγει κύριος, καὶ **συντελέσω** ἐπὶ τὸν οἶκον Ἰσραὴλ καὶ ἐπὶ τὸν οἶκον Ἰούδα διαθήκην καινήν, Note the change of words here to finish or complete. [UBS] **συντελέω** end, complete, finish; establish, make (a covenant); carry out, bring about (Ro 9.28) [LS] **συντελέω** συν-τελέω, f. έσω, *to bring quite to an end, complete,*

provided by the new covenant. They would very shortly become ministers of the new covenant.[64]

The covenant is unconditional and does not depend on the kingdom, a kingdom, any aspect of a kingdom, a taste of a kingdom, Israel making some promise, Christ making it at the second coming, etc., etc., or any of these rather odd notions. All these additions and other rather strange teachings make this covenant a conditional covenant.[65]

It seems many believe the church (the church age in some form) existed at the last supper as if the church is the primary recipient, beneficiary, holder, patron, etc., of the new covenant. The fact is the church did not exist at this time, so no one in the church (church age) could fulfill any covenants. The church is not able to fulfill any covenants of any kind. Even partial fulfillments become rather twisted. The church simply did not exist yet and there are no covenants with the church anyway. The church or church age fulfills nothing with covenants. This is not possible for there is no covenant that God made with the church.

Every now and then a statement comes along where some group or someone in the church believes they are fulfilling one of Israel's eternal covenants (or some aspect of the covenants). This is rather foolish to begin with as only the six direct recipients of the eternal covenants can fulfill them.[66]

---

[64] To deny this is to deny what they would be ministering and what they were told. Note well the next section.

[65] While there are good men who place conditions on the unconditional covenants with Israel, as some may not mean to, they are making the unconditional covenants conditional. One should be very wary when one reads, sees, understands etc. some condition being placed on an unconditional covenant. This is in violation of the true nature of the unconditional covenants Jehovah Himself has graciously made with Abraham, Isaac, Jacob, Israel, David, and Christ Himself. Only they can fulfill the eternal, unilateral, unconditional covenants i.e. the Abrahamic, the land, the Davidic, and the new covenants.

[66] The eternal, unconditional, unilateral covenants are only with six direct recipients i.e. Abraham, Isaac, Jacob, Israel, David, and Christ Himself. The One fulfilling these covenants is God Himself and with the direct recipients of the covenants. No one else can fulfill God's covenanted program. God proved Himself over and over again as Israel's covenant keeping LORD.

These recipients are Abraham, Isaac, Jacob, Israel, David, and Christ. Yet it is true there are gracious blessings from the covenants which may come to many. Yet these are gracious blessings not fulfillments of God's covenants with Israel.

For example a man makes a will and bequeaths ten dollars to be given by a bank every time any person enters the bank. He dies and the will goes into effect immediately. Only the bank carrying out the will as directed by the deceased is fulfilling the will or contract. Any person going into the bank and gets the ten dollars is fulfilling nothing in the will or covenant. The bank alone is fulfilling the contract or will that was made with the deceased.   Neither the deceased is fulfilling the will, nor is the one getting the ten dollars fulfilling the will in any aspect. The one getting the ten dollars is fulfilling nothing. The contract is not with him. He may even refuse the ten dollars, and even by taking the ten dollars he is not fulfilling anything, yet he is getting a blessing. The blessing is only available because the bank is fulfilling the contract with the deceased.[67]

God has extended great and gracious blessings through the Abrahamic covenant. Yet only God can fulfill that which He has covenanted with Abraham. God said through the Abrahamic covenant He would bless in several ways, yet those who are blessed or cursed are fulfilling nothing. Only God and God alone can fulfill His unconditional, unilateral, eternal covenants.

He did make these covenants and confirm them with Abraham, Isaac, Jacob, Israel, David, and Christ Himself. Only God can literally fulfill the eternal, unilateral, unconditional covenants. He is the Supreme Fulfiller, and only He can carry this out. To downplay any of this is to violate what Israel's covenant making and keeping God has done with this created nation. Only in national Israel can and will these covenants be

---

[67] God will one day prove to Abraham, Isaac, Jacob, David, Israel, and Messiah, He has completely fulfilled His covenants with them and no one else. He is the covenant keeping LORD.

fulfilled. God will carry out and fulfill what He covenanted with His covenanted people. The new covenant cut by Jesus at the cross makes the new covenant truly unilateral, truly unconditional, and truly eternal. To miss this is to miss the greatest blessing/s of Israel's covenant keeping Creator (Jer. 43:1, 15).[68] Salvation is of the Jews!! And this is spoken by the Greatest One of all. Eternal redemption was covenanted with Israel's covenant keeping LORD and Savior.

Does this mean the disciples were fulfilling the new covenant? Were the disciples fulfilling the new covenant in any possible way? This is not possible. Can they receive blessing/s from the new covenant? They surely can for they are of the house of Israel, all twelve of them. Eternal redemption was now available through the blood of the new covenant. So why are the disciples (who obviously have blessing from the new covenant) not fulfilling the new covenant in any way? This is easy. These are only twelve from the house of Israel. They themselves are not national Israel. This covenant can only be fulfilled in Israel as a nation. This covenant has to be fully operational i.e. literally in effect for the regeneration of national Israel, and it most certainly was. This is why the disciples were asking Him, saying, "Lord, is it at this time You are restoring the kingdom to Israel?" (Acts 1:6). They could not have asked

---

[68] " But now, thus says the LORD, your Creator, O Jacob, And He who formed you, O Israel, "Do not fear, for I have redeemed you; I have called you by name; you are Mine! (Isa 43:1). "I am the LORD, your Holy One, The Creator of Israel, your King." (Isa 43:15). God personally and sovereignly created this nation. The seed lines of Israel were preserved especially to their Messiah. "Neither are they all children because they are Abraham's descendants, but: "through Isaac your descendants will be named." [8] That is, it is not the children of the flesh who are children of God, but the children of the promise are regarded as descendants. [9] For this is a word of promise: "At this time I will come, and Sarah shall have a son." [10] And not only this, but there was Rebekah also, when she had conceived *twins* by one man, our father Isaac; [11] for though *the twins* were not yet born, and had not done anything good or bad, in order that God's purpose cording to *His* choice might stand, not because of works, but because of Him who calls, [12] it was said to her, "The older will serve the younger." [13] Just as it is written, "Jacob I loved, but Esau I hated." [14] What shall we say then? There is no injustice with God, is there? May it never be!" (Rom. 9:8-14).

this unless they knew the Levitical law had been replaced by the new covenant. But, the blessing of eternal redemption is now available as blessing.

The greatest blessing from the new covenant is a completed redemption and that with the nation Israel (the house of Israel and the house of Judah).[69]   God makes this very clear to this nation. "And they shall not teach again, each man his neighbor and each man his brother, saying, 'Know the LORD,' for they shall all know Me, from the least of them to the greatest of them," declares the LORD, "for I will forgive their iniquity, and their sin I will remember no more" (Jer 31:34). Israel will one day accept what God has done for them in their Messiah. One day there will be a regeneration of Israel.

The new covenant made by God with Israel has to be in place and fully operational as a cause for the effect. Some commentators seem to have this reversed. This is why there was and can be a genuine re-offer of the kingdom to Israel as a nation. Several commentators hold there is a re-offer of the kingdom in Acts or even a perpetual offer of the kingdom to Israel. For this to happen, Christ has to be mediating this covenant from heaven, from the true tabernacle, which He is. One day this covenant will be carried out by Christ and fulfilled with the nation Israel. Only God can fulfill this covenant then. Up to then, Christ is mediating this covenant. There will be much more information on this exact area as verses in Hebrews will be examined.

Showing fulfillment/s with the covenants

It is important to draw attention concerning certain fulfillments of God's eternal covenants. The Abrahamic covenant is critical as it is unilateral, eternal, and unconditional. One of the most important aspects of this covenant was the

---

[69] Note this shows both sister nations brought back together. The church or any other group was *ever* called the house of Israel and the house of Judah.

land. God promised Abraham a land forever.[70] "And the LORD appeared to Abram and said, "To your descendants I will give this **land.**" So he built an altar there to the LORD who had appeared to him" (Gen 12:7). "**For all the land which you see, I will give it to you and to your descendants forever**" (Gen 13:15). "He has remembered His covenant forever, The word which He commanded to a thousand generations, [9] *The covenant* which He made with Abraham, And His oath to Isaac. [10] Then He confirmed it to Jacob for a statute, To Israel as an

[70]There are so many vss confirming the covenanted land forever. "Now the LORD said to Abram, "Go forth from your country, And from your relatives And from your father's house, To the **land** which I will show you" (Gen 12:1). "And the LORD appeared to Abram and said, "To your descendants I will give this **land.**" So he built an altar there to the LORD who had appeared to him" (Gen 12:7). "**For all the land which you see, I will give it to you and to your descendants forever**" (Gen 13:15). "Then he believed in the LORD; and He reckoned it to him as righteousness. [7] And He said to him, "I am the LORD who brought you out of Ur of the Chaldeans, to give you this **land** to possess it" (Gen 15:6-7). "And he said, "O Lord God, how may I know that I shall possess it?" (Gen 15:8). God now makes this a blood covenant. Abraham would know this well, but he took a nap. God alone cut the covenant. "On that day the LORD made a covenant with Abram, saying, "To your descendants I have given this **land,** From the river of Egypt as far as the great river, the river Euphrates: [19] the Kenite and the Kenizzite and the Kadmonite [20] and the Hittite and the Perizzite and the Rephaim [21] and the Amorite and the Canaanite and the Girgashite and the Jebusite" (Gen 15:18-21). "And I will establish My covenant between Me and you and your descendants after you throughout their generations for an everlasting covenant, to be God to you and to your descendants after you. [8] "**And I will give to you and to your descendants after you, the land of your sojournings, all the land of Canaan, for an everlasting possession; and I will be their God**" (Gen 17:7-8). "Sojourn in this **land** and I will be with you and bless you, for to you and to your descendants **I will give all these lands,** and **I will establish the oath which I swore to your father Abraham.** [4] "And I will multiply your descendants as the stars of heaven, and **will give your descendants all these lands;** and by your descendants all the nations of the earth shall be blessed" (Gen 26:3-4). "May He also give you the blessing of Abraham, to you and to your descendants with you; **that you may possess the land of your sojournings, which God gave to Abraham**" (Gen 28:4). "And Joseph said to his brothers, "I am about to die, but God will surely take care of you, and bring you up from **this land to the land which He promised on oath to Abraham, to Isaac and to Jacob**" (Gen 50:24). "And I appeared to Abraham, Isaac, and Jacob, as God Almighty, but *by* My name, LORD, I did not make Myself known to them. [4] "And I also established My covenant with them, **to give them the land of Canaan, the land in which they sojourned**" (Exo 6:3). There are many more verses than these presented. The student can easily check for all the verses confirming the land covenanted to Israel forever.

everlasting covenant, [11] Saying, **"To you I will give the land of Canaan As the portion of your inheritance"** (Psalm 105:8-11). Note that Abraham, Isaac, Jacob, and Israel were promised the land forever and only God can fulfill this covenant with them. These patriarchs plus Israel as a nation must possess the land forever to complete the fulfillment of this covenant. Their Lord God will do exactly what He covenanted with them in every detail. Not one jot or tittle will be violated.

There are parts of the Abrahamic covenant which some believe are fulfilled now or partially fulfilled or perhaps are being fulfilled. One has to approach God's Word very carefully to see if this is indeed correct. "Now the LORD said to Abram, "Go forth from your country, And from your relatives And from your father's house, To the land which I will show you; [2] And I will make you a great nation, And I will bless you, And make your name great; And so you shall be a blessing; [3] And I will bless those who bless you, And the one who curses you I will curse. And in you all the families of the earth shall be blessed" (Gen 12:1-3). Note everything begins with the land. The land is really the key issue for this promised land will be given to Abraham and his descendants **forever**. This has not been fulfilled. God has made Israel a great nation in a sense, yet Israel has had a rather checkered history i.e. idolatry, exile/s, rejection of Messiah, etc.. Yet in the future God will dwell among them as their God and Savior. Then they truly will be great. God promised to bless Abraham. God has done this, but the greatest blessing will come when Abraham will be in his land forever as covenanted. So is this completely fulfilled? Abraham has been a blessing but not to all.

This covenant began immediately when God spoke, for it was unconditional. This covenant did not depend on the obedience of Abraham in any sense. "And I will bless those who bless you, And the one who curses you I will curse" (Gen. 12:3). Did God bless those who blessed Abraham? Yes, He surely did and still does. Did God curse those who cursed Abraham? Yes, He did and still does. Is his part of the

covenant fulfilled? No, and it won't be until Abraham is in the
land forever. Genesis 12:1-3 was called a covenant in Acts
3:25. "It is you who are the sons of the prophets, and of the
covenant which God made with your fathers, saying to
Abraham, 'And in your seed all the families of the earth shall be
blessed" (Acts 3:25).[71] The context of this verse is Peter
preaching to Israel to repent (change their mind) about the
Christ. Peter was allowed to heal a certain man who had been
lame from his mother's womb. People took note of this and
wondered what happened.

> "Peter replied "Men of Israel, why do you marvel
> at this, or why do you gaze at us, as if by our own
> power or piety we had made him walk? [13] "The
> God of Abraham, Isaac, and Jacob, the God of our
> fathers, has glorified His servant Jesus, *the one*
> whom you delivered up, and disowned in the
> presence of Pilate, when he had decided to release
> Him. [14] "But you disowned the Holy and Righteous
> One, and asked for a murderer to be granted to you,
> [15] but put to death the Prince of life, *the one* whom
> God raised from the dead, *a fact* to which we are
> witnesses" (Acts 3:12-15). "Repent therefore and
> return, that your sins may be wiped away, in order
> that times of refreshing may come from the
> presence of the Lord; [20] and that He may send Jesus,
> the Christ appointed for you, [21] whom heaven must
> receive until *the* period of restoration of all things
> about which God spoke by the mouth of His holy
> prophets from ancient time. [22] "Moses said, 'The

---

[71] **Acts 3:25** "It is you who are the sons of the prophets, and of the covenant which
God made with your fathers, saying to Abraham, 'And in your seed **all the families
of the earth shall be blessed.**' ὑμεῖς ἐστε οἱ υἱοὶ τῶν προφητῶν καὶ τῆς διαθήκης ἧς
διέθετο ὁ θεὸς πρὸς τοὺς πατέρας ὑμῶν λέγων πρὸς Ἀβραάμ· καὶ ἐν τῷ σπέρματί σου
[ἐν]ευλογηθήσονται πᾶσαι αἱ πατριαὶ τῆς γῆς. **Are all the families of the earth
blessed at this time? Have all the families of the earth been blessed at this time?**

Lord God shall raise up for you a prophet like me from your brethren; to Him you shall give heed in everything He says to you. [23] 'And it shall be that every soul that does not heed that prophet shall be utterly destroyed from among the people.' [24] "And likewise, all the prophets who have spoken, from Samuel and *his* successors onward, also announced these days. [25] **"It is you who are the sons of the prophets, and of the covenant which God made with your fathers, saying to Abraham, 'And in your seed all the families of the earth shall be blessed.'** [26] "For you first, God raised up His Servant, and sent Him to bless you by turning every one *of you* from your wicked ways" (Acts 3:19-26).

Note well the context and Peter's use of Gen 12:3 in Acts 3:25. Israel is being rebuked as a nation for not receiving the blessing of the seed of Abraham. Can this be any kind of fulfillment? Peter is speaking to those in Israel. Is this a fulfillment of any kind? Observe 3:25 "For you first, God raised up His Servant, and sent Him to bless you by turning every one *of you* from your wicked ways.' This isn't even fulfilled in Israel. All the families of the earth are to be blessed. It does not seem many families of the earth are very interested. While some in Israel have received blessing, how can one assume all the families in Israel have received blessing in his seed? It would be hard to prove that there is a completed fulfillment in and with the Abrahamic covenant in any way. There are no partial fulfillments.

The Davidic covenant promised David and his seed an eternal throne and kingdom. "When your days are complete and you lie down with your fathers, I will raise up your descendant after you, who will come forth from you, and I will establish his kingdom. [13] "He shall build a house for My name, and **I will establish the throne of his kingdom forever**. [14] "I will be a father to him and he will be a son to Me; when he commits iniquity, I will correct him with the rod of men and the strokes of the sons of men, [15] but My lovingkindness shall not depart from him, as I took *it* away from Saul, whom I removed from before you. [16] "And **your house and your kingdom shall endure before Me forever; your throne shall be established forever**" (2 Sam. 7:12-16).

The Davidic covenant established Israel's throne and kingdom forever. The new covenant promised Israel eternal redemption. "And they shall not teach again, each man his neighbor and each man his brother, saying, 'Know the LORD,' for they shall all know Me, from the least of them to the greatest of them," declares the LORD, "**for I will forgive their iniquity, and their sin I will remember no more**" (Jer 31:34). "And not through the blood of goats and calves, but through His own blood, He entered the holy place once for all, **having obtained eternal redemption**" (Heb 9:12). "And for this reason He is the mediator of a new covenant, in order that since a death has taken place for the redemption of the transgressions that were *committed* under the first covenant, **those who have been called may receive the promise of the eternal inheritance**" (Heb 9:15).

- The Abrahamic covenant covenanted a land forever
- The land covenant covenanted the tenure of the land forever
- The Davidic covenant covenanted a throne and kingdom forever
- The new covenant covenanted eternal redemption

God will fulfill the Abrahamic covenant when Abraham, Isaac, Jacob, and Israel are in their land forever. God will fulfill the Davidic covenant with David when David's true Seed and Heir Apparent to David's literal throne is ruling from David's covenanted literal throne forever in the covenanted land forever in the covenanted kingdom forever. The new covenant will be fulfilled by God with Israel when Israel as a nation is in their covenanted land with their covenanted King forever on His covenanted throne forever, enjoying and being blessed by their covenanted eternal redemption as a nation forever. Until then, none of these covenants are being fulfilled by God. Again, there is no kingdom and throne as defined by these covenants at the present time. Any taste of a kingdom now is simply a conjured-up thought.

If the church is in the kingdom, or the church is a taste of the kingdom, or there is a form of the kingdom already, it would be hard to prove with Jesus' view of the church. Note well the seven churches of Revelation. This was given almost 2,000 years ago, so maybe things have improved? "But I have *this* against you, that you have left your first love. 'Remember therefore from where you have fallen, and repent and do the deeds you did at first; or else I am coming to you, and will remove your lamp stand out of its place-- unless you repent" (Rev 2:4-5). Was this church the taste of the kingdom? Smyrna was basically the martyred church and in abject poverty. Is this the taste? What about Pergamum? "But I have a few things against you, because you have there some who hold the teaching of Balaam, who kept teaching Balak to put a stumbling block before the sons of Israel, to eat things sacrificed to idols, and to commit *acts of* immorality" (Rev. 2:14). Or Thyatira "But I have *this* against you, that you tolerate the woman Jezebel, who calls herself a prophetess, and she teaches and leads My bond-servants astray, so that they commit *acts of* immorality and eat things sacrificed to idols" (Rev. 2:20). "And to the angel of the church in Sardis write: He who has the seven Spirits of God, and the seven stars, says this: 'I know your deeds, that you have a name that you are alive, but you are dead" (Rev 3:1). Or Laodicea "So because you are lukewarm, and neither hot nor cold, I will spit you out of My mouth" (Rev 3:16). Spit you out of my mouth is really ready to vomit. So which church represents a taste of the kingdom? Christ's view of the church does not augur for a better church 2,000 years later. To even hint there is a form of the kingdom already, one certainly could not prove this by Christ's words and critique of His church. There is no way the church is any form of the kingdom, and thank God it is not! Until Israel as a nation is in their covenanted land under their covenanted King on His covenanted throne, there is no kingdom whatsoever! But, this is His kingdom we are to pray for and seek (Mat. 6:10, 33).[72] Until then there is no kingdom, no one is building this kingdom, and no one is able to build this kingdom. This is the kingdom to be prayed for,[73] there is no

[72] Matthew 6:10 'Thy kingdom come. Thy will be done, On earth as it is in heaven" ἐλθέτω ἡ βασιλεία σου· γενηθήτω τὸ θέλημά σου, ὡς ἐν οὐρανῷ καὶ ἐπὶ γῆς· Matthew 6:33 "But seek first His kingdom and His righteousness; and all these things shall be added to you" ζητεῖτε δὲ πρῶτον τὴν βασιλείαν [τοῦ θεοῦ] καὶ τὴν δικαιοσύνην αὐτοῦ, καὶ ταῦτα πάντα προστεθήσεται ὑμῖν. Very strange how so many believe they are in the kingdom or are building the kingdom or have some aspect of His kingdom now, etc.etc.. When in fact we are to seek this kingdom earnestly and pray for it to come. The prayer without acknowledging a coming kingdom rather contracts what was taught by Christ Himself. Also, by seeking this kingdom first is acknowledgment of the priorities set by Christ Himself. He is saying this is so vital, seek this for this is God's will i.e. His coming kingdom. When His kingdom comes His will will be done on earth!

[73] "Pray, then, in this way: 'Our Father who art in heaven, Hallowed be Thy name. 'Thy kingdom come. Thy will be done, On earth as it is in heaven. 'Give us this day our daily bread. 'And forgive us our debts, as we also have forgiven our debtors. 'And do not lead us into temptation, but deliver us from evil" (Mat. 6:9-13). οὕτως οὖν προσεύχεσθε ὑμεῖς· Πάτερ ἡμῶν ὁ ἐν τοῖς οὐρανοῖς· ἁγιασθήτω τὸ ὄνομά σου· ἐλθέτω ἡ βασιλεία σου· γενηθήτω τὸ θέλημά σου, ὡς ἐν οὐρανῷ καὶ ἐπὶ γῆς· τὸν ἄρτον ἡμῶν τὸν ἐπιούσιον δὸς ἡμῖν σήμερον· καὶ ἄφες ἡμῖν τὰ ὀφειλήματα ἡμῶν, ὡς καὶ ἡμεῖς ἀφήκαμεν τοῖς ὀφειλέταις ἡμῶν· καὶ μὴ εἰσενέγκῃς ἡμᾶς εἰς πειρασμόν, ἀλλὰ ῥῦσαι ἡμᾶς ἀπὸ τοῦ πονηροῦ. Matthew 6:10 'Thy kingdom come. Thy will be done, On earth as it is in heaven. ἐλθέτω ἡ βασιλεία σου· γενηθήτω τὸ θέλημά σου, ὡς ἐν οὐρανῷ καὶ ἐπὶ γῆς· Note this is Your kingdom and all the imperative/s in this prayer, yet it starts with a jussive as 3rd person command calling on God to bring glory to Himself and let the kingdom come or Lord bring in that kingdom. Oh Lord bring in Your kingdom. This is the real thrust of this prayer. Then His will, will be done!! A prayer without praying for His kingdom is really not prayer. Christ taught to pray for His covenanted kingdom. There is no kingdom at this time, at least the covenanted kingdom referred to here. The believer has been transferred from the kingdom of darkness to the kingdom of light, this is true, but this is not the kingdom which is to be sought by all men. "But seek first His kingdom and His righteousness; and all these things shall be added to you" (Mat 6:33). "The desire for God's kingdom—Your kingdom come—is based on the assurance that God will fulfill all His covenant promises to His people." Barbieri, L. A., & Jr. (1985). Matthew. In J. F. Walvoord & R. B. Zuck (Eds.), *The Bible Knowledge Commentary: An Exposition of*

taste of this kingdom now, and there is no 'already' part of this covenanted kingdom now.

These literal covenants can only be fulfilled by, in and with Abraham, Isaac, Jacob, Israel, David, and Christ in the land.

"For the promise to Abraham or to his descendants that he would be heir of the world was not through the Law, but through the righteousness of faith" (Rom 4:13). "The Jews also considered the Mosaic Law, a special revelation of God's standards for human conduct, as the basis for their special standing before God. Therefore Paul turned next to it, declaring, **It was not through Law** ("not" is emphasized by its position at the beginning of the Gr. sentence) **that Abraham and his offspring** (lit., "seed") **received the promise that he would be heir of the world.** God's promise in Genesis 12:1–3 preceded the giving of the Law by several centuries (cf. Gal. 3:17). Being "heir of the world" probably refers to "all peoples on earth" (Gen. 12:3), "all nations" (Gen. 18:18), and "all nations on earth" (Gen. 22:18), for through Abraham and his descendants all the world is blessed. He is thus their "father" and they are his heirs. These promises of blessing are given to those to whom God has imputed **righteousness**, and this, Paul added once again, is **by faith**. Believers of all ages are "Abraham's seed," for they enjoy the same spiritual blessing (justification) which he enjoyed (Gal. 3:29). (However, God has not abrogated His promises to Abraham about his physical, believing descendants, the regenerate nation Israel, inheriting the land [Gen. 15:18–21; 22:17]. These promises still stand; they will be fulfilled in the Millennium.)[74]

the Scriptures (J. F. Walvoord & R. B. Zuck, Ed.) (Mt 6:5–15). Wheaton, IL: Victor Books.
[74] Witmer, J. A. (1985). Romans. In J. F. Walvoord & R. B. Zuck (Eds.), *The Bible Knowledge Commentary: An Exposition of the Scriptures* (J. F. Walvoord & R. B. Zuck, Ed.) (Ro 4:13). Wheaton, IL: Victor Books.

Are there blessings in and from the covenants? There are many, but there are no fulfillments. All these covenants will be fulfilled in the kingdom. Is eternal redemption accomplished by the new covenant being fulfilled? No! It will be beginning with the regeneration of Israel. Are there blessings from the unilateral, eternal, unconditional covenants? Yes, there are many. Are there blessings from the new covenant? Yes, and it all began with the twelve disciples at the last supper.

Remember one thing, in the future God will show Abraham that He has fulfilled every tittle which He covenanted with Abraham. In the future God will show Isaac that He has fulfilled every tittle which He covenanted with Abraham. In the future God will show Jacob that He has fulfilled every tittle which He covenanted with Abraham. In the future God will show Israel that He has fulfilled every tittle which He covenanted with Abraham. In the future God will show Christ that He has fulfilled every tittle which He covenanted with Abraham.[75] In the future God will show David that He has fulfilled every tittle which He covenanted with David. In the future God will show Israel that He has fulfilled every tittle which He covenanted with David. In the future God will show Israel that He has fulfilled every tittle which He covenanted with Israel.

The disciples became ministers of the new covenant

"And when He had said this, He showed them both His hands and His side. The disciples therefore rejoiced when they saw the Lord. [21] Jesus therefore said to them again, "Peace *be* with you; as the Father has sent Me, I also send you." [22] And when He had said this, He breathed on them, and said to them, "Receive the Holy Spirit. [23] "If you forgive the sins of any, *their*

---

[75] "Now the promises were spoken to Abraham and to his seed. He does not say, "And to seeds," as *referring* to many, but *rather* to one, "And to your seed," that is, Christ." (Gal 3:16)

sins have been forgiven them; if you retain the *sins* of any, they have been retained" (John 20:20-23).[76]

Only God can forgive sins and the disciples understood this full well. The church did not exist at this time, and the church cannot forgive sin--only God. The disciples were to preach the precious free gift of the forgiveness of sins. This was available to all i.e. "the many." If anyone received this free gift, the disciples could declare him as forgiven. If anyone rejected the free gift of forgiveness of sins, the disciples could declare his sin was retained. Jesus' disciples were to preach the forgiveness of sins. They understood this from Christ's teaching at the last supper based exclusively by means of His precious blood of the new covenant. This was very special to them because it had application to them.

These disciples needed two very specific things to carry out the great commission. They needed the supernatural empowerment of God and a complete biblical understanding and teaching of the forgiveness of sins. If they were to preach and declare this, especially that people were forgiven, they would have to fully comprehend everything for accurately presenting the gospel.

They understood this perfectly because Christ taught this specifically to them and for them at the last supper. They understood clearly what all this was about. They knew Levitical law and they knew there was a coming new covenant. They did not question Christ at the last supper. They certainly

---

[76] The disciples understood very well that only God could forgive sin. They understood that they personally had this forgiveness by means of Christ's blood of the new covenant. They understood this ="And when He had taken a cup and given thanks, He gave *it* to them, saying, "Drink from it, all of you; for this is My blood of the covenant, which is poured out for many **for forgiveness of sins**" (Matthew 26:27-28). "And when He had taken a cup, *and* given thanks, He gave *it* to them; and they all drank from it. And He said to them, **"This is My blood of the covenant, which is poured out for many"** (Mar 14:23-24). "And in the same way *He took* the cup after they had eaten, saying, **"This cup which is poured out for you is the new covenant in My blood"** (Luke 22:20). This was being poured out for them and they understood that. Nothing has changed this. There was direct application for them from the new covenant. They became ministers of the new covenant.

did not know how or when the new covenant was to come
about, but Christ made this very clear for them.
"For this is My blood of the covenant, which is poured
out for many for forgiveness of sins" (Matthew 26:28). "And
when He had taken a cup and given thanks, He gave *it* to them,
saying, "Drink from it, all of you; for this is My blood of the
covenant, which is poured out for many for forgiveness of sins"
(Matthew 26:27-28). "And when He had taken a cup, *and*
given thanks, He gave *it* to them; and they all drank from it.
And He said to them, "This is My blood of the covenant, which
is poured out for many" (Mar 14:23-24). "And in the same way
He took the cup after they had eaten, saying, "This cup which is
poured out for you is the new covenant in My blood" (Luke
22:20).[77] This is what they knew about a completed
redemption. Christ taught them this. Christ shed His literal
blood for this. Christ shed His literal blood for the redemption
promised in the new covenant.
    Were His disciples His ministers of the new covenant?
They understood they were His ministers of the new covenant
blood for the forgiveness of sins for them and for the many.
They certainly weren't ministers of the old covenant.
    The forgiveness of sins is the completed redemption
provided by Christ by His blood of the new covenant. There

---

[77] Mat. 26:27καὶ λαβὼν ποτήριον καὶ εὐχαριστήσας ἔδωκεν αὐτοῖς λέγων· πίετε ἐξ
αὐτοῦ πάντες,[28] τοῦτο γάρ ἐστιν τὸ αἷμά μου τῆς διαθήκης τὸ περὶ πολλῶν
ἐκχυννόμενον εἰς ἄφεσιν ἁμαρτιῶν. Mark 14:23 καὶ λαβὼν ποτήριον
εὐχαριστήσας ἔδωκεν αὐτοῖς, καὶ ἔπιον ἐξ αὐτοῦ πάντες. Mk. 14:24 καὶ εἶπεν αὐτοῖς·
τοῦτό ἐστιν τὸ αἷμά μου τῆς διαθήκης τὸ ἐκχυννόμενον ὑπὲρ πολλῶν.Lu22:20 καὶ τὸ
ποτήριον ὡσαύτως μετὰ τὸ δειπνῆσαι, λέγων· τοῦτο τὸ ποτήριον = ἡ καινὴ διαθήκη
ἐν τῷ αἵματί μου τὸ ὑπὲρ ὑμῶν ἐκχυννόμενον. Note well they understood no other
truth than this cup represented the new covenant by mean of His blood and this was
for the forgiveness of sins. This forgiveness was not only for them but for the many.
Christ is stressing the forgiveness of sin provided in the new covenant. His is
literally taking on this covenant as His very own. He is the Testator of His very own
covenant and last will. As the Son of God, the Creator of the ages, He alone can do
this especially with His own blood, The new covenant is a blood covenant set in full
motion by Christ's very own literal blood.

was nothing to contradict, change, or modify any of this information. They understood full well the connection of Christ's blood with the new covenant and forgiveness of sin. To separate His blood from the new covenant for forgiveness of sin/s would be tantamount to changing the whole message of a completed redemption. All this can be easily understood by just reading the context of exactly what the disciples were taught at the last supper.

If Christ has changed or modified any of this information over the almost 50 days with them, it seems very certain that we would have something else on record. We most certainly do have to accept the fact and details which are provided by God's inerrant Word. To violate any of this seems to be just playing games with the Text.

There was no way in which the disciples were ministering the blood of Christ apart from the blood of the new covenant for forgiveness of sin. This would be a great, great stretch as it is impossible to separate Christ's blood from the new covenant. Not only would the disciples not have understood a separation, this would contradict Christ's very teaching to them and for them.

It must be remembered that Matthew, Mark, Luke and John are basically Old Testament. Until Christ dies the law is fully operational. At the death of Christ the law is replaced by the new covenant. What is important here is what Christ taught and the apostles understood. Later, with the New Testament epistles Paul will not contradict or change one tittle of any of this. In fact Paul and other New Testament writers will take this whole matter of the new covenant to a much higher level as will be noted.

Concluding observations

At the moment of Christ's death on the cross, His literal blood of the literal new covenant became fully efficacious.

Again His blood is inseparable from the blood of the new
covenant. There appears to be immediate proof of this at the
moment He breathed His last breath and then just after His
resurrection. "And Jesus cried out again with a loud voice, and
yielded up *His* spirit. And behold, the veil of the temple was
torn in two from top to bottom, and the earth shook; and the
rocks were split, and the tombs were opened; and many bodies
of the saints who had fallen asleep were raised; and coming out
of the tombs **after His resurrection** they entered the holy city
and appeared to many" (Mat 27:50-53).[78]
        The disciples did not have God's fully completed
inerrant Word. They had a complete Old Testament i.e. the
Hebrew and the LXX. So until the Text was fully complete
(both testaments) there was a need for confirmation of God's
Word and what He had declared. Christ would be raised from
the dead in three days, so the disciples and others would have
that full confirmation. His resurrection literally confirms
everything i.e. Who He is and What He did! "Paul, a bond-
servant of Christ Jesus, called *as* an apostle, set apart for the
gospel of God, which He promised beforehand through His
prophets in the holy Scriptures, concerning His Son, who was
born of a descendant of David according to the flesh, who was
declared the Son of God with power by the resurrection from
the dead, according to the Spirit of holiness, Jesus Christ our
Lord" (Rom 1:1-4). "*He* who was delivered up because of our
transgressions, and was raised because of our justification"
(Rom 4:25). Again, His resurrection verifies everything
concerning the truth of Israel's Messiah.
        The veil was torn open providing the way into the
earthly temple or tabernacle which was forbidden before His

---

[78] Matthew 27:50 ὁ δὲ Ἰησοῦς πάλιν κράξας φωνῇ μεγάλῃ ἀφῆκεν τὸ πνεῦμα. ⁵¹ Καὶ
ἰδοὺ τὸ καταπέτασμα τοῦ ναοῦ ἐσχίσθη ἀπ᾽ ἄνωθεν ἕως κάτω εἰς δύο καὶ ἡ γῆ
ἐσείσθη καὶ αἱ πέτραι ἐσχίσθησαν, ⁵² καὶ τὰ μνημεῖα ἀνεῴχθησαν καὶ πολλὰ σώματα
τῶν κεκοιμημένων ἁγίων ἠγέρθησαν, ⁵³ καὶ ἐξελθόντες ἐκ τῶν μνημείων **μετὰ τὴν
ἔγερσιν αὐτοῦ** εἰσῆλθον εἰς τὴν ἁγίαν πόλιν καὶ ἐνεφανίσθησαν πολλοῖς (Mat 27:50-
53). The Text supports 'after His resurrection'.

last breath. It was now fully open for everyone.[79] Then the rocks were split and the tombs were opened. The reaction was very clear. "Now the centurion, and those who were with him keeping guard over Jesus, when they saw the earthquake and the things that were happening, became very frightened and said, "Truly this was the Son of God! And many women were there looking on from a distance, who had followed Jesus from Galilee, ministering to Him, among whom was Mary Magdalene, *along with* Mary the mother of James and Joseph, and the mother of the sons of Zebedee" (Mat. 27:54-56). "At the time of Jesus' death, three momentous events occurred. First, **the curtain of the temple was torn in two from top to bottom**. This curtain separated the holy place from the holy of holies in the temple (Heb. 9:2–3). The fact that this occurred from top to bottom signified that God is the One who ripped the thick curtain. It was not torn from the bottom by men ripping it. God was showing that the way of access into His presence was now available for everyone, not simply the Old Testament high priest (Heb. 4:14–16; 10:19–22). Second, at Christ's death a strong earthquake occurred, splitting **rocks** (Matt. 27:51). Truly the death of Christ was a powerful, earthshaking event with repercussions affecting nature even man."[80]

While there is immediate confirmation of what was transacted on His cross, there will be much more just after His resurrection. Christ appeared to His disciples and many others for about forty days. But note the group that was raised just after His resurrection. "And behold, the veil of the temple was torn in two from top to bottom, and the earth shook; and the

---

[79] But everyone must come by faith by believing Who He is and what He did. Eternal redemption is exclusively by means of the body and the blood of Jesus Christ. His blood is now eternally that of Israel's new covenant for the forgiveness of sins. Salvation is of the Jews. By Christ's own words: "You worship that which you do not know; we worship that which we know, for salvation is from the Jews" (John 4:22).

[80] Barbieri, L. A., & Jr. (1985). Matthew. In J. F. Walvoord & R. B. Zuck (Eds.), *The Bible Knowledge Commentary: An Exposition of the Scriptures* (J. F. Walvoord & R. B. Zuck, Ed.) (Mt 27:51–53). Wheaton, IL: Victor Books.

rocks were split, and the tombs were opened; and **many bodies of the saints** who had fallen asleep were raised; and coming out of the tombs **after His resurrection they entered the holy city and appeared to many**" (Mat. 27:52-53). Many commentators overlook this group or simply do not realize the essential nature of this biblical witness. As the tombs were opened perhaps for a day or so, these saints were then raised from the dead. This is no small issue especially directly connected in context with Christ's resurrection.[81]

So what is exactly happening with this particular resurrection? Not only would these saints draw attention to their resurrection, but this event gives greater focus to Christ's resurrection. Think of all these saints going around Jerusalem and being witnesses appearing to many. The magnitude of this witness cannot be minimized. All that is said in the Text is these saints were raised from the dead, entered the city, and appeared to many. There is

---

[81] "A third event mentioned was recorded only by Matthew. **The tombs** of **many holy** (righteous) **people** (v. 52) were opened, probably at a Jerusalem cemetery. The NIV suggests that these saints were resurrected when Jesus died and then went into Jerusalem **after Jesus' resurrection**. A number of commentators agree with this view. Many others, however, say that since Christ is the firstfruits of the dead (1 Cor. 15:23), their resurrection did not occur till He was raised. In this view, the phrase "after Jesus' resurrection" goes with the words **were raised to life** and **came out of the tombs**. This is possible in the Greek, and is suggested in the KJV and the NASB. The tombs, then, **broke open** at Christ's death, probably by the earthquake, thus heralding Christ's triumph in death over sin, but the bodies were not raised till Christ was raised. These people returned to Jerusalem, (**the Holy City**) where they were recognized by friends and family. Like Lazarus (John 11:43–44), Jairus' daughter (Luke 8:52–56), and the widow of Nain's son (Luke 7:13–15), they too passed through physical death again. Or some say they may have been raised with glorified bodies like the Lord's. Walvoord suggests this event was "a fulfillment of the Feast of the Firstfruits of harvest mentioned in Leviticus 23:10–14. On that occasion, as a token of the coming harvest, the people would bring a handful of grain to the priest. The resurrection of these saints, occurring after Jesus Himself was raised, is a token of the coming harvest when all the saints will be raised" (Walvoord, *Matthew: Thy Kingdom Come*, p. 236)." Barbieri, L. A., & Jr. (1985). Matthew. In J. F. Walvoord & R. B. Zuck (Eds.), *The Bible Knowledge Commentary: An Exposition of the Scriptures* (J. F. Walvoord & R. B. Zuck, Ed.) (Mt 27:51–53). Wheaton, IL: Victor Books.

nothing else recorded. It may be these saints did not fully understand what had happened. It makes no difference. The witness of Christ's resurrection was a powerful testimony going out to many at that moment. Up to this point everything being revealed by God was continually confirmed by two or three witnesses.[82] This was a biblical principle for confirmation of biblical truth being revealed by God. Once God's Word was complete, there was no need for further revelational confirmation. (*When God's revelation was completed, there was no more need for more confirmation by these specific revelational gifts*) (1 Cor. 8:10-13).[83] It must be noted again that His resurrection boldly confirms all the truth concerning Israel's Messiah. There were many happenings at the death of Christ with His resurrection confirming and witnessing to the fact of His death and resurrection. The disciples needed this, all Jerusalem needed

---

[82] Deuteronomy 19:15 "A single witness shall not rise up against a man on account of any iniquity or any sin which he has committed; on the evidence of two or three witnesses a matter shall be confirmed. Matthew 18:16 "But if he does not listen *to you*, take one or two more with you, so that by the mouth of two or three witnesses every fact may be confirmed. 2 Corinthians 13:1 This is the third time I am coming to you. Every fact is to be confirmed by the testimony of two or three witnesses. 1 Timothy 5:19 Do not receive an accusation against an elder except on the basis of two or three witnesses. Hebrews 10:28 Anyone who has set aside the Law of Moses dies without mercy on *the testimony of* two or three witnesses.
[83] " Love never fails; but if *there are gifts of* **prophecy,** they will be done away; if *there are* **tongues,** they will cease; if *there is* **knowledge,** it will be done away. 9 For we **know** in part, and we **prophesy** in part; 10 but when the **perfect** comes, the partial will be done away" (1 Cor. 13:8-10). Ἡ ἀγάπη οὐδέποτε πίπτει· εἴτε δὲ **προφητεῖαι,** καταργηθήσονται· εἴτε **γλῶσσαι,** παύσονται· εἴτε **γνῶσις,** καταργηθήσεται. 9 ἐκ μέρους γὰρ γινώσκομεν καὶ ἐκ μέρους προφητεύομεν· 10 ὅταν δὲ ἔλθῃ **τὸ τέλειον,** τὸ ἐκ μέρους καταργηθήσεται. The gifts of prophecy, tongues, and knowledge are all revelational. They have this in common and they were 'in part'. But, when the complete comes ὅταν δὲ ἔλθῃ **τὸ τέλειον** , then the partial would be done away. These verses are still excellent verses for the truth of cessationism. For an excellent treatment of 1 Cor. 13:8-10 please refer to "A Reexamination of 1 Corinthians 13:8-13", Myron J. Houghton *BSac* 153:611 (Jul 96) p. 345*ff.*

this, and all men need this. All this confirms the fact "Truly this was the Son of God!"

Conclusion

The most important issues were raised concerning His last supper. It is impossible to divorce, separate, etc. Christ' blood of the new covenant from the forgiveness of sins of the new covenant. Christ taught this and without doubt His disciples understood this. The new covenant was not only ratified and inaugurated, but put in full operation at the death of Christ. Christ Himself cut the new covenant. At the moment of His death, His blood of the new covenant became literally efficacious for the forgiveness of sins for the disciples, even Judas. At the moment of His death, His blood of the new covenant became literally efficacious for the forgiveness of sins for the many, this means everyone. Christ taught this and made this very obvious. However, this does not at all mean that the new covenant was fulfilled in any way whatsoever, now, not yet, or partially in any other conceivable language. Fulfillment remains entirely in the future with Christ on David's throne in the covenanted land of Israel.

The fact that the offer and efficacy of Christ's atonement was available or efficacious for the many even Judas, emphatically supports and proves unlimited atonement. There is no such teaching in the Text as limited atonement. His disciples fully understood the atonement for the many. They became His ministers of the new covenant.

Chapter III

This Cup is the New Covenant
1 Cor. 11:23-26

"For I received from the Lord that which I also delivered to you, that the Lord Jesus in the night in which He was betrayed took bread; [24] and when He had given thanks, He broke it, and said, "This is My body, which is for you; do this in remembrance of Me." [25] In the same way *He took* the cup also, after supper, saying, "This cup is the new covenant in My blood; do this, as often as you drink *it*, in remembrance of Me." [26] For as often as you eat this bread and drink the cup, you proclaim the Lord's death until He comes" (1 Cor. 11:23-26).[84]

The body of Christ

Paul was given revelation from the Lord which He gave directly to the Corinthians. 'For I received from the Lord that which I also delivered to you' and 'to you' directly relates to the Corinthians. The concern here is not what Paul may have quoted from another source; his Source was the Lord Jesus Christ. Jesus was relating faultless information to Paul. Who else but Christ could tell Paul exactly what to say to the church at Corinth? As the Text is inerrant, the concern is what is

---

[84] Ἐγὼ γὰρ παρέλαβον ἀπὸ τοῦ κυρίου, ὃ καὶ παρέδωκα ὑμῖν, ὅτι ὁ κύριος Ἰησοῦς ἐν τῇ νυκτὶ ᾗ παρεδίδετο ἔλαβεν ἄρτον [24] καὶ εὐχαριστήσας ἔκλασεν καὶ εἶπεν· τοῦτό μού ἐστιν τὸ σῶμα τὸ ὑπὲρ ὑμῶν· τοῦτο ποιεῖτε εἰς τὴν ἐμὴν ἀνάμνησιν. [25] ὡσαύτως καὶ τὸ ποτήριον μετὰ τὸ δειπνῆσαι λέγων· τοῦτο τὸ ποτήριον ἡ καινὴ διαθήκη ἐστὶν ἐν τῷ ἐμῷ αἵματι· τοῦτο ποιεῖτε, ὁσάκις ἐὰν πίνητε, εἰς τὴν ἐμὴν ἀνάμνησιν. [26] ὁσάκις γὰρ ἐὰν ἐσθίητε τὸν ἄρτον τοῦτον καὶ τὸ ποτήριον πίνητε, τὸν θάνατον τοῦ κυρίου καταγγέλλετε ἄχρι οὗ ἔλθῃ.

recorded and not who quoted what and when.[85] This was direct revelation from the Lord concerning the Lord's night in which He was betrayed at the last supper.[86] The first observation is that the emphasis is on 'the night He was betrayed.' While this is known as the last supper, Christ was making clear that the emphasis is on the night He was betrayed. Actually, only one disciple betrayed Him yet this carried over to the whole issue of His being taken that night and then the crucifixion. No matter what, He is drawing attention to this exact issue in relating His last supper to the church at Corinth.

He took the bread and broke it in pieces to give the bread to them. He did not say this is my body broken for you,[87]

---

[85] One would wonder of those who argue from the dating of the Text and who quoted who when, or what was quoted by whom when, etc. etc. esp. when information is given by direct revelation from the Lord. This portion of the Text was given by the Lord directly. Is inerrancy in question? For by such methodologies there seems to be a question of Divine inspiration of the Text. If the Text is Divinely inspired there can be no error. So, such methodologies put great doubt on those who dwell therein.

[86] *I Corinthians 11:23* **For I received of the Lord** (ἐγο γαρ παρελαβον ἀπο του Κυριου [*ego gar parelabon apo tou Kuriou*]). Direct claim to revelation from the Lord Jesus on the origin of the Lord's Supper. Luke's account (Luke 22:17–20) is almost identical with this one. He could easily have read I Corinthians before he wrote his Gospel. See 15:3 for use of both παρελαβον [*parelabon*] and παρεδωκα [*paredōka*]. Note παρα [*para*] in both verbs. Paul received the account from (παρα— ἀπο [*para—apo*]) the Lord and passed it on from himself to them, a true παραδοσις [*paradosis*] (tradition) as in 11:2. **He was betrayed** (παρεδιδετο [*paredideto*]). Imperfect passive indicative (irregular form for παρεδιδοτο [*paredidoto*], Robertson, *Grammar*, p. 340). Same verb as παρεδωκα [*paredōka*] (first aorist active indicative just used for "I delivered"). Robertson, A. (1933). *Word Pictures in the New Testament* (1 Co 11:23). Nashville, TN: Broadman Press.

[87] *I Corinthians 11:24* **When he had given thanks** (εὐχαριστησας [*eucharistēsas*]). First aorist active participle of εὐχαριστεω [*eucharisteō*] from which word our word Eucharist comes, common late verb (see on 1:14). **Which is for you** (το ὑπερ ὑμων [*to huper humōn*]). Κλωμενον [*Klōmenon*] (broken) of the Textus Receptus (King James Version) is clearly not genuine. Luke (22:19) has διδομενον [*didomenon*] (given) which is the real idea here. As a matter of fact the body of Jesus was not broken (John 19:36). The bread was broken, but not the body of Jesus. **In remembrance of me** (εἰς την ἐμην ἀναμνησιν [*eis tēn emēn anamnēsin*]). The objective use of the possessive pronoun ἐμην [*emēn*]. Not my remembrance of you, but your remembrance of me. Ἀναμνησις [*Anamnēsis*], from ἀναμιμνησκω [*anamimnēskō*], to remind or to recall, is an old word, but only here in N.T. save

for His body was never broken. In fact man could not kill Him, as He made it very clear that no man could take His life.[88] As He gave the bread to each of them He clearly identified the bread as His body. 'He took bread; and when He had given thanks, He broke it, and said, this is My body, which is for you.'[89] This bread was strictly an element (not a sacrament) representing His body being given in place for them i.e. the disciples. This bread had direct application to His disciples and this was taught by Christ Himself. Did this bread representing His body have the same direct application for the church at Corinth? The context permits no other such teaching/s.

As the disciples understood full well this was His body given for them, the church at Corinth understood this was for them also. 'For as often as you eat this bread and drink the cup, you proclaim the Lord's death until He comes.' Jesus was teaching this in the Text to the church at Corinth. The context clearly reveals there is no other conclusion. This is what the Corinthians were taught by Paul, and this is what they understood. This last supper was given by direct revelation to the Corinthians. There was no other Text which would or could contradict what Jesus was revealing through His apostle Paul to the Church at Corinth.

The Church at Corinth was taught that His body was given for them (they are part of the many or all). The bread represented His body which was given for them. This creates a

Luke 22:19 which see. Robertson, A. (1933). *Word Pictures in the New Testament* (1 Co 11:24). Nashville, TN: Broadman Press.
[88] "For this reason the Father loves Me, because I lay down My life that I may take it again.""No one has taken it away from Me, but I lay it down on My own initiative. I have authority to lay it down, and I have authority to take it up again. This commandment I received from My Father" (John 10:17-18).
[89] See the appendix on 1 Cor. 11:23-26. τοῦτό μού ἐστιν τὸ σῶμα τὸ ὑπὲρ ὑμῶν. Note well the ἐστιν defining the body as His own as a predicate nominative. This may seem insignificant but note the articulations. This is my body 'that' τὸ for you ὑπὲρ ὑμῶν. This was His body represented by the bread being give with direct application to His disciples and Judas was there. Unlimited atonement is being taught in the Text.

principle and an application directly to them. "For as often as you (the Church at Corinth) eat this bread and drink the cup, you proclaim the Lord's death until He comes" (1 Cor. 11:26). They were to eat this bread proclaiming the Lord's death.

The bread=His body was for them also as it had been for His disciples. All this was given by direct revelation of the Lord. "Paul proceeded to remind the Corinthians of what they knew but had denied by their actions. Whether this teaching came to Paul directly (by a vision; cf. Gal. 1:12) or indirectly (by men; 1 Cor. 15:1), it came with the Lord's authority. The bread represented the incarnate body of Christ unselfishly assumed (Phil. 2:6–7) and unselfishly given on the cross for the benefit of others (2 Cor. 8:9; Phil. 2:8), that kept needing to be remembered (cf. 1 Cor. 4:8–13)."[90]

The blood of Christ

It was proven very clearly that the body of Christ represented by the element of bread had direct application to the church at Corinth. This second part regarding the blood of Christ was given in equal and perhaps even more clarity. There is really no issue here at all; in fact there is great clarity for the church at Corinth and for all churches in general.

By direct revelation, "In the same way *He took* the cup also, after supper, saying, "This cup is the new covenant in My blood." There is really no mystery here except by those who create one. Christ clearly says this cup is the new covenant. Each cup at the Passover (His last supper) had some special name or significance representing a certain blessing or teaching spoken directly by God to His people Israel.[91] Christ Himself

[90] Lowery, D. K. (1985). 1 Corinthians. In J. F. Walvoord & R. B. Zuck (Eds.), *The Bible Knowledge Commentary: An Exposition of the Scriptures* (J. F. Walvoord & R. B. Zuck, Ed.) (1 Co 11:23–24). Wheaton, IL: Victor Books.
[91] It is recommended to reaearch teachings on the last supper or the Passover Haggadah. There are some very excellent Messianic Passover presentations which will cover this. The cups had represented promises God spoke to His people Israel. The cup of sanctification-I will bring you out from under the burdens of the Egyptians; the cup of judgment or deliverance-I will deliver you from slavery; the

makes it very obvious 'this cup is the new covenant.' Note the construction which is similar to Luke τοῦτο τὸ ποτήριον ἡ καινὴ διαθήκη.[92] There is no verb[93] as there is in 'this is My body.'[94]

While the verb is implied which can be normal, there appears to be emphasis perhaps making this construction appositional. 'This cup is the new covenant' might be more fully represented 'this cup = the new covenant.' This would be with great design and significance for the disciples by Christ naming and defining the cup. The context not only supports this but the naming of the cup would be highly regarded as it is officially defined by the Sovereign Definer. They would always know the cup=His blood of the new covenant and absolutely nothing else. They would know that cup and no other. That is all that they would know and understand by direct revelation of God in the flesh directly to them.

As there is no verb, the representation would have been perfectly clear to His disciples by naming what the actual cup fully represented. This would be quite in line with what was taught by the bread. As the bread represented His body so the cup in itself represented the new covenant.

Note also the position of the ἐστὶν in τοῦτο τὸ ποτήριον= ἡ καινὴ διαθήκη ἐστὶν ἐν τῷ ἐμῷ αἵματι 'this cup = the new covenant **is** in My blood.' Many fail to see the significance of this. "The position of ἐστιν [estin] before ἐν τῳ αἵματι [en tōi haimati] (in my blood) makes it a secondary or additional predicate and not to be taken just with διαθηκη [diathēkē] (covenant or will)."[95] The emphasis of 'is in my

---

cup of redemption-I will redeem you with an outstretched arm; the cup of praise or restoration-I will take you to be my people, and I will be your God. The first cup is part of the Kiddush or thanksgiving. This is the cup of sanctification.
[92] See appendix on Luke.
[93] as ἐστιν
[94] τοῦτό μού **ἐστιν** τὸ σῶμα Please see appendix on 1 Cor. 11:23-26.
[95] *I Corinthians 11:25***After supper** (μετα το δειπνησαι [*meta to deipnēsai*]). Μετα [*Meta*] and the articular aorist active infinitive, "after the dining" (or the supping) as in Luke 22:20. **The new covenant** (ἡ καινη διαθηκη [*hē kainē diathēkē*]). For

blood' makes 'this cup = the new covenant **is** in or by means of My blood.' This would take this quote or truth to a whole new level or the level it should be by definition. Confirmation is being attained that the new covenant was fully established, confirmed, ratified, inaugurated, i.e. set into full operation by the blood of Christ at the cross. Other Scripture will not only confirm this but prove beyond any reason that this covenant is fully operational exclusively by Christ's infinitely efficacious blood.[96]

There is the false argument that 'for you' is not in the quote 'this cup is the new covenant in My blood' as it is 'this is My body, which is **for you**.' So some believe the application of the new covenant blood is still futuristic especially for the disciples and that is what is being quoted.[97] The fallacy with this is Jesus made it very clear it was for them, the disciples as proved earlier.

By way of reminder: "For this is My blood of the covenant, which is poured out **for many for forgiveness of sins**" (Mat 26:28). "And when He had taken a cup, *and* given thanks, He gave *it* to them; and they all drank from it. 24 And He said to them, "**This is My blood of the covenant**, which is

διαθηκη [*diathēkē*] see on Matt. 26:28. For καινος [*kainos*] see on Luke 5:38 and Luke 22:20. **The position of ἐστιν [*estin*] before ἐν τω αἱματι [*en tōi haimati*] (in my blood) makes it a secondary or additional predicate and not to be taken just with διαθηκη [*diathēkē*] (covenant or will).** As oft as ye drink it (ὁσακις ἀν πινητε [*hosakis an pinēte*]). Usual construction for general temporal clause of repetition (ἀν [*an*] and the present subjunctive with ὁσακις [*hosakis*]). So in verse 26. Robertson, A. (1933). *Word Pictures in the New Testament* (1 Co 11:25). Nashville, TN: Broadman Press.

[96] To believe Israel has to do something similar like the Mosaic covenant required, as a bilateral covenant, makes one wonder if anyone has read the Text or understands the nature of man. To believe anything else has to happen to put the new covenant into operation plays down the efficacy of the blood of Christ. The only way some see fit to do this is bifurcate Christ's blood i.e. the blood of Christ made separate from His blood of the new covenant for forgiveness of sin or final redemption. This appears to make a rather convoluted hermeneutic.

[97] This also has been discussed. This also plays down the new covenant application of forgiveness of sins to the disciples, to the Corinthians, and to the whole church by association.

poured out **for many**" (Mark 14:23-24). "And in the same way *He took* the cup after they had eaten, saying, "This cup which is poured out **for you** is the new covenant in My blood" (Luke 22:20). The quote 'for you' is in the Lukan Text and is very clear. There is no issue except for those who create them. Each gospel was emphasizing something related to the writing in context. The 'for you' is very prominent in Luke. Note Matthew said this was for many, Mark said for many, and Luke said for *you*. Does this present such a grave problem?

There is the issue of what Christ was stressing in 1 Cor. 11:25, "this cup = the new covenant **is** in My blood." The emphasis to the Corinthians was not that 'the cup or the blood of the new covenant' was not *for them* (which it obviously was), but the great truth and value of Christ's literal blood was that it accomplished the completed blood atonement of the new covenant. All this is only accomplished by means of His blood, nothing else! Christ was stressing His body for them as substitution and His blood of the new covenant for atonement.

There is power and value in His blood. The fulfilling of His covenant only with Israel will be the result of its having been operational, not the cause of it being put into operation.[98] His blood truly set the new covenant promise of eternal redemption available to the disciples and to the many (all). This includes the Corinthians. If this were not so don't you think He would have told them? Was He so cryptic in speaking and revealing these truths through Paul that they would only understand the blood of the new covenant was not for them? Would this be an enigma or a deception? It appears He is revealing great truth and exactly what He wants them to know.

Again, there is a sense of bifurcating the blood of Christ and this may come close to denying the immediate efficacy of His blood for eternal redemption only promised in the new covenant. There are teachings which seem to have this design.

---

[98] Some of these teachings seem to promote His kingdom as the cause not the new covenant prior to.

Christ's body and blood as an ordinance

There appear to be some division/s in the church (church age) as to certain ordinances or regulations.[99] As this is not the issue here, the only one being addressed is communion or celebrating the last supper. Paul was addressing the church at Corinth and the section of 1 Cor. 11:23-25 is very explicit. Paul made this very explicit: "For I received from the Lord that which I also delivered **to you**." It appears God the Holy Spirit wanted this portion very clear and understandable. As this church had many issues, they were to be very attentive to this.

Communion is set up in and by this Text to the Corinthian church as an ordinance. If they were to make proclamation of Him, His death, and His coming again (proves resurrection), they needed to understand certain things very well. With the ordinance of the last supper, the church or local church in general is making proclamation of Him, His work and His coming again.

- "This is My body, which is for you; **do this** in remembrance of Me" (1Co 11:23),
- "This cup is the new covenant in My blood; **do this**, as often as you drink *it*, in remembrance of Me" (1Co 11:23)

Note the similarities of the two statements. Both forms of 'do this' may easily be a present imperative plural. So this is more of a command in context to the last supper. All this is explained in detail exactly what everything represented. Christ made this very clear to Paul by special revelation. "Do this, as often as you drink *it*, in remembrance of Me." [26] For as often as you eat this bread and drink the cup, you proclaim[100] the Lord's death until He comes."

---

[99] Rules or regulations
[100] καταγγέλλετε verb indicative present active 2nd person plural from καταγγέλλω

This is what He wants for His church. If there were any ordinances which have direct principle and application to the church, this is it. And this would be by Divine decree. Unfortunately, the Corinthians appeared to be mocking the Lord's Supper when they gathered together as a church.[101] Paul had no praise for them in this.

The testimony of this ordinance was the proclamation of His death until He comes. If the church at Corinth was not performing the Lord's Supper properly, the proclaiming of the Lord's death until He comes would be severely flawed. If the church today is not performing the Lord's Supper properly, the proclaiming of the Lord's death until He comes is also severely flawed. The church was to minister the ordinance of the body and the blood of the new covenant. The Text is not misleading in any of this ordinance for the church.

Conclusion

The church is to celebrate or proclaim the body and blood of Christ Jesus until He comes. "And when He had given thanks, He broke it, and said, **"This is My body**, which is **for you;** do this in remembrance of Me. In the same way *He took* the cup also, after supper, saying, **"This cup is the new covenant in My blood**; **do this**, **as often as you drink** *it*, in remembrance of Me." For as often as you eat this bread and

---

[UBS] **καταγγέλλω** (aor. κατήγγειλα ; aor. pass. κατηγγέλην) proclaim, make known, preach; teach, advocate (customs)

[101] " But in giving this instruction, I do not praise you, because you come together not for the better but for the worse. [18] For, in the first place, when you come together as a church, I hear that divisions exist among you; and in part, I believe it. [19] For there must also be factions among you, in order that those who are approved may have become evident among you. [20] Therefore when you meet together, it is not to eat the Lord's Supper, [21] for in your eating each one takes his own supper first; and one is hungry and another is drunk. [22] What! Do you not have houses in which to eat and drink? Or do you despise the church of God, and shame those who have nothing? What shall I say to you? Shall I praise you? In this I will not praise you" (1Co 11:17-22).

drink the cup, you proclaim the Lord's death until He comes"
(1Cor. 11:24-26).

- The bread = His body (substitutionary atonement)
- The cup = the new covenant by His blood (eternal atonement)
- His body and blood

The bread represents His body, and the cup represents the new covenant by means of His blood. It is so clear the church partakes of the body and the blood of Jesus Christ. His body was given in substitution for the sinner. His blood is the blood of the new covenant which procures eternal redemption. The church clearly celebrates and proclaims His body and His blood of the new covenant. The church is to do this until He comes. There is no doubt.

Chapter IV

Ministers of the New Covenant
2 Cor. 3:6

"Who also made us adequate *as* servants of a new covenant, not of the letter, but of the Spirit; for the letter kills, but the Spirit gives life" (2 Cor. 3:6).[102]

Second Corinthians is a more comforting epistle compared to the first.[103] Paul had great love for the Corinthians. "You are our letter, written in our hearts, known and read by all men; being manifested that you are a letter of Christ, cared for by us, written not with ink, but with the Spirit of the living God, not on tablets of stone, but on tablets of human hearts" (2 Cor. 3:2-3).
Paul and the apostles knew that Jesus Christ would make their ministry effective. They were not sufficient of themselves. "And such confidence we have through Christ toward God. Not that we are adequate in ourselves to consider anything as *coming* from ourselves, but our adequacy is from God" (2 Cor. 3:4-5).
They were ministers of a new covenant. Their sufficiency was from God "Who also made us adequate *as* servants of a new covenant, not of the letter, but of the Spirit; for the letter kills, but the Spirit gives life" (2 Cor. 3:6). Paul was defining the nature of the ministry in contrast to ministry

---

[102] ὃς καὶ ἱκάνωσεν ἡμᾶς διακόνους καινῆς διαθήκης, οὐ γράμματος ἀλλὰ πνεύματος· τὸ γὰρ γράμμα ἀποκτέννει, τὸ δὲ πνεῦμα ζῳοποιεῖ.
[103] Paul had great love for the Corinthians. His first letter to them was quite condemnatory. The second is more comforting. Now only a small faction remains opposed to him. He is confident, however, that this small faction will come around and respond to his ministry.

under the old covenant. They were servants of the new covenant.[104]

- servants of a new covenant (the only covenant that gives life is the new covenant)
- not of the letter (the letter of the law kills)
- but of the Spirit (they ministered by God's Holy Spirit)
- for the letter kills (the Mosaic law was a ministry of death)
- but the Spirit gives life (God the Holy Spirit gives life)

Paul clarifies the difference in ministry by contrasting the two ministries. "But if the ministry of death, in letters engraved on stones, came with glory, so that the sons of Israel could not look intently at the face of Moses because of the glory of his face, fading *as* it was, how shall the ministry of the Spirit fail to be even more with glory" (2 Cor. 3:7-8). "The glory of the ministry – its message of grace... Its message was spiritual and life-giving. As the gospel of grace is energized by the Holy Spirit, it is contrasted with the law of Moses, a code written on stone. The power of the minister of the new covenant does not lie in the letter of the law, the old covenant, which convicts of sin and serves only to manifest our death, but in the Spirit of God who grants us eternal life. The old legal covenant that kills is thus 'the ministry that brought death,' 7, 'that condemns men,' 9, since it merely points out our sin. The new covenant of grace 'gives life,' 6, as a 'ministry of the Spirit,' 8, and as a 'ministry that brings righteousness,' since it also provides for

---

[104] **Who also made us sufficient for such confidence** (ὅς καὶ ἱκανωσεν ἡμᾶς [*hos kai hikanōsen hēmas*]). Late causative verb from ἱκανος [*hikanos*] (verse 5) first aorist active indicative, "who (God) rendered us fit." In N.T. only here and Col. 1:12. **As ministers of a new covenant** (διακονους καινης διαθηκης [*diakonous kainēs diathēkēs*]). Predicate accusative with ἱκανωσεν [*hikanōsen*]. For διαθηκη [*diathēkē*] see on Matt. 26:28 and for διακονος [*diakonos*] on Matt. 20:26 and for καινης [*kainēs*] (fresh and effective) on Luke 5:38. Only God can make us that. Robertson, A. (1933). *Word Pictures in the New Testament* (2 Cor. 3:6). Nashville, TN: Broadman Press.

the removal of our sin, 9. One is graven on stones, 7; the other on the human heart. One is glorious, 7; the other is much more glorious, 8–11."[105]

Paul was not ministering condemnation through the law but the righteousness which only flows from Christ's blood of the new covenant providing eternal redemption and transformation (2 Cor. 3:18).[106] This is very clear, emphatic, and in context. To say Paul was not ministering the new covenant misses the whole point of what he is discussing with the Corinthians. He is establishing the fact that his whole ministry was based on the new covenant and the righteousness which flows from it. "For if the ministry of condemnation has glory, much more does the ministry of righteousness abound in glory" (2 Cor. 3:9).

Note the dramatic contrast Paul is making between those who minister the law and those who minister the new covenant. Paul was concerned about those who were still ministering the old system, and this was what the Judaizers were doing (and many do today). Paul and the apostles had the ministry of righteousness which flows from the new covenant. Paul had this confidence and he knew he and the other apostles were servants or ministers of the new covenant:

- For if the ministry of condemnation has glory=the Law
- much more does the ministry of righteousness abound in glory=the new covenant

"Paul's **confidence** was founded not on human resources but on divine ones. He was confident in the Corinthians because the Holy **Spirit** had worked in them. Their faith rested on God's power (1 Cor. 2:1–5).

---

[105] Unger, M. F. (2005). *The new Unger's Bible handbook* (Rev. and updated ed.) (530). Chicago: Moody Publishers.
[106] " But we all, with unveiled face beholding as in a mirror the glory of the Lord, are being transformed into the same image from glory to glory, just as from the Lord, the Spirit" (2Cor. 3:18).

Likewise his own sufficiency and **competence** in the ministry was derived wholly **from God** (cf. 1 Tim. 1:12). Paul's emphasis on the **New Covenant** implies that his opponents were ministers of the Old Covenant. The Mosaic Covenant was a written revelation of the righteousness God asked of Israel (e.g., Ex. 19–23). It was accepted with an oath of obedience and a blood sacrifice (Ex. 24). When Israel proved unable and unwilling to remain faithful to that covenant, God graciously intervened and promised a New Covenant (Jer. 31:31–34; 32:40), new (*kainēs*) both in time and in quality. It was inaugurated by Christ in His sacrifice on the cross (Luke 22:20), and is entered into by faith (Phil. 3:9) and lived out in dependence on the Spirit (Rom. 7:6; 8:4). (However, the physical and national aspects of the New Covenant which pertain to Israel have not been appropriated to the church. Those are yet to be fulfilled in the Millennium. The church today shares in the soteriological aspects of that covenant, established by Christ's blood for all believers [cf. Heb. 8:7–13].) Reliance on human rather than divine authority in letters of commendation was shortsighted and dangerous (2 Cor. 3:1–3). Even more so was the attempt to fulfill God's righteousness apart from divine enablement. Those who did so found that **the letter kills** (cf. Rom. 7:10–11). But those who trust in Christ find that **the Spirit gives life** (cf. Rom. 8:2)"[107]

---

[107] Lowery, D. K. (1985). 2 Corinthians. In J. F. Walvoord & R. B. Zuck (Eds.), *The Bible Knowledge Commentary: An Exposition of the Scriptures* (J. F. Walvoord & R. B. Zuck, Ed.) (2 Co 3:4–18). Wheaton, IL: Victor Books.

Conclusion

Paul made it very clear that God made him and the apostles ministers[108] of the new covenant. What the old covenant could not do, weak as it was through the flesh, God could do through the new covenant which imparts the life-giving Spirit.

The church is also a ministry of the new covenant. The church is not a ministry of the law but of His righteousness. "God declares righteous those who believe in His Son, and then the Holy Spirit empowers the believer to live righteously. This first work of God is called justification, and the second is called sanctification."[109] The dispensation of grace or the church age is rooted in the new covenant. The church celebrates the new covenant. Praise God for His blood of the new covenant.

- "For this is **My blood of the covenant**, which is poured out for many for forgiveness of sins" (Mat 26:28).

- "And He said to them, "This is **My blood of the covenant**, which is poured out for many" (Mar 14:24).

- "And in the same way *He took* the cup after they had eaten, saying, "**This cup which is poured out for you is the new covenant in My blood**" (Luke 22:20).

- "In the same way *He took* the cup also, after supper, saying, '**This cup is the new covenant in My blood; do this**, as often as you drink *it*, in remembrance of Me' (1 Cor. 11:25).

Again, praise God for His blood of the new covenant. The church's ministry stems completely from the new covenant.

---

[108] His ministry was based on the new covenant as was his salvation.

[109] The Nelson Study Bible, Nelson Ministry Services Special Edition, Thomas Nelson Publishers, Nashville, 1997, p.1948.

Chapter V

Change of Priesthood and Law
Heb. 7:12

"For when the priesthood is changed,[110] of necessity there takes place a change of law also" (Hebrews 7:12).[111]

The Lord promised a final 'forever' priesthood. "The LORD has sworn and will not change His mind, "Thou art a priest forever According to the order of Melchizedek" (Psalm 110:4). "In the simplest manner, the author argued for the imperfection of **the Levitical priesthood** on the basis of God's promise (recorded in Ps. 110:4) that a new Priest would arise belonging to an order other than Aaron's. Since there was **a change of the priesthood**, it follows that the whole legal system on which the Levitical institutions were predicated also had to be changed. Here the writer virtually affirmed the Pauline truth that "you are not under Law" (Rom. 6:14), though he approached it from a different angle."[112]

It was impossible for Israel to have a change in the priesthood under the Mosaic or the Levitical law. 'To change

---

[110] The priesthood being changed (μετατιθεμενης της ἱεροσυνης [*metatithemenēs tēs hierosunēs*]). Genitive absolute with present passive participle of μετατιθημι [*metatithēmi*], old word to transfer (Gal. 1:6). A change (μεταθεσις [*metathesis*]). Old substantive from μετατιθημι [*metatithēmi*]. In N.T. only in Heb. (7:12; 11:5; 12:27). God's choice of another kind of priesthood for his Son, left the Levitical line off to one side, forever discounted, passed by "the order of Aaron" (την ταξιν Ἀαρων [*tēn taxin Aarōn*]). Robertson, A. (1933). *Word Pictures in the New Testament* (Heb 7:12). Nashville, TN: Broadman Press.
[111] μετατιθεμένης γὰρ τῆς ἱερωσύνης ἐξ ἀνάγκης καὶ νόμου μετάθεσις γίνεται (Heb. 7:12)
[112] Hodges, Z. C. (1985). Hebrews. In J. F. Walvoord & R. B. Zuck (Eds.), *The Bible Knowledge Commentary: An Exposition of the Scriptures* (J. F. Walvoord & R. B. Zuck, Ed.) (Heb 7:11–14). Wheaton, IL: Victor Books.

the priesthood' was asking Israel to abandon the priesthood which was required by the Law. The emphasis here is on the priesthood being changed. If the priesthood is/was changed (which was impossible under Law), then there was only one conclusion, the Law was changed.

The word 'changed'

"For when the priesthood is *changed*, of necessity there takes place a change of law also" (Heb 7:12). There is an issue with the word changed 'for when the priesthood is *changed*'[113] which needs to be addressed. Change has a basic meaning of 'to make different or become different.' There is nothing completely wrong with this definition, but there is more an essence of a change from one place or one thing to another. This would have the possible significance of a transfer,[114] a removal, a substitution, or maybe a replacement. The better

---

[113] μετατιθεμένης verb participle present passive genitive feminine singular from μετατίθημι [UBS] μετατίθημι (aor. μετέθηκα ; aor. pass. μετετέθην) remove, take back; take up (of Enoch); **change (of priesthood)** ; distort (Jd 4); middle voice, desert, turn away (Ga 1.6) [Fri] μετατίθημι 1aor. μετέθηκα; 1aor. pass. μετετέθην; (1) **literally, as causing a change from one place to another** *transfer, bring to, transplant* (HE 11.5b); passive *be taken, be transferred* (HE 11.5a); of a body transferred to another burial place *be brought back* (AC 7.16); (2) figuratively; (a) *change, alter* (HE 7.12); in a bad sense *pervert* (JU 4); (b) middle, **as changing one's loyalty as a follower** *turn from, desert, become apostate* (GA 1.6) [LS] μετατίθημι μετα-τίθημι, f. -θήσω: aor. ἱ μετ-έθηκα, aor. 2 -έθην:-*to place among,* τῷ κ' οὔτι τόσον κέλαδον μετέθηκεν (v. 1. μεθέηκεν) then *he would* not *have caused* so much noise *among* us, Od. II. *to place differently,* 1. in local sense, *to transpose,* Plat. 2. *to change, alter,* of a treaty, Thuc., Xen.; μ. τὰς ἐπωνυμίας ἐπὶ ὑός *to change* their names *and call them* after swine, Hdt; μ. τι ἀντί τινος *to put* one thing *in place* of another, *substitute*.

[114] μετατίθημι 1. **to convey from one place to another, *put in another place, transfer*** τὴν χεῖρα ἐπί τι *transfer your hand to something...* Of Enoch *be taken up, translated, taken away (to heaven)* 2. **to effect a change in state or condition,** *change, alter* ... τὴν τοῦ θεοῦ ἡμῶν χάριτα εἰς ἀσέλγειαν *pervert the grace of our God to dissoluteness* **Jude 4.** Pass. μετατιθεμένης τῆς ἱερωσύνης *when the priesthood is changed,* i.e. passed on to another **Hb 7:12** ...of the transfer of the office of high priest to another person)... 3. **to have a change of mind in allegiance, *change one's mind, turn away*** Arndt, W., Danker, F. W., & Bauer, W. (2000). *A Greek-English lexicon of the New Testament and other early Christian literature* (3rd ed.) (642). Chicago: University of Chicago Press.

meaning might be transfer or removal. "Change means removal (12:17). If the Levitical priesthood had been able to bring people to perfection, then a superior priest from the order of Melchizedek would not have been needed." [115]   If the Melchizedek priesthood removed the Levitical priesthood, then the Mosaic law has also been removed. There was not a change into something else. The implication is that one would be removed and replaced by the other. No matter what, there was 'the removal or transfer' being brought about by the Lord especially with the priesthood. He brought this about and no one else.

Also, God made it clear that a new covenant which He would make would not be like the old covenant. "Behold, days are coming," declares the LORD, "when I will make a new covenant with the house of Israel and with the house of Judah, *not like the covenant* which I made with their fathers in the day I took them by the hand to bring them out of the land of Egypt, My covenant which they broke, although I was a husband to them declares the LORD" (Jer. 31:31-32).   If there were simply a 'change' the context would not have included something totally different referred to as 'not like that.' There was not a change from one form to another, but a removal of one and replaced by another. The basic meaning used in Heb. 7:12 can easily support this especially when referenced with Jer. 31:31-32.

But nothing was said about another tribe being 'priests.' "For the one concerning whom these things are spoken belongs to another tribe, from which no one has officiated at the altar. [14] For it is evident that our Lord was descended from Judah, a tribe with reference to which Moses spoke nothing concerning priests" (Heb 7:13). "The Levitical priesthood was superseded by the fact that our Lord descended from Judah. That tribe had no role in the Levitical institutions, and the things God had said about the new Priest applied to One from Judah, which is proof

[115] The Nelson Study Bible, Nelson Ministry Services Special Edition; Thomas Nelson Publishers: Nashville, 1997. Page 2086.

that a change was made."[116] The Levitical priesthood was imperfect. The priests were a continuous problem and presenting many problems for themselves and the people they represented.

"The Aaronic priesthood was limited. The Levitical priesthood lacked 'perfection' in the sense of finality of function and completeness of operation and effect. It could neither remove sin, nor grant righteousness or favor and position with God, 11a. This lack of perfection is recognized: (1) in the need which existed for 'another priest,' i.e., one of a different order, the order of Melchizedek, 11b; (2) in the necessity of a change in the law with which the Aaronic priesthood was unseparably bound, 12; and (3) in the need for a change in the exclusive regulations of the law which limited the priesthood to the tribe of Levi, and thereby excluded Christ on the human plane from serving, since He was from the tribe of Judah, 13–14a. Moses gave no priestly authority to Judah, 14b. 15–22. The Melchizedek priesthood is final. Christ's priesthood, after the order of Melchizedek, is final and complete because of: (1) its superior nature, 15 (cf. 4–11); (2) its qualification by the power of an indissoluble life and not by physical regulations, 16; (3) its institution by the authority of the Word of God, 17; (4) its bringing in a better hope with immediate access to God, 19; (5) its finalization by a divine oath establishing and ordaining Christ's eternal priesthood, 20–21; (6) Christ, the guarantee of a new and better covenant by

---

[116] Hodges, Z. C. (1985). Hebrews. In J. F. Walvoord & R. B. Zuck (Eds.), *The Bible Knowledge Commentary: An Exposition of the Scriptures* (J. F. Walvoord & R. B. Zuck, Ed.) (Heb 7:11–14). Wheaton, IL: Victor Books.

virtue of the oath's better validity, 22 (Jer 31:31–33; Mt 26:28; 1 Cor 11:25)."[117]

Christ's heavenly priesthood is of a better order and is ministered through a better covenant. The old has been replaced by the superior and the new. No priest in the Levitical or Aaron's line ever sat down on a throne. The old covenant or Law was ministered by priests from an earthly tabernacle or temple. The new covenant is the ministry of the perfect High Priest from the true tabernacle in heaven. All this proves the superiority of the new priesthood and the new covenant.

Conclusion
God changed the priesthood by removing the earthly priesthood. He replaced this priesthood with His perfect High Priest (Psalm 110:4). The Lord Jesus Christ is the High Priest functioning at this time in the true heavenly tabernacle. "For when the priesthood is changed, of necessity there takes place a change of law also" (Heb. 7:12). By necessity if there is a change of priesthood, then there is a change of law. God replaced the Levitical priesthood by the perfect High Priest. The law has been replaced by the new covenant. The new High Priest is ministering the new covenant from the true temple. We have such a High Priest ministering eternal redemption promised in the new covenant.[118]

---

[117] Unger, M. F. (2005). *The new Unger's Bible Handbook* (Rev. and updated ed.) (610). Chicago: Moody Publishers.

[118] "And when He had taken a cup and given thanks, He gave *it* to them, saying, "Drink from it, all of you; for this is My blood of the covenant, which is poured out for many for forgiveness of sins" (Matthew 26:27-28). "And when He had taken a cup, *and* given thanks, He gave *it* to them; and they all drank from it. And He said to them, "This is My blood of the covenant, which is poured out for many" (Mar 14:23-24). "And in the same way *He took* the cup after they had eaten, saying, "This cup which is poured out for you is the new covenant in My blood" (Luke 22:20).

Chapter VI

The Better Covenant
Hebrews 8:6

"But now He has obtained a more excellent ministry, by as much as He is also the mediator of a better covenant, which has been enacted on better promises" (Hebrews 8:6).[119]

The writer of Hebrews has drawn attention to the present ministry of the Lord Jesus Christ as Mediator of a better covenant. His focus is on the true High Priest Who is functioning as the High Priest in the true tabernacle, and His current ministry as the Mediator of a better covenant which has better promises.

[119] Hebrews 8:6 νυν[ὶ] δὲ διαφορωτέρας τέτυχεν λειτουργίας, ὅσῳ καὶ κρείττονός ἐστιν διαθήκης μεσίτης, ἥτις ἐπὶ κρείττοσιν ἐπαγγελίαις νενομοθέτηται.**But now** (νυν δε [*nun de*]). Logical use of νυν [*nun*], as the case now stands, with Jesus as high priest in heaven. **Hath he obtained** (τετυχεν [*tetuchen*]). Perfect active indicative of τυγχανω [*tugchanō*] with the genitive, a rare and late form for τετευχεν [*teteuchen*] (also τετευχηκεν [*teteuchēken*]), old verb to hit the mark, to attain. **A ministry the more excellent** (διαφορωτερας λειτουργιας [*diaphorōteras leitourgias*]). "A more excellent ministry." For the comparative of διαφορος [*diaphoros*] see 1:4. This remark applies to all the five points of superiority over the Levitical priesthood. **By how much** (ὁσῳ [*hosōi*]). Instrumental case of the relative ὁσος [*hosos*] between two comparative adjectives as in 1:4. **The mediator** (μεσιτης [*mesitēs*]). Late word from μεσος [*mesos*] (amid) and so a middle man (arbitrator). Already in Gal. 3:19f. and see I Tim. 2:5. See Heb. 9:15; 12:24 for further use with διαθηκη [*diathēkē*]. **Of a better covenant** (κρειττονος διαθηκης [*kreittonos diathēkēs*]). Called "new" (καινης, νεας [*kainēs, neas*]) in 9:15; 12:24. For διαθηκη [*diathēkē*] see Matt. 26:28; Luke 1:72; Gal. 3:17, etc. This idea he will discuss in 8:7–13. **Hath been enacted** (νενομοθετηται [*nenomothetētai*]). Perfect passive indicative of νομοθετεω [*nomotheteō*] as in 7:11 which see. **Upon better promises** (ἐπι κρειττοσιν ἐπαγγελιαις [*epi kreittosin epaggeliais*]). Upon the basis of (ἐπι [*epi*]). But how "better" if the earlier were also from God? This idea, alluded to in 6:12–17, Will be developed in 10:19 to 12:3 with great passion and power. Thus it is seen that "better" (κρεισσων [*kreissōn*]) is the keynote of the Epistle. At every point Christianity is better than Judaism. Robertson, A. (1933). *Word Pictures in the New Testament* (Heb 8:6). Nashville, TN: Broadman Press.

"Now the main point in what has been said *is
this*: **we have such a high priest,** who has taken
His seat at the right hand of the throne of the
Majesty in the heavens, a **minister** in the
sanctuary, and **in the true tabernacle**, which the
Lord pitched, not man. For every high priest is
appointed to offer both gifts and sacrifices; hence
it is necessary that this *high priest* also have
something to offer. **Now if He were on earth,
He would not be a priest at all,** since there are
those who offer the gifts according to the Law;
who serve a copy and shadow of the heavenly
things, just as Moses was warned *by God* when
he was about to erect the tabernacle; for, "See,"
He says, "that you make all things according to
the pattern which was shown you on the
mountain." **But now He has obtained a more
excellent ministry,** by as much as **He is also the
mediator of a better covenant, which has been
enacted on better promises**" (Heb. 8:1-6).

Note the concentration given to the present ministry of
Christ as the now functioning High Priest and Mediator. This is
not a future ministry as the tenses all indicate in the Text, but a
very present ministry. He has obtained this ministry now and
this is His present ministry. He mediates to us a better
covenant. He does not mediate the old covenant or law. The
new High Priest demands a better covenant. He has now
obtained this more perfect ministry.

"Hath he obtained (τετυχεν [*tetuchen*]). Perfect
active indicative of τυγχανω [*tugchanō*] with the
genitive, a rare and late form for τετευχεν
[*teteuchen*] (also τετευχηκεν [*teteuchēken*]), old
verb to hit the mark, to attain. A ministry the

more excellent (διαφορωτερας λειτουργιας
[*diaphorōteras leitourgias*]). "A more excellent
ministry." For the comparative of διαφορος
[*diaphoros*] see 1:4. This remark applies to all
the five points of superiority over the Levitical
priesthood."[120]

These points are obvious but need to be stressed.

- We have such a high priest
- A minister in the sanctuary, and in the true tabernacle
- Now if He were on earth, He would not be a priest at all
- But now He has obtained a more excellent ministry
- He is also the mediator of a better covenant
- The better covenant is obviously the new covenant

The position and prominence of this High Priest is the
focal point of these verses (Heb. 8:1-6). The accentuation is on
this flawless High Priest and Mediator in the true tabernacle.
There should be no attention given by anyone to an earthly
priesthood and tabernacle in any sense. Why look to the
inferior of earthly things when one has full access to the
superior and infinitely perfect? Why contemplate the mundane
when the true High Priest has obtained a more excellent
ministry in the true tabernacle? Why contemplate an old
covenant (the Mosaic Law) when this High Priest is mediating a
better covenant?

"The main 'point' in what has been said is that
Christ 'sat down at the right hand of the throne
of the Majesty in heaven,' completely
superseding the Levitical priesthood. He is
infinitely above all other priests, exercising His

[120] Robertson, A. (1933). *Word Pictures in the New Testament* (Heb 8:6). Nashville,
TN: Broadman Press.

priesthood in heaven, not on earth (10:12). The high priest, even when he entered the holiest annually, only *stood* for a moment before the *symbol* of God's throne. By contrast, our Lord *ever sits* on the throne of the Majesty on high till His enemies are made His footstool (Ps 110:1). Further, Christ sits as a minister in the sanctuary – the administrator of the holy things in the real tabernacle in heaven. The early tabernacle was a mere foreshadow of the heavenly, being pitched not by man but by the Lord."[121]

The writer of Hebrews was continually stressing the need of not going back to the old (the old system of the priesthood, earthly tabernacle, sacrifices, etc). The old is just a mere shadow. Why even look to these things for anything? There were even warnings given by the Author turning back to the old ways of the earthly law and priesthood. How could anyone do this when their Messiah is the true High Priest and Mediator? He is the One mediating the better covenant. In case the readers were in doubt, the Author of Hebrews spells out the better covenant for them (Heb. 8:8-12). They cannot miss the better covenant in any sense.

The better covenant is the new covenant of Jeremiah (Jer. 31:31-34). To miss this is to completely miss the current ministry of the Lord Jesus Christ. He is now mediating this covenant in the true tabernacle. Again, the true Author spells this out word for word *literally*. It is virtually impossible to miss this *in any sense*. "For if that first *covenant* had been faultless, there would have been no occasion sought for a second" (Heb. 8:7). What is this second covenant He is currently mediating? The Writer spells it out!

---

[121] Unger, M. F. (2005). *The New Unger's Bible Handbook* (Rev. and updated ed.) (610–611). Chicago: Moody Publishers.

"For finding fault with them, He says, "Behold, days are coming, says the Lord, When I will effect a new covenant With the house of Israel and with the house of Judah; Not like the covenant which I made with their fathers On the day when I took them by the hand To lead them out of the land of Egypt; For they did not continue in My covenant, And I did not care for them, says the Lord. For this is the covenant that I will make with the house of Israel After those days, says the Lord: I will put My laws into their minds, And I will write them upon their hearts. And I will be their God, And they shall be My people. And they shall not teach everyone his fellow citizen, And everyone his brother, saying, 'Know the LORD,' For all shall know Me, From the least to the greatest of them. For I will be merciful to their iniquities, And I will remember their sins no more" (Heb. 8:8-12). [122]

That better covenant was stated word for word. The fact that He has obtained this excellent ministry as Mediator should cause the reader of Hebrews to focus on Him in the true tabernacle. Not only should the focus be on Him but also His excellent ministry as the Mediator of the new covenant.

---

[122] "Behold, days are coming," declares the LORD, "when I will make a new covenant with the house of Israel and with the house of Judah, [32] not like the covenant which I made with their fathers in the day I took them by the hand to bring them out of the land of Egypt, My covenant which they broke, although I was a husband to them," declares the LORD. [33] "But this is the covenant which I will make with the house of Israel after those days," declares the LORD, "I will put My law within them, and on their heart I will write it; and I will be their God, and they shall be My people. [34] "And they shall not teach again, each man his neighbor and each man his brother, saying, 'Know the LORD,' for they shall all know Me, from the least of them to the greatest of them," declares the LORD, "for I will forgive their iniquity, and their sin I will remember no more" (Jer. 31:31-34).

Conclusion

Christ, the High Priest, is currently mediating the new covenant in the true tabernacle. All this is obviously explicit and conclusive. If a consistent literal hermeneutic is used there can be no other conclusion. 'But *now* He has obtained a more excellent ministry, by as much as He is also the mediator of a better covenant, which has been enacted on better promises" (Hebrews 8:6).[123]

---

[123]Hebrews 8:6 νυν[ì] δὲ διαφορωτέρας τέτυχεν λειτουργίας, ὅσῳ καὶ κρείττονός ἐστιν διαθήκης μεσίτης, ἥτις ἐπὶ κρείττοσιν ἐπαγγελίαις νενομοθέτηται. The νυν[ì] δὲ is drawing a very dramatic emphasis in context. 'But now' He has obtained. **"But now** (νυν δε [*nun de*]). Logical use of νυν [*nun*], as the case now stands, with Jesus as high priest in heaven. **Hath he obtained** (τετυχεν [*tetuchen*]). Perfect active indicative of τυγχανω" Robertson, A. (1933). *Word Pictures in the New Testament* (Heb 8:6). Nashville, TN: Broadman Press.

Chapter VII

Christ the High Priest in the Perfect Tabernacle
Heb. 9:11

"But when Christ appeared[124] *as* a high priest of the good things to come, *He entered* through the greater and more perfect tabernacle, not made with hands, that is to say, not of this creation" (Heb. 9:11).

Christ arrived as a high priest and entered the true and perfect tabernacle. This is the true tabernacle which is in heaven. The writer has emphasized this truth several times to the readers. He wanted them to fully understand that Christ is now functioning as the true high priest in the true tabernacle.

"Now the main point in what has been said *is this*: we have such a high priest, who has taken His seat at the right hand of the throne of the Majesty in the heavens, a minister in the sanctuary, and in the true tabernacle, which the Lord pitched, not man. For every high priest is appointed to offer both gifts and sacrifices; hence it is necessary that this *high priest* also have something to offer. Now if He were on earth, He would not be a priest at all, since there are those who offer the gifts according to the Law; who serve a copy and shadow of the heavenly things, just as Moses was warned *by God* when he was about to erect the

---

[124] παραγενόμενος verb participle aorist middle nominative masculine singular from παραγίνομαι [UBS] παραγίνομαι (aor. παρεγενόμην, subj. παραγένωμαι) come, arrive; appear; come to one's defense, stand by (2 Tm 4.16). The root word has the meaning of come or arrives; and with the aorist participle the normal rendering would have the meaning of has come or has arrived. Perhaps when Christ came or arrived He entered...

tabernacle; for, "See," He says, "that you make all
things according to the pattern which was shown you
on the mountain" (Heb 8:1-5).

He is presently functioning as the high priest of the good
things 'to come.' There is a variant (manuscript differences)
with the good things 'to come.' [125] There are several
translations based on the variants. "But when Christ appeared
as a high priest of **the good things that have come**, then
through the greater and more perfect tent (not made with hands,
that is, not of this creation)" (ESV); "But when Christ appeared
as a high priest of **the good things to come**, *He entered* through
the greater and more perfect tabernacle, not made with hands,
that is to say, not of this creation" (NAS); "But when Christ
came as high priest of **the good things that are now already
here**, he went through the greater and more perfect tabernacle
that is not made with human hands, that is to say, is not a part of
this creation" (NIV).

This does not create that great an issue. Robertson
presents an excellent resolution. **"Of the good things to come**

[125] **Having come** (παραγενομενος [*paragenomenos*]). Second aorist middle
participle of παραγινομαι [*paraginomai*]. This is the great historic event that is the
crux of history. "Christ came on the scene, and all was changed" (Moffatt). **Of the
good things to come** (των μελλοντων ἀγαθων [*tōn mellontōn agathōn*]). But B D
read γενομενων [*genomenōn*] (that are come). It is a nice question which is the true
text. Both aspects are true, for Christ is High Priest of good things that have already
come as well as of the glorious future of hope. Westcott prefers γενομενων
[*genomenōn*], Moffatt μελλοντων [*mellontōn*]. **Through the greater and more
perfect tabernacle** (δια της μειζονος και τελειοτερας σκηνης [*dia tēs meizonos kai
teleioteras skēnēs*]). Probably the instrumental use of δια [*dia*] (II Cor. 2:4; Rom.
2:27; 14:20) as accompaniment, not the local idea (4:14; 10:20). Christ as High Priest
employed in his work the heavenly tabernacle (8:2) after which the earthly was
patterned (9:24). **Not made with hands** (οὐ χειροποιητου [*ou cheiropoiētou*]). Old
compound verbal for which see Mark 14:58; Acts 7:48; 17:24. Cf. Heb. 8:2. Here in
the predicate position. **Not of this creation** (οὐ ταυτης της κτισεως [*ou tautēs tēs
ktiseōs*]). Explanation of οὐ χιεροποιητου [*ou chieropoiētou*]. For κτισις [*ktisis*] see II
Cor. 5:17; Rom. 8:19. For the idea see II Cor. 4:18; Heb. 8:2. This greater and more
perfect tabernacle is heaven itself (9:24). Robertson, A. (1933). *Word Pictures in the
New Testament* (Heb 9:11). Nashville, TN: Broadman Press.

(τῶν μελλόντων ἀγαθῶν [*tōn mellontōn agathōn*]). But B D
read γενομενων [*genomenōn*] (that are come). It is a nice
question which is the true text? Both aspects are true, for Christ
is High Priest of good things that have already come as well as
of the glorious future of hope."[126] The greater issue presented
here is that Christ has appeared or come already. He is also
functioning as the high priest now. His present ministry is in
the true tabernacle. "Christ's appearance as High Priest
fulfilled the types of both the Melchizedek and the Aaronic
priesthoods in bringing 'the good things that are already here,'
11a. He fulfilled the type of the high priest's entering the holiest
once a year (Lev 16) by having entered *once for all* into the real
holy place in the tabernacle in heaven, 11b. There He presented
His own infinitely efficacious blood on the heavenly mercy
seat, showing His one sacrifice to be incomparably superior to
the *many continued* sacrifices of the blood of goats and calves
12a (cf. 9:13–14). This once- for-all sacrifice secured eternal
redemption, not merely a temporary covering and passing over
of sin for the time being, as under the old covenant, 12b.
'Eternal redemption' has reference to the safety and security
which the believer possesses in Christ, and his future eternal
glorification."[127]

The eternal redemption promised is through His blood of
the new covenant. He is now ministering this new covenant in
the true tabernacle. In fact, the new covenant can only be
ministered in the true tabernacle where all now have access to
God. This ministry will come to earth one day in the kingdom
and be fulfilled in and with Israel. "This eternal redemption,
purchased by Christ's own blood, purifies not only externally
and ceremonially (as did the Levitical sacrifices on the Day of
Atonement), but inwardly and vitally for service rendered to a

[126] This greater and more perfect tabernacle is heaven itself (9:24). Robertson, A.
(1933). *Word Pictures in the New Testament* (Heb 9:11). Nashville, TN: Broadman
Press.
[127] Unger, M. F. (2005). *The new Unger's Bible handbook* (Rev. and updated ed.)
(612). Chicago: Moody Publishers.

'living God.' If the sprinkling of ceremonially defiled persons with animal blood and the ashes of a red heifer (Num 19:16–18) could purify outwardly to any degree, to how much greater degree shall the blood of Christ effect inward cleansing and obtain an eternally complete salvation.?"[128]

This truly defines the things that have come. This also defines things that will come in His kingdom when all the eternal, unconditional, unilateral covenants will be fulfilled. Then it will truly be 'Thy/Your kingdom has come.'

There is one more issue which might be looked at. "But when Christ appeared *as* a high priest of the good things to come, **He entered through the greater and more perfect tabernacle**, not made with hands, that is to say, not of this creation." The term 'He entered through' might be better rendered: " It is not likely the writer meant to say that **Christ ... went through the greater and more perfect tabernacle**, since this cannot be distinguished from "the most holy place" which He entered according to verse 12. It is probably better to take the original word translated "through" (*dia*) and connect it with **came as High Priest of the good things that are already here** (or, per most Gr. Mss. "the good things which were to come"). In that case, instead of "through" the word can be translated "in connection with" and the total statement expresses the idea that Christ's high-priesthood is linked with "the greater and more perfect tabernacle" rather than the "earthly" one previously described (vv. 1–5)."[129] "The preposition would be better translated 'with reference to' rather than 'through."[130]

---

[128] Unger, M. F. (2005). *The new Unger's Bible handbook* (Rev. and updated ed.) (612). Chicago: Moody Publishers.

[129] Hodges, Z. C. (1985). Hebrews. In J. F. Walvoord & R. B. Zuck (Eds.), *The Bible Knowledge Commentary: An Exposition of the Scriptures* (J. F. Walvoord & R. B. Zuck, Ed.) (Heb 9:11–12). Wheaton, IL: Victor Books.

[130] Χριστὸς δὲ παραγενόμενος ἀρχιερεὺς τῶν γενομένων ἀγαθῶν **διὰ** τῆς μείζονος καὶ τελειοτέρας σκηνῆς οὐ χειροποιήτου, τοῦτ' ἔστιν οὐ ταύτης τῆς κτίσεως, [UBS] διά prep. with: (1) gen. **through, by means of,** with; during, throughout (διὰ παντός continually); through, among, throughout; (2) acc. because of, on account of, for the

Conclusion

Christ is now ministering in the true tabernacle in heaven. His ministry is that of mediating His new covenant. "How much more will the blood of Christ, who through the eternal Spirit offered Himself without blemish to God, cleanse your conscience from dead works to serve the living God? [15] And for this reason He is the mediator of a new covenant, in order that since a death has taken place for the redemption of the transgressions that were *committed* under the first covenant, those who have been called may receive the promise of the eternal inheritance" (Heb 9:14-15). "When Christ **entered the most holy place once for all by His own blood** (v. 12; cf. Christ's blood in v. 14; 10:19, 29; 13:20) rather than by animal blood, He likewise demonstrated the superiority of His service because His blood had **obtained eternal redemption**. Thus the value of His sacrifice is immeasurably greater than the animal offerings of the Levitical arrangements. A perfect ransom price had been paid for human "redemption," and because it need not be paid again (this sacrificial act was "once for all," *ephapax;* cf. 7:27; 10:10) that redemption is an "eternal" one. 9:13–14. This "eternal redemption" through which the blessings of the New Covenant (cf. 8:10–12) have reached all believers, should affect the way believers serve God. Old-Covenant rituals served for the **ceremonially unclean** and only made them **outwardly clean**. But **the blood of Christ** can do much more."[131]

---

sake of; through, by (rarely); διὰ τοῦτο therefore, for this reason; διὰ (τό) with inf. because; διὰ τί why?

[131] Hodges, Z. C. (1985). Hebrews. In J. F. Walvoord & R. B. Zuck (Eds.), *The Bible Knowledge Commentary: An Exposition of the Scriptures* (J. F. Walvoord & R. B. Zuck, Ed.) (Heb 9:11–14). Wheaton, IL: Victor Books.

Chapter VIII

The Testator and His Will
Heb. 9:16-17

"For where a covenant is, there must of necessity
be the death of the one who made it. For a
covenant is valid *only* when men are dead, for it
is never in force while the one who made it
lives" (Heb. 9:16-17). [132]

The writer of Hebrews is making it very obvious that the
new covenant is in full force or operation, and it is being
mediated by the High Priest and Mediator the Lord Jesus Christ.
The writer also makes it very clear that this mediation is taking
place in the heavenlies in the true tabernacle where they now
have access. When the veil was torn, there was not only access
to the earthly tabernacle for all, [133] but to the real tabernacle
which was in heaven. Christ is there now functioning now as
the true High Priest. It was not possible to go back to the old
priesthood, to the old tabernacle, to the law, to the blood of
animals, or to anything connected with the old system of
worship. They have now come to the new and living way by a
perfect sacrifice which cleanses eternally and makes the
worshipper fit to come into the true holy of holies.
    This was a big step for any Hebrew to leave the old
system of worship (biblical Judaism) and come to an entirely
new system of worship by the new and living way. Everything
with the old was 'physical' i.e. the earthly temple, earthly

---

[132] Hebrews 9:16 Ὅπου γὰρ διαθήκη, θάνατον ἀνάγκη φέρεσθαι τοῦ διαθεμένου· [17]
διαθήκη γὰρ ἐπὶ νεκροῖς βεβαία, ἐπεὶ μήποτε ἰσχύει ὅτε ζῇ ὁ διαθέμενος.
[133] "And behold, the veil of the temple was torn in two from top to bottom, and the
earth shook; and the rocks were split" (Mat 27:5); "And the veil of the temple was
torn in two from top to bottom (Mar 15:38); "the sun being obscured; and the veil of
the temple was torn in two" (Luke 23:45).

priesthood, earthly sacrifices, etc., but now they had to come by faith to the true way provided by the blood of the new covenant.[134] They had to know this new covenant was in full operation or in force for them to come. The writer of Hebrews makes this clear in several ways but this may be the most important. "For a covenant is valid *only* when men are dead, for it is never in force while the one who made it lives."

When a person dies their 'will' goes into effect at the exact time of his death. The very moment of death the 'will' becomes effective. This is why the coroner's official time of death is so important especially with wills. The timing has to be very exact.

"For a covenant is valid *only* when men are dead, for it is never in force while the one who made it lives." The same word for covenant is easily used for 'will'[135] and in this case it is. "**Where there hath been death** (ἐπι νεκροις [*epi nekrois*]). "In the case of dead people." A will is only operative then."[136] "In opening the new unit of thought, the writer employed a swift semantic shift in which he treated the Greek word for "covenant" (*diathēkē*) in the sense of **a will**. While "covenants" and "wills" are not in all respects identical, the author meant

---

[134] Probably why the 'hall of faith' is in this epistle i.e. Hebrews 11.

[135] **A testament** (διαθηκη [*diathēkē*]). The same word occurs for covenant (verse 15) and will (verse 16). This double sense of the word is played upon also by Paul in Gal. 3:15f. We say today "The New Testament" (*Novum Testamentum*) rather than "The New Covenant." Both terms are pertinent. **That made it** (του διαθεμενου [*tou diathemenou*]). Genitive of the articular second aorist middle participle of διατιθημι [*diatithēmi*] from which διαθηκη [*diathēkē*] comes. The notion of will here falls in with κληρονομια [*klēronomia*] (inheritance, I Peter 1:4) as well as with θανατος [*thanatos*] (death). **Of force** (βεβαια [*bebaia*]). Stable, firm as in 3:6, 14. **Where there hath been death** (ἐπι νεκροις [*epi nekrois*]). "In the case of dead people." A will is only operative then. **For doth it ever avail while he that made it liveth?** (ἐπει μη ποτε ἰσχυει ὁτε ζῃ ὁ διαθεμενος; [*epei mē pote ischuei hote zēi ho diathemenos?*]). This is a possible punctuation with μη ποτε [*mē pote*] in a question (John 7:26). Without the question mark, it is a positive statement of fact. Aleph and D read τοτε [*tote*] (then) instead of ποτε [*pote*]. The use of μη [*mē*] in a causal sentence is allowable (John 3:18, ὁτι μη [*hoti mē*]). Robertson, A. (1933). *Word Pictures in the New Testament* (Heb 9:16). Nashville, TN: Broadman Press.

[136] Robertson, A. (1933). *Word Pictures in the New Testament* (Heb 9:16). Nashville, TN: Broadman Press.

that in the last analysis the New Covenant is really a
testamentary disposition. Like human wills, all the
arrangements are secured by the testator and its beneficiaries
need only accept its terms. Treating the New Covenant in this
way, the author argued that its **force**—like that of all human
wills—depends on **the death of the one who made it**. That is
when it **takes effect.**[137]
    A will goes into full force at the death of the testator.
Even if the deceased has 'no will' (intestate) at the legal time of
death, the court will carry out 'a will' by decree of the court.
The exact time of death determined by the coroner determines
the time the will goes into full force. There is no delay! The
will may be contested by heirs or anyone, but the will takes full
effect at death of the testator.
    This is the most important issue being presented here.
The 'will' is never in force or effect while the one who made
the will lives. This is really the key for understanding the
outworking of the new covenant by Christ Himself. As long as
He lived the new covenant was not operative as a formal will or
contract. God said there was a time coming when He would
make a new covenant not like the one He made before (the
Mosaic covenant). "Behold, days are coming," declares the
LORD, "when I will make a new covenant with the house of
Israel and with the house of Judah, **not like the covenant** which
I made with their fathers in the day I took them by the hand to
bring them out of the land of Egypt, My covenant which they
broke, although I was a husband to them," declares the LORD"
(Jer. 31:31-34). As the Mosaic covenant was initiated by blood,
we find that Christ claimed this covenant as His own which
would be enacted or initiated by His blood. 'For this is My
blood of the covenant '(Matthew 26:28); This is My blood of
the covenant' (Mark 14:24); 'This cup which is poured out for
you is the new covenant in My blood' (Luke 22:20).

[137] Hodges, Z. C. (1985). Hebrews. In J. F. Walvoord & R. B. Zuck (Eds.), *The Bible Knowledge Commentary: An Exposition of the Scriptures* (J. F. Walvoord & R. B. Zuck, Ed.) (Heb 9:16–17). Wheaton, IL: Victor Books.

This is the new covenant which is not like the Mosaic covenant. The Mosaic covenant was bilateral, conditional, and temporal. The new covenant was unilateral, unconditional, and eternal. The new covenant promised eternal forgiveness or redemption to Israel. There was a time coming under this covenant, He would not even remember their sins. "For I will forgive their iniquity, and their sin I will remember no more."[138] The Law promised death for not keeping the covenant. The new covenant promised forgiveness of sin. The new covenant would never be in force while the one who made it lives. At the death of the testator, the new covenant went into effect when Jesus yielded up His spirit or breathed His last (breath).[139] All four gospels record the very moment of His death (the separation of the soul from the body). At that very

[138]**Jeremiah 31:31** "Behold, days are coming," declares the LORD, "when I will make a new covenant with the house of Israel and with the house of Judah, [32] not like the covenant which I made with their fathers in the day I took them by the hand to bring them out of the land of Egypt, My covenant which they broke, although I was a husband to them," declares the LORD. [33] "But this is the covenant which I will make with the house of Israel after those days," declares the LORD, "I will put My law within them, and on their heart I will write it; and I will be their God, and they shall be My people. [34] "And they shall not teach again, each man his neighbor and each man his brother, saying, 'Know the LORD,' for they shall all know Me, from the least of them to the greatest of them," declares the LORD, **"for I will forgive their iniquity, and their sin I will remember no more."** (Jer 31:31 NAS).
[139] Luke noted four things that occurred at the time Jesus died. First, two symbolic events took place while Jesus was on the cross. **Darkness came over the whole land** for three hours, from **the sixth hour (noon) until the ninth hour** (3:00 P.M.). Jesus had already told those who arrested Him that "this is your hour—when darkness reigns" (22:53). Darkness was reigning because of His crucifixion. The other symbolic event was the tearing **in two** of **the curtain of the temple**, which separated the holy of holies from the rest of the temple. The curtain divided people from the place where God had localized His presence. The tearing from top to bottom (Matt. 27:51) symbolized the fact that now, because of Jesus' death, people had freer access to God as they no longer had to go through the sacrificial system (cf. Rom. 5:2; Eph. 2:18; 3:12). Jesus was the only Sacrifice needed to enable people to have a proper relationship with God. Second, Luke noted that Jesus' death occurred because He willed it. Breathing **His last** (Luke 23:46), He voluntarily gave up His life (John 10:15, 17–18). Martin, J. A. (1985). Luke. In J. F. Walvoord & R. B. Zuck (Eds.), *The Bible Knowledge Commentary: An Exposition of the Scriptures* (J. F. Walvoord & R. B. Zuck, Ed.) (Lk 23:44–49). Wheaton, IL: Victor Books.

moment His blood becomes efficacious and the new covenant went into full operation.

> "And Jesus cried out again with a loud voice, **and yielded up *His* spirit**" (Mat 27:50). "And Jesus uttered a loud cry, **and breathed His last**. And the veil of the temple was torn in two from top to bottom. And when the centurion, who was standing right in front of Him, saw the way He breathed His last, he said, "Truly this man was the Son of God!" (Mar 15:37-38). "And Jesus, crying out with a loud voice, said, "Father, into Thy hands I commit My spirit." And having said this, **He breathed His last**. (Luke 23:46). "When Jesus therefore had received the sour wine, He said, "It is finished!" And He bowed His head, **and gave up His spirit**" (John 19:30).

- **yielded up *His* spirit** (Mat 27:50).
- **and breathed His last** (Mark 15:37)
- **He breathed His last**. (Luke 23:46)
- **and gave up His spirit**" (John 19:30)

At that exact moment 'His last breath' the new covenant went into effect. Jesus had claimed the new covenant as His by means of His blood.

- Matthew 26:28: For this is My blood of the covenant
- Mark 14:24: This is My blood of the covenant
- Luke 22:20: This cup which is poured out for you = the new covenant in My blood

Jesus could claim the new covenant as the Son of God for He made it (Heb. 11:3). The One Who created the ages[140]

---

[140] Hebrews 11:3 By faith we understand that the <u>worlds</u> were prepared by the word of God, so that what is seen was not made out of things which are visible. Πίστει

certainly made the covenants. And the covenants are the key for understanding God's entire program for man and this creation. These are His contracts with man especially with Israel. The new covenant can only be fulfilled by Israel for it is only made or contracted with Israel. The fact is the new covenant is unilateral, eternal, and unconditional means only God can fulfill it.

Conclusion

The writer of Hebrews is confirming that the new covenant is unquestionably in force, that it is completely operative. For a 'will' goes into effect immediately upon the death of the One Who made it. The writer of Hebrews is pointing to Christ as Testator of the new covenant. He has been raised from the dead to execute His own will. Who else could execute His own will but the true Testator of the new covenant?

He made it, claimed it as His last will and testament. He paid it in full with His blood. He was raised from the dead and is executing His covenant as the Mediator of the/His new covenant. This is truly the greatness of His blood of the new covenant. "For where a covenant is, there must of necessity be the death of the one who made it. For a covenant is valid *only* when men are dead, for it is never in force while the one who made it lives" (Heb. 9:16-17). While He lived, the new covenant was not in force. When He died, it went into full force.

νοοῦμεν κατηρτίσθαι τοὺς αἰῶνας ῥήματι θεοῦ, εἰς τὸ μὴ ἐκ φαινομένων τὸ βλεπόμενον γεγονέναι. The ages are much greater than the physical creation. The ages contain the physical creation. Most just see substance, matter, things, etc. But the emphasis here is on the greater, for the greater contains the lesser.

Chapter IX

Blood Put the New Covenant in Force
Heb. 9:18

Therefore even the first *covenant* was
not inaugurated without blood' (Heb.
9:18)[141]

This verse compares two blood covenants. Covenants
are actually contracts. The first covenant referred to in this
verse is the Mosaic covenant. This covenant that God made
with Israel was conditional, temporal, and bilateral. It was
conditional in that it had conditions to be met. It was temporal
in the sense it was made in time and would end in time. And it
was bilateral in that it had two sides or two parties that
contracted to keep their part of the covenant. The "Mosaic
covenant (Ex 20:1–31:18) was the legal covenant, given solely
to Israel. It consisted of the commandments (Ex 20:1–26); the
judgments (social) (Ex 21:1; 24:11) and the ordinances
(religious); (Ex 24:12–31:18); also called the law. It was a
conditional covenant of works, a ministry of 'condemnation'
and 'death' (2 Cor. 3:7–9), designed to lead the transgressor
(convicted thereby as a sinner) to Christ."[142] This covenant was
truly a ministry of death-- not of life. Both parties were to keep
their part of the contract completely and flawlessly.

What inaugurated[143] or put this covenant into full force
and fully operational was the blood. It was by means of the
blood that put this covenant into full operation-- nothing else.

---

[141] ὅθεν οὐδὲ ἡ πρώτη χωρὶς αἵματος ἐγκεκαίνισται· (Heb. 9:18)
[142] Unger, M. F. (2005). *The New Unger's Bible Handbook* (Rev. and updated ed.)
(613). Chicago: Moody Publishers.
[143] ἐγκεκαίνισται verb indicative perfect passive 3rd person singular from ἐγκαινίζω
; [UBS] ἐγκαινίζω put into force, inaugurate; open (He 10.20); [Fri] ἐγκαινίζω (or
ἐνκαινίζω) 1aor. ἐνεκαίνισα; pf. pass. ἐγκεκαίνισμαι (or ἐνκεκαίνισμαι); (1) *make*

"Then He said to Moses, "Come up to the LORD, you and Aaron, Nadab and Abihu and seventy of the elders of Israel, and you shall worship at a distance. [2] "Moses alone, however, shall come near to the LORD, but they shall not come near, nor shall the people come up with him." [3] **Then Moses came and recounted to the people all the words of the LORD and all the ordinances; and all the people answered with one voice, and said, "All the words which the LORD has spoken we will do!"** [4] And Moses wrote down all the words of the LORD. Then he arose early in the morning, and built an altar at the foot of the mountain with twelve pillars for the twelve tribes of Israel. [5] And he sent young men of the sons of Israel, and they offered burnt offerings and sacrificed young bulls as peace offerings to the LORD. [6] And Moses took half of the blood and put *it* in basins, and the *other* half of the blood he sprinkled on the altar. [7] Then he took the book of the covenant and read *it* in the hearing of the people; and they said, "All that the LORD has spoken we will do, and we will be obedient!" [8] **So Moses took the blood and sprinkled *it* on the people, and said, "Behold the blood of the covenant, which the LORD has made with you in accordance with all these words'** (Exodus 24:1-8). [144]

---

new, renew; as opening a way not there before *open, dedicate* (HE 10.20); (2) as solemnly bringing a covenant into effect *put into effect, inaugurate, establish* (HE 9.18)

[144] Ex. 24:6–8. The blood was divided into two parts. One half was swung by Moses upon the altar (זָרַק to swing, shake, or pour out of the vessel, in distinction from הִזָּה to sprinkle) the other half he put into basins, and after he had read the book of the covenant to the people, and they had promised to do and follow all the words of Jehovah, he sprinkled it upon the people with these words: *"Behold the blood of the covenant, which Jehovah has made with you over all these words."* As several animals were slaughtered, and all of them young oxen, there must have been a considerable quantity of blood obtained, so that the one half would fill several basins, and many persons might be sprinkled with it as it was being swung about. The

The Mosaic Law was a true blood covenant. The fact
that the verb 'inaugurated' ἐγκεκαίνισται[145] is a perfect
passive indicative makes this 'inaugurating' something that
happened in the past and the results or effects continue. This
means this blood covenant, the Mosaic Law, went into effect
and was inaugurated and ratified immediately by the blood.
Nothing else put this bilateral, conditional, temporal covenant
into full operation. Sometimes the terms 'blood sprinkling' is

division of the blood had reference to the two parties to the covenant, who were to be
brought by the covenant into a living unity; but it had no connection whatever with
the heathen customs adduced by *Bähr* and *Knobel,* in which the parties to a treaty
mixed their own blood together. For this was not a mixture of different kinds of
blood, but it was a division of one blood, and that *sacrificial* blood, in which animal
life was offered instead of human life, making expiation as a pure life for sinful man,
and by virtue of this expiation restoring the fellowship between God and man which
had been destroyed by sin. But the sacrificial blood itself only acquired this
signification through the sprinkling or swinging upon the altar, by virtue of which the
human soul was received, in the soul of the animal sacrificed for man, into the
fellowship of the divine grace manifested upon the altar, in order that, through the
power of this sin-forgiving and sin-destroying grace, it might be sanctified to a new
and holy life. In this way the sacrificial blood acquired the signification of a vital
principle endued with the power of divine grace; and this was communicated to the
people by means of the sprinkling of the blood. As the only reason for dividing the
sacrificial blood into two parts was, that the blood sprinkled upon the altar could not
be taken off again and sprinkled upon the people; the two halves of the blood are to
be regarded as one blood, which was first of all sprinkled upon the altar, and then
upon the people. In the blood sprinkled upon the altar, the natural life of the people
was given up to God, as a life that had passed through death, to be pervaded by His
grace; and then through the sprinkling upon the people it was restored to them again,
as a life renewed by the grace of God. In this way the blood not only became a bond
of union between Jehovah and His people, but as the blood of the covenant, it became
a vital power, holy and divine, uniting Israel and its God; and the sprinkling of the
people with this blood was an actual renewal of life, a transposition of Israel into the
kingdom of God, in which it was filled with the powers of God's spirit of grace, and
sanctified into a kingdom of priests, a holy nation of Jehovah (Ex. 19:6). And this
covenant was made "upon all the words" which Jehovah had spoken, and the people
had promised to observe. Consequently it had for its foundation the divine law and
right, as the rule of life for Israel. Keil, C. F., & Delitzsch, F. (1996). *Commentary
on the Old Testament* (Ex 24:6–8). Peabody, MA: Hendrickson.
[145] ἐγκεκαίνισται verb indicative perfect passive 3rd person singular from ἐγκαινίζω
; [UBS] ἐγκαινίζω put into force, inaugurate; open (He 10.20);

used to prove or show this covenant (or other blood covenants) is in full operation with the parties involved. The same verb is used in Heb. 10:20 "since therefore, brethren, we have confidence to enter the holy place by the blood of Jesus, [20] by a new and living way which He **inaugurated** for us through the veil, that is, His flesh" (Heb. 10:19-20).[146] The new and living was fully open immediately at the death of Christ. "At any rate because of the coming of Christ in the flesh we have the new way opened for access to God (Heb. 2:17f.; 4:16)."[147] There was and could be no delay with this inauguration. If there were any delay with this inauguration or ratification, God would have made this very obvious in His Word.

"The description of all that Christ is and has done is found in the preceding argument of this epistle. Confidence (assurance, boldness) is enjoined for these fellow Hebrew believers as they enter the very presence of God because: (1) the blood of Christ – eternally acceptable to God and totally sufficient – has made such access possible, 19; (2) Jesus has inaugurated a new and living way through the veil into the immediate presence of God, 20; and (3) we have a High Priest, superior to all other priests, who serves 'over the house of God,' the real sanctuary in heaven, 21 (see notes on 9:11–12, 23–24). Such privileges enable the believer to 'draw near [come to God intimately and frequently] with a sincere heart in full

---

[146] Ἔχοντες οὖν, ἀδελφοί, παρρησίαν εἰς τὴν εἴσοδον τῶν ἁγίων ἐν τῷ αἵματι Ἰησοῦ,
[20] ἣν ἐνεκαίνισεν ἡμῖν ὁδὸν πρόσφατον καὶ ζῶσαν διὰ τοῦ καταπετάσματος, τοῦτ᾽ ἔστιν τῆς σαρκὸς αὐτοῦ, **ἐνεκαίνισεν** verb indicative aorist active 3rd person singular from **ἐγκαινίζω** [UBS] ἐγκαινίζω put into force, inaugurate; open (He 10.20)
[147] Robertson, A. (1933). *Word Pictures in the New Testament* (Heb 10:20). Nashville, TN: Broadman Press.

assurance of faith,' freed from the doubts of an evil
conscience and cleansed from defilement."[148]

Conclusion
A blood covenant is put into full effect and operation by
the blood. To inaugurate or ratify has the same effective
meaning biblically. The blood covenant was put into full
operation immediately and there was no delay.
If there were any delay in these two covenants in any
sense being put into full operation, God would have made this
not only very clear, but given the grounds for the delay. For
this delay, if there were one, would be contrary to the
outworking of His blood covenants with man. 'Therefore even
the first *covenant* was not inaugurated without blood' (Heb.
9:18).[149]   Therefore even the first covenant was not put into
force or literally begun without blood.

[148] Unger, M. F. (2005). *The new Unger's Bible handbook* (Rev. and updated ed.)
(615–616). Chicago: Moody Publishers.
[149] ὅθεν οὐδὲ ἡ πρώτη χωρὶς αἵματος ἐγκεκαίνισται· (Heb 9:18)

Chapter X

He Established the New Covenant
Heb. 10:9

"Then He said, "Behold, I have come to do Thy will." He takes away[150] the first in order to establish[151] the second" (Heb. 10:9).[152]

"Therefore, when He comes into the world, He says, "Sacrifice and offering Thou hast not desired, But a body Thou hast prepared for Me; [6] In whole burnt offerings and *sacrifices* for sin Thou hast taken no pleasure. [7] "Then I said, 'Behold, I have come (In the roll of the book it is written of Me) To do Thy will, O God" (Heb 10:5-7).

In context 'I have come to do Thy will' is the Son's sacrifice of Himself. By doing this He takes away the first in order to establish the second. What is the first? In context the writer of Hebrews has been continually warning the readers they cannot go back to the old Mosaic system for anything. This was their tutor to lead them to the One who would finally bring eternal redemption. This eternal redemption was exclusively by the blood of the new covenant.

---

[150] [UBS] ἀναιρεῖ verb indicative present active ἀναιρέω (fut. ἀνελῶ, 3 sg. ἀνελεῖ ; aor. ἀνεῖλα, subj. ἀνέλω, inf. ἀνελεῖν, opt. 3 sg. ἀνέλοι ; aor. pass. ἀνῃρέθην) do away with, kill, destroy; condemn to death (Ac 26.10) ; **annul, abolish** (He 10.9); midd. adopt (Ac 7.21)

[151] **στήσῃ,** verb subjunctive aorist active 3rd person singular from ἵστημι [UBS] ἵστημι and ἱστάνω …set, place, put; establish, set up, make stand; put forward; fix (a day of judgment); pay, count out (money);

[152] Hebrews 10:9 τότε εἴρηκεν· ἰδοὺ ἥκω τοῦ ποιῆσαι τὸ θέλημά σου. ἀναιρεῖ τὸ πρῶτον ἵνα τὸ δεύτερον στήσῃ, Note the articulation referring to identity they would obviously know as the first replaced by 'the second.' The only second is a system based on the blood of the covenant. The only covenant which is based on His blood is the blood of the new covenant.

The writer had drawn attention to the new covenant in many ways. The most prevalent would be in chapter eight (Heb. 8:7-13). [153] "For if that first *covenant* had been faultless, there would have been no occasion sought for a second" (Heb. 8:7). "When He said, 'A new *covenant*,' He has made the first obsolete. But whatever is becoming obsolete and growing old is ready to disappear" (Heb. 8:13).

Why go back to an old system (the first) that was passing away? The passing away was referring to the system that was dying, for its remnants were still there but the remnants were dead. It was an antique with no results but a completely dead system. Remnants may remain even from cremation, but there is no life. The system was totally dead and replaced. Israel as a nation never fully kept the Levitical system in any sense.

This old dead system was replaced with God's perfect sacrifice. "Christ's perfect sacrifice annuls the old order. The Father's dissatisfaction with the Levitical ritual, 8, is contrasted with His will for the Son, 9. This will involved the Son's sacrifice of Himself in order to establish the new covenant of perfect redemption. It also has resulted in the formation of a new company of redeemed, those who are positionally

---

[153] " **For if that first *covenant* had been faultless, there would have been no occasion sought for a second.** [8] For finding fault with them, He says, "Behold, days are coming, says the Lord, When I will effect a new covenant With the house of Israel and with the house of Judah; [9] Not like the covenant which I made with their fathers On the day when I took them by the hand To lead them out of the land of Egypt; For they did not continue in My covenant, And I did not care for them, says the Lord. [10] "For this is the covenant that I will make with the house of Israel After those days, says the Lord: I will put My laws into their minds, And I will write them upon their hearts. And I will be their God, And they shall be My people. [11] "And they shall not teach everyone his fellow citizen, And everyone his brother, saying, 'Know the LORD,' For all shall know Me, From the least to the greatest of them. [12] "For I will be merciful to their iniquities, And I will remember their sins no more." [13] **When He said, "A new *covenant*," He has made the first obsolete. But whatever is becoming obsolete and growing old is ready to disappear**" (Heb 8:7-13).

sanctified (set apart unto God as holy) through the once-for-all offering of Christ's own body."[154]

He takes away the first in order to establish the second. "The writer then expounded the text he had just quoted. In the words **He sets aside the first to establish the second** (v. 9), the author referred to the setting aside of the Old-Covenant sacrifices which did not ultimately satisfy God. What was established was God's will, and it was **by that will** that **we have been made holy through the sacrifice of the body of Jesus Christ once for all** (*ephapax;* cf. 7:27; 9:12). The words rendered "made holy" involve a single Greek word (*hēgiasmenoi*) often rendered "sanctify" (cf. 10:14, 29). Here it occurs in a tense that makes it plain, along with the rest of the statement, that the sanctification is an accomplished fact. Nowhere in Hebrews does the writer refer to the "progressive sanctification" of a believer's life. Instead sanctification is for him a functional equivalent of the Pauline concept of justification. By the sanctification which is accomplished through the death of Christ, New-Covenant worshipers are perfected for guilt-free service to God (cf. 2:11)."[155]

Conclusion

God has literally taken away the first. God has literally established the second.

"Then He said, "Behold, I have come to do Thy will." He takes away the first in order to establish the second" (Heb. 10:9).[156]

---

[154] Unger, M. F. (2005). *The new Unger's Bible Handbook* (Rev. and updated ed.) (614). Chicago: Moody Publishers.

[155] Hodges, Z. C. (1985). Hebrews. In J. F. Walvoord & R. B. Zuck (Eds.), *The Bible Knowledge Commentary: An Exposition of the Scriptures* (J. F. Walvoord & R. B. Zuck, Ed.) (Heb 10:8–10). Wheaton, IL: Victor Books.

[156] "Then He said, "Behold, I have come to do Thy will." He takes away *the first* in order to establish *the second*" (Heb. 10:9). **Note well the articulation:** τότε εἴρηκεν· ἰδοὺ ἥκω τοῦ ποιῆσαι τὸ θέλημά σου. ἀναιρεῖ **τὸ πρῶτον** ἵνα **τὸ δεύτερον** στήσῃ, The ἵνα clause is purpose with the subjunctive. [UBS] **ἀναιρεῖ** verb indicative present active **ἀναιρέω** (fut. ἀνελῶ, 3 sg. ἀνελεῖ ; aor. ἀνεῖλα, subj. ἀνέλω, inf. ἀνελεῖν, opt. 3 sg. ἀνέλοι ; aor. pass. ἀνῃρέθην) do away with, kill, destroy; condemn to death (Ac 26.10) ; **annul, abolish** (He 10.9); midd. adopt (Ac 7.21)**στήσῃ,** verb

The readers knew exactly what the first was as well as the second. They were in jeopardy of going back to the first.

subjunctive aorist active 3rd person singular from ἵστημι [UBS] ἵστημι and ἱστάνω
...set, place, put; establish, set up, make stand; put forward; fix (a day of judgment); pay, count out (money);

Chapter XI

Treat Unclean the Blood of the Covenant
Heb. 10:29

"How much severer punishment do you think he
will deserve who has trampled under foot the
Son of God, and has regarded as unclean the
blood of the covenant by which he was
sanctified, and has insulted the Spirit of grace?"
(Heb. 10:29).[157]

Note the severity of the warning to the Hebrew
believers. These were believers who were going back to the old
system or contemplating going back to the Mosaic system. The
warnings of turning from the Person and work of Christ appears
to be the constant warning throughout Hebrews. This takes
different directions as that presented here.

The context is calling attention to those who go on
sinning willfully especially after receiving the truth of all Christ
has done for them. "For if we go on sinning willfully after
receiving the knowledge of the truth, there no longer remains a
sacrifice for sins, but a certain terrifying expectation of
judgment, and the fury of a fire which will consume the
adversaries. Anyone who has set aside the Law of Moses dies
without mercy on *the testimony of* two or three witnesses" (Heb.
10:26-28). "Under the Old Covenant, if an Israelite spurned the
Mosaic Law and at least **two or three witnesses** verified his
actions, he was put to death." [158]

---

[157] Hebrews 10:29 πόσῳ δοκεῖτε χείρονος ἀξιωθήσεται τιμωρίας ὁ τὸν υἱὸν τοῦ θεοῦ
καταπατήσας καὶ τὸ αἷμα τῆς διαθήκης κοινὸν ἡγησάμενος, ἐν ᾧ ἡγιάσθη, καὶ τὸ
πνεῦμα τῆς χάριτος ἐνυβρίσας;
[158] Hodges, Z. C. (1985). Hebrews. In J. F. Walvoord & R. B. Zuck (Eds.), *The Bible
Knowledge Commentary: An Exposition of the Scriptures* (J. F. Walvoord & R. B.
Zuck, Ed.) (Heb 10:28–29). Wheaton, IL: Victor Books.

There is no longer a sacrifice for sins for anyone who turns back to the law, after receiving the knowledge of the truth. By doing so, this same person has also:

- trampled underfoot the Son of God,
- regarded as unclean the blood of the covenant by which he was sanctified
- insulted the Spirit of grace.

Trampling underfoot the Son of God is turning away from the redemption of the Eternal Son Who has provided the only way to God. "Jesus said to him, "I am the way, and the truth, and the life; no one comes to the Father, but through Me. [7] "If you had known Me, you would have known My Father also; from now on you know Him, and have seen Him" (John 14:6-7). The Son of God is the One Who has paid the penalty for all sin.

If one turns his faith from the blood of the covenant back to the law and its sacrifices, then he regards the blood of the covenant by which he was sanctified as unclean. It is His blood of the new covenant that sanctifies. These believers were already declared fully sanctified. "For by one offering He has perfected for all time those who are sanctified" (Heb 10:14). By turning back, the believer has declared the blood of the covenant as unclean.

The final charge is insulting the Spirit of grace. God the Holy Spirit is the One who has brought the unbeliever to belief. These were very serious charges. "The charge placed against these rejectors included: (1) trampling underfoot (spurning and treating shamefully) the Son of God, who purchased so great salvation; (2) rejecting as common and unholy the covenant blood of Christ by which the believer is consecrated; and (3) insulting the Holy Spirit who imparts the gracious blessing of God."[159]

One of the charges which has been leveled against a believer who has turned back to the law has to be clarified. Remember the Author was speaking of a much more severe punishment. 'How much severer punishment do you think he will deserve?'[160]

As has been shown, these charges or violations have very definite meaning. What is of interest here is those who regarded as unclean the blood of the covenant by which he was sanctified.[161] It is not the blood that sanctified or the covenant that sanctified but 'the blood of the covenant.' The writer is placing the emphasis on 'the blood of the covenant' that does the sanctifying. It is not the blood of animals or any other blood which does this. It is only the blood of the covenant or covenanted blood which sanctifies forever.

[159] Unger, M. F. (2005). *The new Unger's Bible handbook* (Rev. and updated ed.) (616). Chicago: Moody Publishers.

[160] "How much (ποσῳ [posōi]). Instrumental case of degree or measure. An argument from the less to the greater." Robertson, A. (1933). *Word Pictures in the New Testament* (Heb 10:29). Nashville, TN: Broadman Press.

[161] "The words "sanctified him" refer to true Christians. Already the writer to the Hebrews has described them as "made holy (Gr. 'sanctified') through the sacrifice of the body of Jesus Christ once for all" (10:10) and as "made perfect forever" through this sanctifying work (v. 14). Some seek to evade this conclusion by suggesting that Christ is the One referred to here as "sanctified" or that the person only *claims* to be sanctified. But these efforts are foreign to the writer's thought and are so forced that they carry their own refutation. The author's whole point lies in the seriousness of the act. To treat "the blood of the covenant" (which actually sanctifies believers) as though it were an "unholy" (*koinon*, "common") thing and to renounce its efficacy, is to commit a sin so heinous as to dwarf the fatal infractions of the Old Covenant. To this, an apostate adds the offense of insulting **the Spirit of grace** who originally wooed him to faith in Christ. This kind of spiritual rebellion clearly calls for a much worse punishment than the capital penalty that was inflicted under the Mosaic setup. But again the writer was not thinking of hell. Many forms of divine retribution can fall on a human life which are worse than immediate death. In fact, Jeremiah made just such a complaint about the punishment inflicted on Jerusalem (Lam. 4:6, 9). One might think also of King Saul, whose last days were burdened with such mental and emotional turmoil that death itself was a kind of release." Hodges, Z. C. (1985). Hebrews. In J. F. Walvoord & R. B. Zuck (Eds.), *The Bible Knowledge Commentary: An Exposition of the Scriptures* (J. F. Walvoord & R. B. Zuck, Ed.) (Heb 10:28–29). Wheaton, IL: Victor Books.

The modifier here is what is so essential. If all that was implied was 'blood' they could respond that the blood of animals can do this. But the blood of animals could not do this eternally. So the distinction has to be made clear that this is the blood of the covenant.[162] "This being true, the author then argued from the lesser to the greater. If defiance of an inferior covenant could bring such retribution, what about defiance of the New Covenant which, as he had made clear, is far superior? The answer can only be that the punishment would be substantially greater in such a case. In order to show that this is so, the writer then placed defection from the faith in the harshest possible light. An apostate from the New Covenant **has trampled the Son of God underfoot** and **has treated as an unholy thing the blood of the covenant** (cf. "blood of the eternal covenant," 13:20) **that sanctified him.**"[163]

Comments concerning modifiers

"How much severer punishment do you think he will deserve who has trampled under foot **the Son of God**, and has regarded as unclean[164] **the blood of the covenant** by which he was sanctified, and has insulted **the Spirit of grace**? Note the modifiers: the Son **of the God**, the blood **of the covenant,** the

[162] Hebrews 10:29 πόσῳ δοκεῖτε χείρονος ἀξιωθήσεται τιμωρίας ὁ τὸν υἱὸν τοῦ θεοῦ καταπατήσας καὶ **τὸ αἷμα τῆς διαθήκης** κοινὸν ἡγησάμενος, ἐν ᾧ ἡγιάσθη, καὶ τὸ πνεῦμα τῆς χάριτος ἐνυβρίσας; Note the construction with the articulation. The writer was referring continually to one particular covenant. Only the blood of the covenant = the new covenant sanctified eternally.
[163] Hodges, Z. C. (1985). Hebrews. In J. F. Walvoord & R. B. Zuck (Eds.), *The Bible Knowledge Commentary: An Exposition of the Scriptures* (J. F. Walvoord & R. B. Zuck, Ed.) (Heb 10:28–29). Wheaton, IL: Victor Books.
[164] [UBS] **κοινός**, ή, όν common, in common; common, profane; defiled, unclean; κοινός, ή, όν ...primarily 'common' ...pertaining to being of mutual interest or shared collectively, *communal, common*...pertaining to being of little value because of being common, *common, ordinary, profane... consider something ordinary* Hb 10:29...*have never eaten anything common or unclean* ... Hb 10:29 Arndt, W., Danker, F. W., & Bauer, W. (2000). *A Greek-English lexicon of the New Testament and other early Christian literature* (3rd ed.) (552). Chicago: University of Chicago Press.

Spirit **of the grace.** The prepositional modifiers cannot be ignored. This is not any Son but the Son of **(the)** God. It is not just any blood; it is the blood of **(the)** covenant. It is not just the Spirit but the Spirit of **(the)** grace.[165] The last reference is to God the Holy Spirit Who applies His grace for both salvation and sanctification.

Note it is the blood of the covenant by which he (the reader) was sanctified. This obviously proves the new covenant's blood is that which sanctified and the blood of the covenant is fully operational. This is direct principle and application and cannot be understood as totally futuristic. This can be the only deduction from the context.

The Hebrew believers were fully culpable at the time of the writing of Hebrews for their treatment of the blood of the covenant. By not handling the blood of the covenant correctly they were treating the blood as unclean.[166] The covenant's blood was totally effective. These believers were turning to other blood as that of animals of the old system. This shows that the new covenant blood is the source of that which sanctifies. No other blood can do this. This is His blood of the new covenant. It would be insulting to God to go back to the blood of animals after receiving blessings especially that of sanctification.[167]

[165] πόσῳ δοκεῖτε χείρονος ἀξιωθήσεται τιμωρίας ὁ τὸν υἱὸν **τοῦ θεοῦ** καταπατήσας καὶ τὸ αἷμα **τῆς διαθήκης** κοινὸν ἡγησάμενος, ἐν ᾧ ἡγιάσθη, καὶ τὸ πνεῦμα **τῆς χάριτος** ἐνυβρίσας (Heb. 10:29). Note the emphasis with the articulation.

[166] [UBS] **κοινός**, ή, όν common, in common; common, profane; defiled, unclean; κοινός, ή, όν ...primarily 'common' ...pertaining to being of mutual interest or shared collectively, *communal, common*...pertaining to being of little value because of being common, *common, ordinary, profane... consider something ordinary* Hb 10:29...*have never eaten anything common or unclean* ... Hb 10:29 Arndt, W., Danker, F. W., & Bauer, W. (2000). *A Greek-English lexicon of the New Testament and other early Christian literature* (3rd ed.) (552). Chicago: University of Chicago Press.

[167] **Wherewith he was sanctified** (ἐν ᾧ ἡγιάσθη [*en hōi hēgiasthē*]). First aorist passive indicative of ἁγιάζω [*hagiazō*]. It is an unspeakable tragedy that should warn every follower of Christ not to play with treachery to Christ (cf. 6:4–8). **An unholy thing** (κοινόν [*koinon*]). Common in the sense of uncleanness as Peter used it in Acts 10:14. Think of one who thus despises "the blood of Christ wherewith he was

The bifurcation or separation of these modifiers is not possible for proper exegesis and interpretation. Divorcing the modifiers from any Text divorces the intended meaning of the true Author and does damage to a proper interpretation. This appears to be done by some interpreters which cause great confusion and a lack of understanding for proper exegesis.

Conclusion

'For if we go on sinning willfully after receiving the knowledge of the truth, there no longer remains a sacrifice for sins, but a certain terrifying expectation of judgment, and the fury of a fire which will consume the adversaries" (Heb. 10:26-27). If believers turn from Christ, especially His blood of the covenant, back to law, there remains a severer punishment.[168]

sanctified." And yet there are a few today who sneer at the blood of Christ and the gospel based on his atoning sacrifice as "a slaughter house" religion! **Hath done despite** (ἐνυβρισας [*enubrisas*]). First aorist active participle of ἐνυβριζω [*enubrizō*], old verb to treat with contumely, to give insult to, here only in the N.T. It is a powerful word for insulting the Holy Spirit after receiving his blessings (6:4). Robertson, A. (1933). *Word Pictures in the New Testament* (Heb 10:29). Nashville, TN: Broadman Press.

[168] **How much** (ποσῳ [*posōi*]). Instrumental case of degree or measure. An argument from the less to the greater, "the first of Hillel's seven rules for exegesis" (Moffatt). **Think ye** (δοκειτε [*dokeite*]). An appeal to their own sense of justice about apostates from Christ. **Sorer** (χειρονος [*cheironos*]). "Worse," comparative of κακος [*kakos*] (bad). **Punishment** (τιμωριας [*timōrias*]). Genitive case with ἀξιωθησεται [*axiōthēsetai*] (first future passive of ἀξιοω [*axioō*], to deem worthy). The word τιμωρια [*timōria*] originally meant vengeance. Old word, in LXX, only here in N.T. **Who hath trodden under foot the Son of God** (ὁ τον υιον του θεου καταπατησας [*ho ton huion tou theou katapatēsas*]). First aorist active articular participle of καταπατεω [*katapateō*], old verb (Matt. 5:13) for scornful neglect like Zech. 12:3. See same idea in Heb. 6:6. **Wherewith he was sanctified** (ἐν ᾧ ἡγιασθη [*en hōi hēgiasthē*]). First aorist passive indicative of ἁγιαζω [*hagiazō*]. It is an unspeakable tragedy that should warn every follower of Christ not to play with treachery to Christ (cf. 6:4–8). **An unholy thing** (κοινον [*koinon*]). Common in the sense of uncleanness as Peter used it in Acts 10:14. Think of one who thus despises "the blood of Christ wherewith he was sanctified." And yet there are a few today who sneer at the blood of Christ and the gospel based on his atoning sacrifice as "a slaughter house" religion! **Hath done despite** (ἐνυβρισας [*enubrisas*]). First aorist active participle of ἐνυβριζω [*enubrizō*], old verb to treat with contumely, to give insult to, here only in the N.T. It is a powerful word for insulting the Holy Spirit after receiving his

"But again the writer was not thinking of hell. Many forms of divine retribution can fall on a human life which are worse than immediate death. In fact, Jeremiah made just such a complaint about the punishment inflicted on Jerusalem (Lam. 4:6, 9). One might think also of King Saul, whose last days were burdened with such mental and emotional turmoil that death itself was a kind of release."[169]

The new covenant is not only operational but there are judgments for those who do not treat the blood of the covenant with absolute reverence. The writer has singled out this blood. This is not just any blood but the blood of the covenant by definition.

blessings (6:4). Robertson, A. (1933). *Word Pictures in the New Testament* (Heb 10:29). Nashville, TN: Broadman Press.

[169] Hodges, Z. C. (1985). Hebrews. In J. F. Walvoord & R. B. Zuck (Eds.), *The Bible Knowledge Commentary: An Exposition of the Scriptures* (J. F. Walvoord & R. B. Zuck, Ed.) (Heb 10:28–29). Wheaton, IL: Victor Books.

118 The Greatness of His Blood

Chapter XII

Blood of the Eternal Covenant
Heb. 13:20

"Now the God of peace, who brought up
from the dead the great Shepherd of the
sheep through the blood of the eternal
covenant, *even* Jesus our Lord" (Heb.
13:20)

The writer of Hebrews presents a most powerful
benediction. This verse brings together the God of peace, the
great Shepherd, the blood of the eternal covenant, and Jesus our
LORD. The writer is drawing attention to His resurrection. His
resurrection may be alluded to by the writer (Heb. 1:3)[170] yet
this is the only direct mention of Jesus' resurrection in this
epistle. This verse stresses His resurrection confirming all
being mentioned is true based on the God of peace raising Him
from the dead.[171]

---

[170] "And He is the radiance of His glory and the exact representation of His nature,
and upholds all things by the word of His power. **When He had made purification
of sins,** He sat down at the right hand of the Majesty on high" (Heb 1:3).
[171] **"The God of peace** (ὁ θεος της εἰρηνης [*ho theos tēs eirēnēs*]). God is the author
and giver of peace, a Pauline phrase (6 times) as in I Thess. 5:23. **Who brought
again from the dead** (ὁ ἀναγαγων ἐκ νεκρων [*ho anagagōn ek nekrōn*]). Second
aorist active articular participle of ἀναγω [*anagō*] (cf. Rom. 10:7), the only direct
mention of the resurrection of Jesus in the Epistle, though implied often (1:3, etc.).
That great shepherd of the sheep (τον ποιμενα των προβατων τον μεγαν [*ton
poimena tōn probatōn ton megan*]). This phrase occurs in Isa. 63:11 except τον μεγαν
[*ton megan*] which the author adds as in 4:14; 10:21. So here, "the shepherd of the
sheep the great one." **With the blood of the eternal covenant** (ἐν αἱματι διαθηκης
αἰωνιου [*en haimati diathēkēs aiōniou*]). This language is from Zech. 9:11. The
language reminds us of Christ's own words in Mark 14:24 (Matt. 26:28=Luke
22:20=I Cor. 11:25) about "my blood of the covenant." Robertson, A. (1933). *Word
Pictures in the New Testament* (Heb 13:20–21). Nashville, TN: Broadman Press.

The God of peace[172] has raised or brought up the great Shepherd of the sheep from the dead. His resurrection proves everything He has declared is absolute truth. His resurrection proves the written Word is absolute truth. "And if Christ has not been raised, your faith is worthless; you are still in your sins. (1Co 15:17); "*He* who was delivered up because of our transgressions, and was raised because of our justification" (Rom 4:25).

The writer has also drawn attention to the 'blood of the eternal covenant.' The only eternal covenant which Hebrews was stressing and has quoted in essence word for word is the new covenant of Jeremiah 31:31-34. This covenant or contract is eternal, unilateral, and unconditional. It is eternal in that it is made only by God from heaven. It is unilateral based on the fact that only God will keep this covenant or contract. It is not dependent on the party with whom God has made the contract. It is unconditional in that there are no conditions, conditional statements, or contingencies which are added or have been added to the contract for its fulfillment. Only God can fulfill this eternal covenant.

The translators appear to use the word 'through' that is 'through the blood of the eternal covenant.' This is unusual for the normal use of the word ἐν which can mean 'in, at near, by, or with.'[173] The more normal use of the preposition is to

---

[172] Romans 15:33 Now the **God of peace** be with you all. Amen. Romans 16:20 And the **God of peace** will soon crush Satan under your feet. The grace of our Lord Jesus be with you. Philippians 4:9 The things you have learned and received and heard and seen in me, practice these things; and the **God of peace** shall be with you. 1 Thessalonians 5:23 Now may the **God of peace** Himself sanctify you entirely; and may your spirit and soul and body be preserved complete, without blame at the coming of our Lord Jesus Christ. Hebrews 13:20 Now the **God of peace**, who brought up from the dead the great Shepherd of the sheep through the blood of the eternal covenant, *even* Jesus our Lord,

[173] Ὁ δὲ θεὸς τῆς εἰρήνης, ὁ ἀναγαγὼν ἐκ νεκρῶν τὸν ποιμένα τῶν προβάτων τὸν μέγαν ἐν αἵματι διαθήκης αἰωνίου, τὸν κύριον ἡμῶν Ἰησοῦν, Note the ἐν and the translation "Now the God of peace, who brought up from the dead the great Shepherd of the sheep **through** the blood of the eternal covenant, *even* Jesus our Lord" (Heb. 13:20). The normal use of is [UBS] ἐν prep. with dat. in, on, at; near, by, before; among, within; by, with; into (= εἰς); to, for (rarely); ἐν τῷ with inf. during, while, as;

translate in this way 'with the blood.' "With the blood of the eternal covenant (ἐν αἵματι διαθηκης αἰωνιου [*en haimati diathēkēs aiōniou*]). This language is from Zech. 9:11.[174] The language reminds us of Christ's own words in Mark 14:24 (=Matt. 26:28=Luke 22:20=I Cor. 11:25) about "my blood of the covenant."[175]

The fact the writer of Hebrews virtually quoted the new covenant gives rise to the prominence being placed on the expression 'with the blood of the eternal covenant.' This is an eternal, unconditional, unilateral blood covenant being confirmed not only by His blood but now by His resurrection. This is further proof to the Hebrew readers that the new covenant not only became fully functional at His death, but also completely validated by His resurrection. They appeared to need this confirmation.

ἐν ὀνόματι ὅτι because (Mk 9.41); ἐν preposition with the dative; the primary idea is *within, in, withinness*, denoting static position or time, but the many and varied uses can be determined only by the context; very rarely would the translation be made 'through'.. that would be more [UBS] διά prep. with: (1) gen. through, by means of, with; during, throughout (διὰ παντός continually); through, among, throughout; (2) acc. because of, on account of, for the sake of; through, by (rarely); διὰ τοῦτο therefore, for this reason; διὰ (τό) with inf. because; διὰ τί why? (UBS).
[174] **Zechariah 9:11** "As for you also, because of the blood of *My* covenant with you, I have set your prisoners free from the waterless pit" (Zech 9:11) "God's faithfulness to His covenants with Israel is His basis for delivering her from worldwide dispersion. The immediate addressees in these verses may have been Jewish exiles still in Babylon, but the covenant-fulfillment theme suggests an ultimate reference to Israel's end-time regathering. At least the nation's future hope (messianic deliverance) was the basis for contemporary encouragement in Zechariah's day. **The blood of My covenant with you** may refer to the sacrifices of the Mosaic Covenant (cf. Ex. 24:8), but could as well relate back to the foundational Abrahamic Covenant which was confirmed with a blood sacrifice (Gen. 15:8–21). **The waterless pit** (an empty cistern used for a dungeon) is probably a figure for the place of exile. The **fortress** refers to Jerusalem. The exiles in Babylon were called **prisoners of hope** because they had God's promise of being regathered. God **will restore twice as much**, that is, His blessings in the Millennium will far exceed anything Israel has ever known." Lindsey, F. D. (1985). Zechariah. In J. F. Walvoord & R. B. Zuck (Eds.), *The Bible Knowledge Commentary: An Exposition of the Scriptures* (J. F. Walvoord & R. B. Zuck, Ed.) (Zec 9:11–12). Wheaton, IL: Victor Books.
[175] Robertson, A. (1933). *Word Pictures in the New Testament* (Heb 13:20–21). Nashville, TN: Broadman Press.

Blood is mentioned over 400 times in the Scriptures. In the New Testament it is mentioned about 97 times. Hebrews mentions blood the most at 23 times.[176] What is significant in Heb. 13:20 is the association of 'the blood' with the resurrection of Christ which is normally referred to as bodily resurrection. Here the stress is on His resurrection yet 'with the blood of the eternal covenant.'[177] The readers were to be encouraged even more by this benediction for their focus should be on the body and blood of Christ.[178]

---

[176] 2:14 Since then the children share in flesh and **blood**, He Himself likewise also partook of the same, that through death He might render powerless him who had the power of death, that is, the devil; 9:7 but into the second only the high priest *enters*, once a year, not without *taking* **blood**, which he offers for himself and for the sins of the people committed in ignorance. 9:12 and not through the **blood** of goats and calves, but through His own **blood**, He entered the holy place once for all, having obtained eternal redemption. 9:13 For if the **blood** of goats and bulls and the ashes of a heifer sprinkling those who have been defiled, sanctify for the cleansing of the flesh, 9:14 how much more will the **blood** of Christ, who through the eternal Spirit offered Himself without blemish to God, cleanse your conscience from dead works to serve the living God? 9:18 Therefore even the first *covenant* was not inaugurated without **blood**. 9:19 For when every commandment had been spoken by Moses to all the people according to the Law, he took the **blood** of the calves and the goats, with water and scarlet wool and hyssop, and sprinkled both the book itself and all the people, 9:20 saying, "This is the **blood** of the covenant which God commanded you." 9:21 And in the same way he sprinkled both the tabernacle and all the vessels of the ministry with the **blood**. 9:22 And according to the Law, *one may* almost *say*, all things are cleansed with **blood**, and without shedding of **blood** there is no forgiveness. 9:25 nor was it that He should offer Himself often, as the high priest enters the holy place year by year with **blood** not his own. 10:4 For it is impossible for the **blood** of bulls and goats to take away sins. 10:19 Since therefore, brethren, we have confidence to enter the holy place by the **blood** of Jesus, 10:29 How much severer punishment do you think he will deserve who has trampled under foot the Son of God, and has regarded as unclean the **blood** of the covenant by which he was sanctified, and has insulted the Spirit of grace? 11:28 By faith he kept the Passover and the sprinkling of the **blood**, so that he who destroyed the first-born might not touch them. 12:4 You have not yet resisted to the point of shedding **blood** in your striving against sin; 12:24 and to Jesus, the mediator of a new covenant, and to the sprinkled **blood**, which speaks better than *the **blood*** of Abel. 13:11 For the bodies of those animals whose **blood** is brought into the holy place by the high priest *as an offering* for sin, are burned outside the camp. 13:12 Therefore Jesus also, that He might sanctify the people through His own **blood**, suffered outside the gate. 13:20 Now the God of peace, who brought up from the dead the great Shepherd of the sheep through the **blood** of the eternal covenant, *even* Jesus our Lord.

[177] This may seem strange yet the writer has put emphasis on 'blood' especially that of Christ and the new covenant.

[178] As it should also be in the church age.

As He has been resurrected 'bodily' it is still His body raised yet changed from the earthly body (1 Cor. 15:38-48).[179] The writer has associated His literal blood with His literal bodily resurrection. At Christ's last breath His blood became totally efficacious for the forgiveness of all sin for all time (Mat. 26:28; Luke 22:20). This is His blood of the new covenant.[180] But observe well that the author of Hebrews has connected the blood of the new covenant with His resurrection. Their focus must be on His body and His blood of the new covenant. All this is inseparable.

His body and blood go together for making atonement. The writer has stressed His resurrection in connection with the blood of the new covenant.[181] Christ's resurrection gives full

[179] "But God gives it a body just as He wished, and to each of the seeds a body of its own. [39] All flesh is not the same flesh, but there is one *flesh* of men, and another flesh of beasts, and another flesh of birds, and another of fish. [40] There are also heavenly bodies and earthly bodies, but the glory of the heavenly is one, and the *glory* of the earthly is another. [41] There is one glory of the sun, and another glory of the moon, and another glory of the stars; for star differs from star in glory. [42] So also is the resurrection of the dead. It is sown a perishable *body*, it is raised an imperishable *body*; [43] it is sown in dishonor, it is raised in glory; it is sown in weakness, it is raised in power; [44] it is sown a natural body, it is raised a spiritual body. If there is a natural body, there is also a spiritual *body*. [45] So also it is written, "The first man, Adam, became a living soul." The last Adam *became* a life-giving spirit. [46] However, the spiritual is not first, but the natural; then the spiritual. [47] The first man is from the earth, earthy; the second man is from heaven. [48] As is the earthy, so also are those who are earthy; and as is the heavenly, so also are those who are heavenly" (1Co 15:38-48).

[180] Just one infinitesimal drop of that precious blood became the source for putting the new covenant into full operation.

[181] "In a lovely benediction which captures a number of the major themes of the epistle (e.g., **peace, blood, covenant**, Resurrection, **Shepherd, equip**), the writer expressed confidence in **our Lord Jesus** as the **Great Shepherd** of New-Covenant people, through whom God was able to effect His will (equip is *katartisai*, "to prepare, make ready for use"; cf. Eph. 4:12) in the readers and in himself. This indeed is what he prayed for his readers." Hodges, Z. C. (1985). Hebrews. In J. F. Walvoord & R. B. Zuck (Eds.), *The Bible Knowledge Commentary: An Exposition of the Scriptures* (J. F. Walvoord & R. B. Zuck, Ed.) (Heb 13:20–21). Wheaton, IL: Victor Books."This prayer of the writer contains essential elements for the spiritual well-being of the Hebrew believers to whom he has been writing: (1) 'the God of peace,' who has established or made peace between man and Himself through the sacrifice of Christ, and who gives peace of mind and soul to those who trust in Him; (2) the hope of resurrection founded on God's raising Christ from the dead; (3) the

assurance of the blood of the new covenant.[182] Again, all this is inseparable.

Conclusion

There is only one new covenant Heb. 8:8-12 (Jer. 31:31-34). There is only One Who was raised from the dead with the blood of the new covenant. His death set in motion the new covenant and the forgiveness of sins by the blood of the new covenant. The resurrection gives absolute proof and assurance to the truth of His blood of the new covenant.

> "And they shall not teach again, each
> man his neighbor and each man his brother,
> saying, 'Know the LORD,' for they shall all
> know Me, from the least of them to the
> greatest of them," declares the LORD, *"for I
> will forgive their iniquity, and their sin I will
> remember no more"* (Jer. 31:34).

This is the promised eternal forgiveness covenanted or contracted exclusively in the new covenant. Christ's very words claiming the new covenant as His own.

> "And in the same way *He took* the cup
> after they had eaten, saying, "This cup which
> is poured out for you is the new covenant in
> My blood" (Luke 22:20); "For this is My

shepherd care of Christ for His own; (4) the assurance of covenant relationship based on Christ's shed blood; (5) a request for each believer's fitness for his task in the will of God – 'equip you'; (6) a request to allow the indwelling Christ to work in the believer that which is pleasing to God. Such matters would have particular relevance for Hebrew believers, who would contrast them with the inferior blessings of Judaism.' Unger, M. F. (2005). *The new Unger's Bible handbook* (Rev. and updated ed.) (623). Chicago: Moody Publishers.

[182] This verse stresses that assurance to the Hebrew believers. They can't go back to the old system and the blood of animals. For if they don't accept His resurrection 'with the blood of the new covenant' they have to go back to the blood of the old.

blood of the covenant, which is poured out for many for forgiveness of sins" (Mat 26:28); "And He said to them, "This is My blood of the covenant, which is poured out for many" (Mar 14:24).

His blood set this covenant into full operation.

"Behold, days are coming," declares the LORD, "when I will make a new covenant with the house of Israel and with the house of Judah, [32] not like the covenant which I made with their fathers in the day I took them by the hand to bring them out of the land of Egypt, My covenant which they broke, although I was a husband to them," declares the LORD. [33] "But this is the covenant which I will make with the house of Israel after those days," declares the LORD, "I will put My law within them, and on their heart I will write it; and I will be their God, and they shall be My people. [34] "And they shall not teach again, each man his neighbor and each man his brother, saying, 'Know the LORD,' for they shall all know Me, from the least of them to the greatest	"Behold, days are coming, says the Lord, When I will effect a new covenant With the house of Israel and with the house of Judah; [9] Not like the covenant which I made with their fathers On the day when I took them by the hand To lead them out of the land of Egypt; For they did not continue in My covenant, And I did not care for them, says the Lord. [10] "For this is the covenant that I will make with the house of Israel After those days, says the Lord: I will put My laws into their minds, And I will write them upon their hearts. And I will be their God, And they shall be My people. [11] "And they shall not teach everyone his fellow citizen, And everyone his brother, saying, 'Know the LORD,' For all shall know Me, From the least to the greatest of them. [12] "For

of them," declares the LORD, "for I will forgive their iniquity, and their sin I will remember no more" (Jer 31:31-34).	I will be merciful to their iniquities, And I will remember their sins no more." (Heb 8:8-12)

- "For this is **My blood of the covenant**, which is poured out for many for forgiveness of sins" (Mat 26:28)
- "And He said to them, "This **is My blood of the covenant**, which is poured out for many" (Mar 14:24)
- **"This cup which is poured out for you is the new covenant in My blood**" (Luke 22:20)
- "For I will forgive their iniquity, and their sin I will remember no more" (Jer. 31:34)
- "Now the God of peace, who brought up from the dead the great Shepherd of the sheep **with the blood of the eternal covenant**, *even* Jesus our Lord" (Heb. 13:20)

His resurrection gives proof and assurance of Who He is and what He did. He is the Son of God. He died for our sins and was raised on the third day. The blood of the new covenant was for the forgiveness of sins. This gives these Hebrew believers as well as all believers great assurance concerning the blood of the new covenant.

Believers cannot turn back to the old (Mosaic system) for anything. They can't go back to the old system and the blood of animals. For if they don't accept His resurrection 'with the blood of the new covenant' they have to go back to the blood of the old. "The readers of Hebrews were wondering whether they should reject Christianity and return to Judaism in the face of increasing persecution. Jesus is the Great Shepherd of the sheep, having laid down His life for them (see John 10:15) and now continues to make intercession for them (7:25).

The New Covenant is an everlasting covenant; it will never become obsolete like the Mosaic covenant (8:13)."[183]

[183] The Nelson Study Bible, Nelson Ministry Services Special Edition; Thomas Nelson Publishers, Nashville, 1997; p. 2101.

Chapter XIII

The Root of the Tree
(Rom. 11:16-17)

"And if the first piece *of dough* be holy, the lump
is also; and if the root be holy, the branches are
too. But if some of the branches were broken
off, and you, being a wild olive, were grafted in
among them and became partaker with them of
the rich root of the olive tree" (Rom. 11:16-
17).[184]

There is continued concern of how Gentiles (especially
in the church age) are connected to God's covenanted program
with His holy people, national Israel. This started very early in
the church, and Paul addressed this in his epistle to the Romans.
To be very specific the question is how do Gentiles in the
church age relate to God's covenants with Israel?

The history of man after the fall and the flood is based
on God's eternal covenanted program with Israel. The eternal,
unilateral, and unconditional covenants were made exclusively
by God with Abraham, Isaac, Jacob, David, and Israel. These
covenants can only be fulfilled exclusively with these named
persons and nation. The question is again, how do Gentiles fit
in? Paul addressed this very issue in Romans chapter 11. Paul
made it very clear that the Gentiles and/or the church do not
replace Israel in any sense. Not only are Israel and the church
completely distinct, their programs are completely distinct. As
an example the church is not a kingdom, not building a
kingdom, not a taste of the kingdom, not a preview of the

---

[184] εἰ δὲ ἡ ἀπαρχὴ ἁγία, καὶ τὸ φύραμα· καὶ εἰ ἡ ῥίζα ἁγία, καὶ οἱ κλάδοι. [17] Εἰ δέ
τινες τῶν κλάδων ἐξεκλάσθησαν, σὺ δὲ ἀγριέλαιος ὢν ἐνεκεντρίσθης ἐν αὐτοῖς καὶ
συγκοινωνὸς τῆς ῥίζης τῆς πιότητος τῆς ἐλαίας ἐγένου,

kingdom, but the church certainly prays for the coming kingdom. Christ is now building His church not a kingdom in any sense. Replacement theology or supersessionism[185] seems to have started very early in the church. Paul made it very obvious that national Israel's future is not only secured, but the future depends on the continued existence and fulfillment of His covenanted program with national Israel. If one tittle of any of these covenants fails to be accomplished, then the entire word of God fails to be true. It is sometimes said that God has a future for Israel. That is more than a gross understatement as the entire future for everyone and the world depends on His keeping His eternal covenants with Israel. If He does not keep His covenanted promises with Israel, why should anyone depend on His promises? More will be said on this later.

Romans chapter nine basically deals with the past history of Israel. Chapter ten addresses present Israel and chapter eleven future Israel. What needs to be determined is the place of Gentiles (or the church) as the wild branches[186] opposed to the natural branches. Very rarely would one graft a wild plant into a cultivated plant.

"And if the first piece *of dough* be holy, the lump is also; and if the root be holy, the branches are too" (Rom. 11:16). Paul gives an explanation of the dough or lump being holy starting with a reference in the Pentateuch. "Then it shall be, that when you eat of the food of the land, you shall lift up an offering to the LORD. 'Of the first of your dough you shall lift up a cake as an offering; as the offering of the threshing floor, so you shall lift it up. 'From the first of your dough you shall

---

[185]The replacement in any sense of Israel with the church is replacement theology. Only dispensationalism holding to a complete distinction between Israel and the church can claim a non-supersession position.
[186]"For if you were cut off from what is by nature **a wild olive tree**, and were grafted contrary to nature into a cultivated olive tree, how much more shall these who are the natural *branches* be grafted into their own olive tree?" (Rom 11:24). Very rarely would a horticulturist graft a wild plant into a cultivated plant.

give to the LORD an offering throughout your generations" (Num 15:19-21).[187] "When the people entered the land of Canaan and began to enjoy its produce, they were to show their devotion to the LORD by presenting to Him a cake[188] baked from the first cutting of the grain."[189] Note well that the first piece (literally the 'first fruits') *of the dough* is holy.[190] Since this is true the lump is 'holy' also. And since the root is holy also are the branches. There are two separate metaphors being used in these verses yet both have the same premise and conclusion. The first piece (fruit/s), the lump, the root, and the branches are all holy by definition. The basic definition of holy is separate or literally separated unto God.

- The first piece = holy = separated unto God
- The lump = holy = separated unto God

- The root = holy = separated unto God
- The branches = holy = separated unto God

How are all the above (holy) separated unto God and when did they become separated unto God? God separated Abraham when He chose him and made an eternal covenant

[187] καὶ ἔσται ὅταν ἔσθητε ὑμεῖς ἀπὸ τῶν ἄρτων τῆς γῆς ἀφελεῖτε ἀφαίρεμα ἀφόρισμα κυρίῳ [20] **ἀπαρχὴν φυράματος** ὑμῶν ἄρτον ἀφαίρεμα ἀφοριεῖτε αὐτό ὡς ἀφαίρεμα ἀπὸ ἅλω οὕτως ἀφελεῖτε αὐτόν [21] **ἀπαρχὴν φυράματος** ὑμῶν καὶ δώσετε κυρίῳ ἀφαίρεμα εἰς τὰς γενεὰς ὑμῶν (Numbers 15:19-21 LXX)
[188]" Then it shall be, that when you eat of the food of the land, you shall lift up an offering to the LORD. [20] 'Of **the first of your dough** you shall lift up a cake as an offering; as the offering of the threshing floor, so you shall lift it up. [21] 'From **the first of your dough** you shall give to the LORD an offering throughout your generations" (Num 15:19-21). Note: both expressions identical from the LXX **ἀπαρχὴν φυράματος**
[189] Merrill, E. H. (1985). Numbers. In J. F. Walvoord & R. B. Zuck (Eds.), *The Bible Knowledge Commentary: An Exposition of the Scriptures* (J. F. Walvoord & R. B. Zuck, Ed.) (Nu 15:17–21). Wheaton, IL: Victor Books.
[190] "And if the first piece *of dough* be **holy**, the lump is also; and if the root be **holy**, the branches are too" (Rom. 15:16). εἰ δὲ ἡ **ἀπαρχὴ** ἁγία, καὶ τὸ φύραμα· καὶ εἰ ἡ ῥίζα **ἁγία**, καὶ οἱ κλάδοι.

with him. This began God's eternal, unconditional, and unilateral covenanted program with Abraham. God made this covenant with Abraham, and this covenant is the basis for God's entire program with man from Genesis to Revelation. God separated Abraham and from him came Isaac, Jacob, David, and Israel as only these are His covenanted people. They are holy or separate/d for God has decreed this by covenants and oaths.

If the first piece is holy, the lump also is holy. The first piece is literally the first fruits. The first fruit was taken from the lump (the dough or baked cake). Paul is discussing in Rom. 11:16f the 'origins' especially that of national Israel.[191] The first fruits could easily be the patriarchs of Israel i.e. Isaac and Jacob.[192] Isaac and Jacob came from the 'lump' or origin which was Abraham. Jacob's name was changed to Israel and from him came the twelve tribes or national Israel (the tree and the branches).[193] But the patriarchs cannot be separated from the

[191] One might say the tree or the branches. The olive tree was a normal term for Israel. Branches might be the individuals of the tree.
[192] **First fruit** (ἀπαρχη [*aparchē*]). See on I Cor. 15:20, 23. The metaphor is from Numb. 15:19f. The LXX has ἀπαρχην φυραματος [*aparchēn phuramatos*], first of the dough as a heave offering. **The lump** (το φυραμα [*to phurama*]). From which the first fruit came. See on 9:21. Apparently the patriarchs are the first fruit. **The root** (ἡ ριζα [*hē riza*]). Perhaps Abraham singly here. The metaphor is changed, but the idea is the same. Israel is looked on as a tree. But one must recall and keep in mind the double sense of Israel in 9:6f. (the natural and the spiritual). Robertson, A. (1933). *Word Pictures in the New Testament* (Ro 11:16–18). Nashville, TN: Broadman Press.
[193] "But *it is* not as though the word of God has failed. For they are not all Israel who are *descended* from Israel" (Rom 9:6). National Israel is an elect and holy nation. But not all Israel are believers. God has always had a remnant who are His chosen within the chosen nation. "The failure of the Jews to respond to the gospel of Christ did not mean **God's Word had failed**. Instead this rejection was simply the current example of the principle of God's sovereign choice established in the Old Testament. Paul reminded his readers of a truth he had presented earlier: **For not all who are descended from Israel are Israel**, that is, spiritual Israel (cf. 2:28–29). Then Paul gave three Old Testament illustrations of God's sovereignty (Isaac and Ishmael, 9:7b–9; Jacob and Esau, vv. 10–13; and Pharaoh, vv. 14–18). The first two show that God made a sovereign choice among the physical descendants of Abraham in establishing the spiritual line of promise. Ishmael, born to Hagar (Gen. 16)—and the six sons of Keturah as well (Gen. 25:1–4)—were Abraham's **descendants** (*sperma*), but they were not counted as **Abraham's children** (*tekna*, "born ones") in

covenants made with them. In fact this defines them and God's entire program with them. "He has remembered His covenant forever, the word which He commanded to a thousand generations, *the covenant* which He made with Abraham, And His oath to Isaac. Then He confirmed it to Jacob for a statute, To Israel as an everlasting covenant, Saying, "To you I will give the land of Canaan As the portion of your inheritance" (Psalm 105:8-11). The land was the basis for the original Abrahamic covenant which was unconditional. It did not depend on Abraham leaving his land or his obedience in any way. There was *no* condition for this covenant.

Abraham as the origin or root, Isaac and Jacob as the first fruits, these patriarchs and the covenants God made with them define Israel. The natural branches of the tree are holy and this refers to national Israel or better the individuals of national Israel. Again, they are holy, separated unto God as His people a holy nation. "And you shall be to Me a kingdom of priests and a holy nation. These are the words that you shall speak to the sons of Israel" (Ex. 19:6). All this is rooted in Abraham and the covenant made with him.

- The first piece = holy = separated unto God=Isaac and Jacob
- The lump = holy = separated unto God=Abraham and the covenant

the line of promise. Instead, as God told Abraham (Gen. 21:12), **It is through Isaac that your offspring will be reckoned** (lit., "in Isaac seed [*sperma*] will be called to you"). Paul repeated the principle for emphasis **in** different **words: It is not the natural children** (lit., "the born ones of the flesh") **who are God's children** (*tekna*, "born ones of God"), **but it is the children** (*tekna*) **of the promise who are regarded as Abraham's offspring** (*sperma*). To be a physical descendant of Abraham is not enough; one must be chosen by God (cf. "chosen" in Rom. 8:33) and must believe in Him (4:3, 22–24). God's assurance that **the promise** would come through Isaac, not Ishmael, was given to Abraham: **At the appointed time I will return, and Sarah will have a son** (a somewhat free quotation of Gen. 18:10 from the LXX." Witmer, J. A. (1985). Romans. In J. F. Walvoord & R. B. Zuck (Eds.), *The Bible Knowledge Commentary: An Exposition of the Scriptures* (J. F. Walvoord & R. B. Zuck, Ed.) (Ro 9:6–9). Wheaton, IL: Victor Books.

- The root = holy = separated unto God=the patriarchs and covenant/s
- The branches = holy = separated unto God=national Israel

Note well that 'some' of the branches were broken off: "But if some of the branches were broken off, and you, being a wild olive, were grafted in among them and became partaker with them of the rich root of the olive tree" (Rom 11:17).[194] The first part of the statement is a first class condition. As some of the natural branches were broken off, this means these natural branches have been removed or taken away from the place of privilege or blessing (the rich root of blessings). Paul made it very clear these natural branches would be re-grafted into the tree which is theirs by God's eternal covenant design.

Some of the branches *were* broken off, 'and you (believing Gentiles) were grafted in.' As these Gentiles have been grafted in they have become partakers of the root of the fatness or the rich root of the olive tree.   From the day of Pentecost, Israel has not been in their natural place of privilege

---

[194] **Branches** (κλαδων [*kladōn*]). From κλαω [*klaō*], to break. **Were broken off** (ἐξεκλασθησαν [*exeklasthēsan*]). First aorist passive indicative of ἐκκλαω [*ekklaō*]. Play on the word κλαδος [*klados*] (branch) and ἐκκλαω [*ekklaō*], to break off. Condition of first class, assumed as true. Some of the individual Jews (natural Israel) were broken off the stock of the tree (spiritual Israel). **And thou** (και συ [*kai su*]). An individual Gentile. **Being a wild olive** (ἀγριελαιος ὢν [*agrielaios ōn*]). This word, used by Aristotle, occurs in an inscription. Ramsay (*Pauline Studies*, pp. 219ff.) shows that the ancients used the wild-olive graft upon an old olive tree to reinvigorate the tree precisely as Paul uses the figure here and that both the olive tree and the graft were influenced by each other, though the wild olive graft did not produce as good olives as the original stock. But it should be noted that in verse 24 Paul expressly states that the grafting of Gentiles on to the stock of the spiritual Israel was "contrary to nature" (παρα φυσιν [*para phusin*]). **Wast grafted in** (ἐνεκεντρισθης [*enekentristhēs*]). First aorist passive indicative of ἐνκεντριζω [*enkentrizō*], to cut in, to graft, used by Aristotle. Belongs "to the higher *Koiné*" (literary *Koiné*) according to Milligan. **Partaker** (συνκοινωνος [*sunkoinōnos*]). Co-partner. **Fatness** (πιοτητος [*piotētos*]). Old word from πιων [*piōn*] (fat), only here in N.T. Note three genitives here "of the root of the fatness of the olive." Robertson, A. (1933). *Word Pictures in the New Testament* (Ro 11:16–18). Nashville, TN: Broadman Press.

and blessing. They are the natural heirs to *all* the covenant blessings never the church and never Gentiles. But the church and Gentiles do receive blessings from the root.

Paul gives warning to the wild branches (Gentiles) being grafted into the place of some of the natural branches. "Do not be arrogant toward the branches; but if you are arrogant, *remember that* it is not you who supports the root, but the root *supports* you" (Rom 11:18). The root has not changed. It is the identical root that defined Israel and all Israel's blessings. There is no reason for anti-Semitism in the church. The church has no right to boast about anything. "*Remember that* it is not you who supports the root, <u>but the root</u> *supports* you" Everything the church has is rooted in the fact God called Abraham, Isaac, Jacob, and Israel and made eternal covenants with them. And from them the Jews, national Israel, came Christ and salvation, for salvation is of the Jews.

Just because some natural branches (Israel) were broken off does not mean Gentiles or the church in the present age or any age replace Israel's covenanted position with God. The wild branches do not replace Israel or the Jews in any sense. Paul made this perfectly clear. "I say then, God has not rejected His people, has He? *May it never be*! For I too am an Israelite, a descendant of Abraham, of the tribe of Benjamin" (Rom 11:1); "Now if their transgression be riches for the world and their failure be riches for the Gentiles, *how much more will their fulfillment be!*" (Rom 11:12); and thus all Israel will be saved; just as it is written, "The Deliverer will come from Zion, He will remove ungodliness from Jacob" (Rom 11:26).

Only the natural branches are the legal natural heirs to the covenants. Yet blessings flow to *all* the branches in the tree. Gentiles easily receive blessings just from the blessings promised in the Abrahamic covenant. "And I will bless those who bless you, and the one who curses you I will curse. And in you all the families of the earth shall be blessed" (Gen 12:3). The complete opposite can happen also, and this was the warning to these Gentiles who were arrogant towards the natural branches.[195] The Gentiles and the church owe basically everything to Israel and God's covenanted plan with them.

There is not one iota of replacement of the church with Israel in any sense. Yet, at this time the church is in a place of privilege and blessing. And one day God will engraft His people back into their natural place as the natural branches. They will truly be once again in the place of great privilege and blessings as God will fulfill all His covenants with them. All the blessings are the result of the holy root. And that holy root began with choosing Abraham and making an eternal, unconditional, unilateral covenant with him.

Conclusion

Blessings flow from God's choosing a people as His own and covenanting His earthly and eternal program with them. All men may participate in these gracious eternal blessings. All these blessings are from His grace through faith. Only by faith are Gentiles grafted into this tree. Jews on the other hand are both physically (seminally) and spiritually the natural branches.[196] The Gentiles were never seminally connected to the root of Abraham. Paul makes this very clear to the Gentiles: "You will say then, "Branches were broken off so

---

[195] Again the warning concerning Gentiles and their arrogance towards the natural heirs or branches: "Do not be arrogant toward the branches; but if you are arrogant, *remember that* it is not you who supports the root, but the root *supports* you" (Rom 11:18). Jesus made it very clear that salvation is of the Jews. This was a stern warning to these Gentile believers. Paul sternly warned these believers. One wonders how many churches believe they have replaced Israel?

[196] "But *it is* not as though the word of God has failed. For they are not all Israel who are *descended* from Israel; (Rom 9:6). While national Israel is His chosen people, not all are His children by faith (see footnote 10). Paul made it very clear that even the Jew who is part of natural Israel seminally must also be a believer.

that I might be grafted in. Quite right, they were broken off for their unbelief, but you stand by your faith. Do not be conceited, but fear; for if God did not spare the natural branches, neither will He spare you" (Rom. 11:19-21).[197] There will be a reminder of God's eternal program in the eternal state in the eternal city.

"It had a great and high wall, with twelve gates, and at the gates twelve angels; and names *were* written on them, which are *those* of the twelve tribes of the sons of Israel" (Rev 21:12). "And the wall of the city had twelve foundation stones, and on them *were* the twelve names of the twelve apostles of the Lamb" (Rev 21:14). Blessings flow through His eternal covenants. Salvation is of the Jews.

---

[197] Romans 11:19 ἐρεῖς οὖν· ἐξεκλάσθησαν κλάδοι ἵνα ἐγὼ ἐγκεντρισθῶ. 20 καλῶς· τῇ ἀπιστίᾳ ἐξεκλάσθησαν, σὺ δὲ τῇ πίστει ἔστηκας. μὴ ὑψηλὰ φρόνει ἀλλὰ φοβοῦ· 21 εἰ γὰρ ὁ θεὸς τῶν κατὰ φύσιν κλάδων οὐκ ἐφείσατο, [μή πως] οὐδὲ σοῦ φείσεται.

APPENDICES

Appendix I

The Biblical Covenants with Israel

The focus in this article is that the unconditional covenants revealed in the Bible are between God and the remnant of Israel and not with the New Testament Church. This is the inevitable deduction that arises out of a consistently applied literal or normative hermeneutics. This emphasis needs to be made more clearly than ever due to the persistent rhetoric of "replacement" theologies, as well as the sad defections from classic dispensationalism by many who were once its friends (Article is from Conservative Theological Journal 9:28 December 2005; copied with permission)

The Importance of Understanding God's Biblical Covenants

God has revealed Himself to man primarily by His inerrant Word and man is accountable to understand what God has revealed. God has revealed Himself and His purposes not in mystery enshrouded with secrecy, but in such a way that man is fully capable and responsible to comprehend what has been revealed. "For God holds us only responsible *for the plain, naked, grammatical sense of the Word,* and not for recondite, hidden senses that the ingenuity or imagination of man may concoct."[1] What are impossible to miss in Scripture are the *biblical covenants* that God has made with the elect nation of Israel, *the Jews.*

God never gave His Word, especially the biblical covenants, to deceive, but to be fully comprehended and understood. The

---

[1] George N. H. Peters, *The Theocratic Kingdom,* 3 vols. (Grand Rapids: Kregel Publications, 1988), 1:130.

Abrahamic, land, Davidic and new covenants are the
fountainhead from which God's entire redemptive kingdom
program springs forth. These covenants clearly reveal:

1) the covenanted people
2) the covenanted nation
3) the covenanted land
4) the covenanted seed
5) the covenanted house
6) the covenanted throne
7) the covenanted kingdom
8) the covenanted king
9) the covenanted reign
10) the covenanted redemption
11) the covenanted cleansing
12) the covenanted Spirit

This list goes on into great depth and detail.[2] In Scripture,
any reference to Israel is always to the covenanted Jewish
nation Israel by God's covenanted design and definition. This is
not only because God simply declared it, but also because
God's biblical covenant promises and oaths are solely for His
directly covenanted people the Jews and no other.[3] These
covenants are the vehicles in which God rests His complete
redemptive, prophetic, and kingdom program.[4] Unless there is a

[2] It must be remembered that the Abrahamic, Land, Davidic and New covenants are
very comprehensive and cover many specific details.
[3] By God's own oath bound covenants with Israel, it is utterly impossible for God to
abandon the nation Israel, *the Jews*. There are many similar passages that can be
referenced here. It seems it would be well advised for any form of *replacement
theology* to be more prudent about what it advocates about the nation Israel
(Deuteronomy 7:6–8; 1 Kings 6:13; Malachi 3:6).
[4] God has revealed His *entire* redemptive kingdom program for Israel that is
biblically covenanted with Israel but includes all men, *the Gentiles, the nations of the
world*. Paul addresses and expounds on this exact issue that is foundationally based
on the Abrahamic covenant; the promise of salvation to the Gentiles or the nations,
that faith alone saves, the offer of grace to the nations is full lodged in the Abrahamic
covenant. See Galatians 3:6–18 especially vs. 8. All biblical prophecy stems from the

thorough knowledge and acceptance of God's biblical covenants, confusion results in the outworking of His total and unified kingdom program as revealed in Scripture. That is why there is much admonition to seek and pray for this coming and restored kingdom (Mat. 6:10; 33; Acts 1:6). If Scripture is consistently understood as grammatically literal - utilizing a normative use of the original languages - there will be a sensible and consistent interpretation, especially concerning these covenants.

God's Biblical Covenants and Consistent Hermeneutics

The covenants that are of most concern are the Abrahamic, the Land, the Davidic, and the New. All but the Mosaic are eternal, unilateral, and unconditional, being dependent on God alone to carry out all the promises spelled out in them. These biblical covenants fully define the Davidic or Messianic throne and kingdom. This kingdom of God or theocracy was fully identified as the covenanted Davidic kingdom and throne, which the Lord adopted as His very own (1 Chron. 17:14; 28:5; 29:23).

Neither Gentile nor the Church were *ever* God's biblically covenanted people or nation in any sense (Eph. 2:11–12).[5] This means at the outset that they are not capable of *fulfilling* any biblical covenants.[6] It does not mean there were not great promises made to all Gentiles. Justification by faith alone was promised to the nations in the original Abrahamic covenant (Gal. 3:8), as well as other blessings, but the Abrahamic covenant itself was never made *with* the Gentiles. As the Land,

---

biblical covenants. His *kingdom program* spoken of in Scripture is always fully derived from His biblically covenanted plan and program with Israel.
[5]This is worked out more fully below. See under "The *Direct Recipients* of the Biblical Covenants."
[6] Being that the covenants are made with Abraham, Isaac, Jacob, Israel, and Jesus, only these direct recipients can fulfill the covenants.

Davidic, and New covenants were not made with the Gentiles or the Church, how is it possible for any of these groups to fulfill or to begin to fulfill these covenants?

God swore to carry out His sovereign and eternal program, purposes, and design in and through chosen individuals. These include Abraham, Isaac, Jacob, David, David's seed and ultimately through the *Jew,* that is, national Israel. Israel is designated as His elect nation and people and they are protected by the biblical covenants as to their continued existence into eternity (Gen. 12:3; Jer. 31:35–37; 33:19–26). If this were not true, then prima facie Scripture lies. This nation was elected by God as direct recipients to the biblical covenants ultimately sealed with His Son's blood (Heb. 9:11–28). No Gentile nation or people has this promised covenanted position and protection. Not even the Church[7] has one covenanted promise such as this, unless one holds to some form of replacement formula for the nation Israel.

To disregard any aspect or detail of the biblical covenants in order to replace God's covenanted people Israel with any people, including the Church, constitutes a total failure in interpretation which does violence to the entire Word of God. Israel is defined and guarded by the biblical covenants. Much of biblical apostasy stems from the belief that any other group or nation can replace Israel or fulfill Israel's covenants and prophecies. The Church is not the natural branch or vine (Rom. 11:17–24). "That the professing Church on earth is 'the true vine' — this is the daring and impious lie of the apostasy. That is 'the olive tree' is a delusion shared by the mass of Christians in the churches of the Reformation. But the teaching of Scripture is explicit, that Christ Himself is the vine, and Israel

---

[7]The Church is Christ's body, that is Jew and Gentile united on an equal basis and something *totally* new (Eph. 2:11–16; esp. 15), and is thus incapable of fulfilling any of Israel's promises. These promises are reserved exclusively for the house of Israel as God's biblically covenanted program can only be fulfilled in them and through the nation Israel.

the olive. For 'God hath not cast away His people whom He foreknew.[8]

The importance of the biblical covenants and their direct relation to the nation Israel cannot be overstated. The oath-bound promises pertaining to the Messianic kingdom set the entire structure for the unity and purpose of God's complete program for the restoration of man (Ps 8). The history of the Church has been notorious for trying to rob Israel and the Heir Apparent of the restored Davidic throne and kingdom, but all the promises in the covenants will be strictly and *literally* fulfilled in every detail.

Traditional dispensationalists are very much concerned with all the *specific details* of all the biblical covenants that have been made with the nation Israel. This also includes the prophecies directly related to the covenants. Non-dispensational systems such as amillennialism and progressive dispensationalism are not concerned with *specific* details and the literalness of covenants or prophecy. The Scriptures are very clear in this matter and consistent in their use and interpretation of the covenants. This includes *all* the prophecies directly related to the covenants in their every detail. This means there is but one Messianic Kingdom and throne being promised by covenant design with Israel. Peters makes these comments on this exact subject:

> "The prophets describe but one Kingdom. The language and whole tenor of the Word is so explicit that both Jews and Gentiles thus understand it... This Kingdom, too, according to the grammatical sense, is one here *on the earth,* not somewhere else, as e.g. in the third heaven or the Universe. Take the most vivid descriptions, such as are contained in Isa. 60, or Dan. 7, etc., and they refer to this Kingdom, *exclusively to this earth,* which, of course, follows naturally *from the*

[8]J. Vernon McGee, *Thru the Bible,* 5 vols. (Nashville: Thomas Nelson, 1983), 5:502–3. Quoting Sir Robert Anderson, *The Hebrew Epistle in the Light of the Types.*

relation that this Kingdom sustains to the Jewish nation and Davidic throne. Any other portraiture of it would be incongruous, and hostile to covenant and fact. If it is one Kingdom, and thus related, it must, of necessity, embrace the following features: (1) Notwithstanding the removal of the Kingdom and the severe tribulation of the nation, *the preservation* of the race must be announced, for otherwise the election would fail and the Kingdom, as predicted, could not be restored. This is done in the most positive manner, as e.g. Jer. 31:35–37, and 33:19-26, Isa. 54:9–10, etc. (2) The *restoration* of the Jews, notwithstanding their sinfulness and punishment, ought to be distinctively presented, because David's Kingdom is based on it. This is also predicted, as e.g. Ezek. 36:22, 24, and ch. 37, Jer., chs. 31, 32, and 33, etc... (3) And as David's throne was in Jerusalem, and was adopted as God's throne, when His Son shall reign, *the city* ought to be specially honored in such a revelation of the Kingdom, seeing that it stands intimately related to it. The Prophets thus distinguish it in the future, as e.g. Jer. 3:17, Isa. 24:23, Joel 3:17, etc... Indeed, all the particulars needed for *a full identification* of *the identical* Kingdom, *once* established but *now* overthrown, are thus given in *the most simple language.*"[9]

What is often missing in the study of theology is a principle of *consistent* literal hermeneutic of Scripture. Without consistent literal interpretation, there will always be major problems especially concerning the details of the covenants. This is why there have been so many problems with prophecy and eschatological issues through Church history. Very few

[9] George N. H. Peters, *The Theocratic Kingdom,* 1:245.

seem to be taking the specifics of the biblical covenants seriously.

The Direct Recipients of the Biblical Covenants

Essential to a comprehension of the biblical covenants is the question *with whom* each covenant is actually made and will be fulfilled. Such may be defined as the *direct recipients* of the covenants. This does not mean other recipients are not included in the covenants as heirs to certain blessings, but only with the *direct heirs* will the covenants be fulfilled. As has been pointed out, all the biblical covenants are ultimately and literally made through Abraham, Isaac, and Jacob (Israel) and his *natural* seed, or directly with the nation Israel (Jer. 31:31–34). Although the covenants are unilateral and unconditional, the covenants must be fulfilled with the directly named recipients or heirs of those covenants. There are those who are heirs to the covenants by simply being *in Christ,* that is the Church, but these are not the direct heirs with whom the covenants can possibly be fulfilled.

The direct recipients or heirs are literally and accurately spelled out in each of the covenants, in fact, so literally and accurately there can be no possibility of anyone questioning with whom the biblical covenants must be fulfilled. Each biblical covenant must be thoroughly examined as to its specific promise/s to the specified recipient. Only then can a literal fulfillment be known. This is often overlooked and not even considered by many students of the Word of God.

As an example, God makes it clear in Genesis 15 that the covenant that He ratified was with Abraham (Gen. 15:18; lit. Abram). The covenant was made directly with Abraham, but note the *direct* recipients, and what was covenanted: "To *your descendants I have given this land."* This does not mean Abraham is not a direct recipient in this promise of the covenant of the land for he most certainly was and will be. Abraham is still a direct recipient and heir to this covenant and this essential point is made throughout the Old Testament. Nevertheless, God also makes it extremely clear that this covenant was specifically to Abraham and *"his seed"* after him throughout *their generations* (Genesis 17:7–9).

Notice that the Abrahamic covenant is *expanded* through progressive revelation but not changed, altered, or abrogated in any way, as regards and its eternal outworking. God now promises *"to be God to you and to your descendants after you,"* also "I will give *to you* and to *your descendants* after you, the land of your sojournings, *all the land of Canaan,* for an *everlasting possession."* The covenant is now extended to Abraham and his seed after him throughout their generations as an everlasting possession.[10]

In the original covenant, the promises were made to Abraham and his seed. Nevertheless, the promises will be made to Abraham and his seed, which is through Isaac, not through Ishmael. It seemed as if Abraham expected Ishmael to be the child through whom God would establish the promises of the covenant. *"But God said, No, but Sarah your wife will bear you a son, and you shall call his name Isaac; and I will establish My covenant with him for an everlasting covenant for his descendants after him"* (Genesis 17:19). The direct recipient is identified as Isaac, through whom the promises must be fulfilled. Nothing has actually changed in the covenant, but it is significant that the direct recipients are now Abraham *and* Isaac and his seed after him.

For the Gentiles or the Church to fulfill the covenants is absolutely impossible unless the covenants are redefined, or one creates different covenants.[11] Gentiles and the Church are *never* identified as the natural branch or seed (Eph. 2:11–12; Rom. 11:11–32; esp. 18–21; Gal. 3:17–18). All the biblical covenants

---

[10] The covenant is also proven to be everlasting, for the land cannot be promised as *'an everlasting possession'* based on a temporal or non-eternal covenant.

[11] A significant point is that there are absolutely no covenants directly made with the Gentiles. Therefore, absolutely no biblical covenants can be fulfilled with the Gentiles or in the Church, which is predominantly Gentile.

are ultimately with Israel, the Jews, and specifically must be finally fulfilled in and through the nation Israel. Literally, everyone is dependent on these biblical covenants made with Israel. This may be humbling for some but biblically true.

While the four biblical covenants have already been inaugurated,[12] there is absolutely no complete fulfillment of any of them. This is not possible because *all* the details of the covenants made with *all* the *direct recipients* have not been fulfilled. Abraham may have received personal blessings, and the Gentiles are truly blessed (Gen. 12:3), but this is totally remote from a complete fulfillment of any of these covenants.

Certain theologies dictate that the biblical covenants and prophecies related to them may be fulfilled or partly fulfilled by or in the Church. This is categorically not possible. Only a dispensational theology has any comprehension of this. A departure from a *complete distinction* made with Israel and the Church (which is the very heart of dispensationalism) has led to many Church-kingdom theories, redefining God's revealed *unity of purpose.*

Church-Kingdom Theories, Covenant Theology, and Unity of Purpose

The Church is often assumed to be the essence, the archetype, being able to fulfill in some manner God's covenanted kingdom plan and program. This is espoused by covenant theology, replacement theology, progressive dispensationalism, or their various counterparts. This can hardly be assumed to be biblically true. For example, even in the first century Christ Himself had some very negative things to say about the first century churches e.g., *"you have left your first love"* (Revelation 2:1; 4); *Note:* all the false teachings in

---

[12]Not all dispensationalists would agree that the biblical covenants have been inaugurated, but most would agree there is no fulfillment of these covenants except with the nation Israel in the covenanted kingdom.

Pergamum and Thyatira (2:12; 14–15; 18–20); to Sardis *"you are dead"* (3:1); to Laodicea *"I will spit you out of My mouth"* (Revelation 3:14–16). It would be a gross misstatement to say things have gotten better in the Church age (1 Tim. 4:1–5; 2 Tim. 4:1–5).

The Church is often assumed to be in the Kingdom of God, or identified as the Kingdom of God in some form. This comes from defining the Kingdom as the rule of Christ in heaven or in the heart, and not as the biblically covenanted restored Jewish Davidic throne and kingdom of Israel from where Christ must rule. This wrong assumption leads to many Church-kingdom theories and theologies. The biblical distinctions between the Church and Israel become continually blurred. Note Berkhof's *immediate* rejection of a restored kingdom of Israel to Israel in the following statement:

"The Kingdom of God is primarily an eschatological concept. The fundamental idea of the Kingdom in Scripture is not that of a restored theocratic kingdom of God in Christ - which is essentially a kingdom of Israel--, as the Premillenarians claim; ... The primary idea of the Kingdom of God in Scripture is that of the rule of God established and acknowledged in the hearts of sinners by the powerful regenerating influence of the Holy Spirit, insuring them of the inestimable blessings of salvation, ~ a rule that is realized in principle on earth, but will not reach its culmination until the visible and glorious return of Jesus Christ. The present realization of it is spiritual and invisible. Jesus took hold of this eschatological concept and made it prominent in his teachings. He clearly taught the present spiritual realization and the universal character of the Kingdom. Moreover, He Himself effected that realization in a measure formerly unknown and greatly increased the present blessings of the Kingdom. At the same time He held out the blessed hope of the future appearance of that Kingdom in external glory and with the perfect blessings of salvation."[13]

Most theologies, except traditional dispensationalism, believe in some form of a "Church-kingdom" theory, not understanding or consistently interpreting the great biblical distinctives between the true nature of Israel and the true nature of the Church. Israel alone is God's biblically covenanted and defined nation and people. This distinction is not only biblical, but grows inevitably out of basic hermeneutics. To ignore these distinctions may be very convenient in a theological system, but falls short of good exegesis, let alone biblical fact. There is vast and cosmic distinction between the Church as the body of Christ and the covenanted Jewish theocracy. The kingdom has very explicit theocratic ordering as demanded by the biblical covenants.

The Church is not like the Kingdom of God once established, *lacking* the Theocratic arrangement once instituted.... The Church is not like the Kingdom once established *overthrown and promised a restoration....* The Church is not the Kingdom, otherwise the disciples were *ignorant* of what they preached... that the Church is the promised Kingdom is opposed *by the covenants* ... the preaching of the Kingdom as nigh and then its *postponement* is against making the Church a Kingdom... The simple fact is, that if we once take the covenanted promises in their plain sense, and view the testimony of Scripture sustaining such a sense, it is *utterly impossible* to convert the Church into the promised Kingdom without a *violation* of propriety and unity of Divine Purpose.[14]

There are those who treat the Church, the reformers, and certain theologies as sacrosanct or with some infallible authority. "The Roman Church took up the idea of Augustine

[13]Louis Berkhof, *Systematic Theology,* 568; 295; 571.
[14]George N. H. Peters, *The Theocratic Kingdom,* 3 vols. (Grand Rapids: Kregel Publications, 1988), 1:612.

and identified the church with the kingdom of God, but it also went a step farther in identifying the kingdom of God with its own ecclesiastical organization. As Berkhof states: 'Augustine viewed the kingdom as a present reality and identified it with the pious and holy, that is, with the church as a community of believers; but he used some expressions which seem to indicate that he also saw it embodied in the episcopally organized Church... In the Reformation the Reformers seem to have returned somewhat to the position of Augustine. This is defined by Berkhof as a denial to the Roman position that the kingdom of God is identical to the visible church, i.e., the whole company of believers. This is essentially the position of amillennial conservatives today."[15]

Nevertheless, the inerrant Word of God is always the authority, not the Church, the reformers, or a theological system. In the history of the Church, there has been division over biblical covenants knowingly or unknowingly. The question is not whether there are covenants, but what *are* the actual covenants, and which ones may have application to the Church and how, and perhaps which ones do not. This great lack of exegesis and discernment frequently relates to replacement theology and/or preterism[16] or various forms of preterism.

Covenant theology replaces or overrides the biblical covenants by two or three undefined covenants that it believes and affirms are biblical.[17] Covenant theologians believe their

---

[15]John F Walvoord, *The Millennial Kingdom* (Grand Rapids: Zondervan, 1959), 99.
[16]The basis definition of *preterism* according to Webster's Encyclopedic Dictionary is "maintaining that the prophecies in the Apocalypse have already been fulfilled.' While the term *preterism* seems to be evolving as relating also to partial preterism, most who are preterists see or understand God's program for Israel as somehow fulfilled or to some degree partially or totally fulfilled. What is tragic is that many preterists are looking only to *prophecy* that is admittedly essential, but they are not confining themselves in any way to biblical covenants from which prophecy emerges especially concerning the Jew or national Israel.
[17]According to Berkhof 'wherever we have the essential elements of a covenant, namely contracting parties, a promise or promises, and a condition, there we have a covenant' (266, B. 3.). He goes on to define the Covenant of Redemption, the basis

covenants are biblical and extant, and the basis for God's program. It is claimed that covenant theology sees or understands that the ultimate goal of man in history is for the glory of God, and without further scrutiny, this claim would be quite acceptable. However, covenant theology analyzed reveals the glory of God *might* be the intended goal, but this goal and glory rests/abides in the Church, that is, in the redemption of the *elect*.[18] Biblically, there are different groups of the elect-- not just one. A scriptural example is God's remnant in the nation Israel. Biblically, the remnant will always be the elect Jews from the elect nation of Israel, unless some theology redefines the nation Israel or the Jew. Therefore, in covenant theology there is effectively one gospel and one covenant. "The Bible teaches that there is but a single gospel by which men can be saved. And because the gospel is nothing but the revelation of the covenant of grace, it follows that there is also but one covenant. This gospel was already in the maternal promise, Gen. 3:15, was preached unto Abraham, Gal. 3:8, and may not be supplanted by any Judaistic gospel, Gal. 1:8, 9."[19] While this is extraordinary reductionism, and certainly simplifies any or all theology especially eschatology, what does one do with 39 books of the Hebrew Scriptures directed primarily to the nation Israel. These theologies have reduced God's plan and purposes

for the Covenant of Grace (270, E. 2.) But he admits that 'it is not easy to determine precisely who the second part is' in the Covenant of Grace (273). To base an entire theological system on covenants defined with no complete and specific clarity would seem to encourage those who hold to such a system to rethink their position on what *the true Biblical covenants* are. Quotes from Louis Berkhof, *Systematic Theology* (Grand Rapid: Eerdmans Publishing, 1979).

[18] "From the point of view of election... According to some theologians the Church is the *community of the elect,* the *coetus electorum.* This definition is apt to be somewhat misleading, however. It applies only to the Church *ideally* considered, the Church as it exists in the idea of God and as it will be completed at the end of the ages, and not to the Church as a present empirical reality. Election includes all those who belong to the body of Christ, irrespective of their present actual relation to it. But the elect who are yet unborn, or who are still strangers in Christ and outside the pale of the Church, cannot be said to belong to the Church *realiter"* -Berkhof, *Systematic Theology,* 567.

[19] Berkhof, 279.

for man down to absolutely nothing. In covenant theology, the covenant of grace dominates the entire theological system, and nothing is allowed to violate it. "The covenant of grace may be defined as that gracious agreement between the offended God and the offending but elect sinner, in which God promises salvation through faith in Christ, and the sinner accepts this believingly, promising a life of faith and obedience."[20] "The idea of a transcendent purpose and provision, which is spoken of in Christian literature as the "Covenant of Grace" or of "Redemption," underlies the whole of Written Revelation."[21] John Walvoord has this to say about the covenant of grace:

"All events of the created world are designed to manifest the glory of God. The error of covenant theologians is that they combine all the many facets of divine purpose in the one objective of fulfillment of the covenant of grace. From a logical standpoint, this is the reductive error — the use of one aspect of the whole as the determining element. The dispensational view of Scripture taken as a whole is far more satisfactory as it allows for the literal and natural interpretation of the great covenants of Scripture, in particular those with Abraham, Moses, David, and with Israel as a whole and explains them in the light of their own historical and prophetical context without attempting to conform them to a theological concept to which they are mostly unsuited. This explanation fully sustains the fundamental thesis of Calvinism, that God is sovereign and all will in the end manifest His glory. The various purposes of God for Israel, for the church which is His body, for the Gentile nations, for the unsaved, for Satan and the wicked angels, for the earth and for the heavens have each their contribution. How impossible

[20]Berkhof, 277.
[21]Roderick Campbell, *Israel and the New Covenant* (Philadelphia: Presbyterian and Reformed Publishing Company, 1954), 25.

it is to compress all of these factors into the mold of the covenant of grace."[22]

While covenant theology may deny salvation or redemption of the elect as the ultimate goal, this is covenant theology's salvific end and purpose, totally based on a covenant or covenants that are believed to be biblical. But to place full confidence in covenants which are not literally spelled out in Scripture, and not to place full confidence in the biblical covenants which are eternal, unconditional, unilateral, and literally and inerrantly spelled out over and over again in Scripture, is to violate most rules of exegesis and interpretation. "Covenant theology is definitely a product of theological theory rather than biblical exposition. While covenant theologians such as Berkhof labor over many Scriptural proofs, the specific formulas of the covenants are inductions from Calvinistic theology which go beyond the Scriptures. Charles Hodge, a covenant theologian, states plainly: God entered into covenant with Adam. This statement does not rest upon any express declaration of the Scriptures."[23] Not only is there great misunderstanding of the biblical covenants, but also concerning their nature and the use or the outworking of the biblical covenants. George Peters comments:

> "The reader will carefully regard this matter, as it is essential to a correct understanding of much Scripture. It is a sad fact, that more ignorance and misunderstanding exist in relation to the covenants than perhaps of any other portion of the Bible. This originates from the manner in which the subject has been handled by theologians of talent and eminence. Instead of confining themselves to the covenants in which man is directly interested and which have been

[22]John F. Walvoord, *The Millennial Kingdom* (Grand Rapids: Zondervan Publishing, 1959), 92.
[23]John F. Walvoord, The Millennial Kingdom, 88.

directly given to him by God, they have much to say concerning "a covenant of Redemption" entered into by the Father and Son from eternity (and undertake to give the particulars of what is not on record), and "a Covenant of Grace" (which embraces the particulars of salvation, etc.) but the distinctive Abrahamic Covenant and the manner in which it is confirmed is left without due consideration. This introduces a series of wild and fanciful interpretations, such as that all nations are now in the position once occupied by the Jewish nation; that God does not regard the Jewish nation with more favor than other nations; that the promises to the Jewish nation are typical, temporary, conditional, etc. Believing that we are under an entire New Covenant (which they cannot point out in the Scriptures, but which they affirm is this or that, viz.: this dispensation or the sacrifice of Christ, or the tender of Salvation to all believers, etc.), they, of course, ignore the *necessity* of our becoming "the seed of Abraham, of our being engrafted, etc. The relationship that believers sustain to the Jewish nation is utterly misapprehended, and inevitable confusion and antagonism arise.... It is painful to notice the discrepancies, amid a show of profound learning and speculation."[24]

All the biblical covenants literally describe and clearly define one covenanted people and nation and that is the Jewish nation Israel. All the biblical covenants taken literally describe but one covenanted Jewish throne and kingdom. All the biblical covenants taken literally describe *a single unity of purpose and design* to events in world history as revealed in the progressive revelation of Scripture. All biblical prophecy about the Messiah will never contradict the biblical covenants, but will arise and flow from them. Prophecy not only flows from the biblical

---

[24]Peters, The Theocratic Kingdom, 1:320.

covenants but also is dependent on them. Against the accusation of being too pedantic or too Jewish concerning biblical covenants, Jesus as the Jewish Messiah has His covenanted position described only by the biblical covenants. This is what the Jewish throne and kingdom are all about, Jesus is the Jewish Messiah as the covenanted Heir to the covenanted Davidic throne and must reign from David's throne over the covenanted Jewish kingdom from Jerusalem. All this is covenanted and prophesied repeatedly throughout all of Scripture.

The biblical covenants must be literally and completely fulfilled in every detail, for Christ must reign in the restored Davidic kingdom for the covenants to be fulfilled. This is why Christ's command to seek this kingdom first (Mat. 6:33) is so essential. This is why Christ taught his disciples to pray as an entreaty for God to bring in His Kingdom (Mat. 6:10). This is why Jesus' genealogy as the son of Man (Dan. 7:13; Mat. 1:1– 17; Luke 3:23–38) is so critical, as only He is by covenant design and definition the Davidic Jewish Heir Apparent to the Jewish throne and kingdom over Israel.

Based on the biblical covenants, especially the Davidic, the Davidic throne and kingdom by covenanted and antitypical design, cannot be changed even minutely without violating the original intent of His archetypal plan, goal, and purpose. If this were possible, which it is not, then perhaps God is not able to carry out His program designed around the Jewish nation Israel, or He has deceived Israel and the nations of the world and never intended to do so. On the other hand, has He completely abandoned His oath-bound covenants sealed with blood sacrifice, even His own Son's blood and swore by His own Person and holiness *"Once I have sworn by My holiness; I will not lie to David'* (Psalm 89:35) to carry out? Assuming this premise, then the original biblical covenants based on God's promises and oaths were never given as antitypical and to be understood as literal to be carried out exactly in every detail as He promised. If any of this were true (which it most definitely is not), that is God departing or abandoning in any sense His original covenants, as certain writers and theologians confidently assert, this would violate, vitiate, and abrogate effectively everything God has declared in His Word. This impugns the very character, nature, and faithfulness of God. How utterly inconceivable is the arrogance and audacity of those who do not just simply accept the promises God has declared and proven to be true by His Word. It would seem many more teachers and students of the Word would be more reticent about making bold assertions about which they are so confident if they relied more on the inerrant words of Scripture and details rather than on any errant theological system.

The biblical covenants and the prophecies related to them define the nation Israel, the Jew and His revealed theocratic program with them. This is the *vital key* for understanding the complete fulfillment of His entire eschatological and redemptive program. To replace Israel in any way with any other people, nation, or theology is to violate the truths and promises of all the biblical covenants and prophecies in the Word of God. The Church is not defined or described in the biblical covenants or prophecies made with Israel. To find fulfillment of Israel's covenants in the Church or church age simply proves very flawed theology lacking any unity of purpose except that found by the enthroned interpreter. Dispensationalism displays biblical unity of purpose.

The Biblical Covenants Mean Exactly What They Say

One thing that is crucial about the biblical covenants God made directly with Abraham, David, and Israel that must be reemphasized is their antitypical nature. This will be an essential element not only in the understanding of these covenants but their actual outworking. When God described the persons involved, the land, the seed, the blessing, the throne, the kingdom, the Spirit, or anything related directly to the biblical covenants, He was not being cryptic or enigmatic speaking in type or allegory.

A type is diametrically opposed to the character and nature of a covenant or contract. If a type or allegory is the style of communication or language God used when He made His promises or covenants, then no concrete and substantive conclusions are possible when interpreting the biblical covenants. God established the oath-bound biblical covenants containing His great promises, which He swore to uphold and carry out fully in every specific detail. When any theological system denies or is not consistent with God's biblical covenants as to their *literal* meaning and outworking, then they also will confuse God's biblically covenanted program for the destiny of man and Israel, especially relating to the kingdom. If God did not really mean what He said in the biblical covenants, that is if He used types or allegories, how is anyone to understand anything in the Word of God?

The many and varied interpretations that arise from exegesis that allows for a virtual plethora of types, allegories, and a redefining of the antitypes prove a lack of understanding of the covenants. If the land is not the land as described in the biblical covenants, or the throne of the kingdom is in the third heaven but not that described in exact detail, then the question has to be which is the type and which is the antitype? There can and never will be a clear answer to these questions, except what will be made evident in the future. "For if we adopt this modernized principle, so prevailing, where then a promise in the covenants to which can be ascribed certainty of meaning? Rejecting the plain one that the letter contains, or more conveniently converting it into a type, the promise may then represent what the ingenuity of man ascribes to it, and conjecture follows.... From Origen to Swedenborg, we are content to abide by the former, as certainly God-given. The truth is that these writers all come to the Word with an unproven hypothesis, viz.: that the church, as now constituted, is the covenanted Messianic Kingdom, and hence all Scripture, including the precise and determinate language of the covenants, must be interpreted to correspond with a prejudged case. Learning and ability must champion a fundamental misconception."[25]

The nature of language is to communicate exactly what is meant, and this is true of the biblical covenants. It is essential to realize magnitude of the clarity of language contained in the biblical covenants. The massive promises God has made that affect the destiny of all mankind are contained therein. These biblical covenants speak of the redemption of man from the curse and the perfected redemptive kingdom as covenanted through the nation Israel. This is a very weighty matter and to divorce the biblical covenants as to their literal language, the normal use of the language and meaning is to void promises that are ultimately sealed with Christ's blood.

"The Kingdom being based on the covenants, the covenants must be carefully examined, and the literal language of the same must be maintained... In all earthly transactions, when a promise, agreement, or contract is entered into by which one party gives a promise of value to another, it is *universally* the custom to explain such a relationship and its promises *by the well-known laws of language* contained in our grammars or in common usage. It would be regarded absurd and trifling to view them in any other light... Why, then, should this universal rule be laid aside when coming to the covenants of the Bible? If it is important in any mere earthly relationship for the parties to *understand* each other, and such a comprehension is based on *the plain grammatical sense* of the language used, is it not equally, yea more, essential in *so weighty a case as this*; and to ensure comprehension of the same is it not most reasonable to expect the same literal language? Indeed, when the covenants embrace *the vital interests* of a nation and *the destiny* of the race and the world, is it not requisite that they should be presented in such a form that the parties to whom they are given can *readily perceive their meaning*, without searching around for another

[25]Peters, 1:291–292.

and very different one to be engrafted upon them, or, without waiting for an Origen or Swedenborg to arise and spiritualize them into a proper conception."[26]

When God described the land to Abraham, He was not speaking of heaven. Now if He were speaking of heaven or some heavenly place, as some seem to believe, then everything God was talking about was not literal as to the antitypical nature one would expect in a contract or covenant. However, God did refer to a specific land that was real, earthly, and tangible. How could anyone possibly understand otherwise unless God made it very clear that He was not speaking of a literal land? This is not reading too much into the overall discussion. There is not one clue in the Scriptures that Abraham believed that the land described in the Abrahamic covenant was to be anything other than a literal land or a literal seed. The literal seed would be in Isaac, Jacob, Israel, and ultimately Christ. This does not mean there would be no other seed such as in Ishmael, but to fulfill the Abrahamic covenant as given by God, this covenant must be fulfilled in the literal seed of Abraham with Sarah. The land promises are just as literal.

Abraham was promised a child, a progeny, or a seed. Sarah and Abraham were not able to have children, but God gave them a seed in Isaac. This seed was very literal and shows God carrying out His Word, a literal true fulfillment of a specific promise made to Abraham. There is not one promise made in Scripture that was not literally made which won't be literally fulfilled especially in the biblical covenants. Promises were never types, but are literal and meant to be so. Promises are antitypical, and the nature of biblical covenants made by God absolutely demands it.

Abraham went to the land, inhabited the land as did many of his descendants, but this certainly does not fulfill all the details of the land promises made in the Abrahamic or the land covenants. Abraham is not the only heir or direct recipient

---

[26]Ibid., 1:290.

spoken of in the Abrahamic covenant. When God described blessing to Abraham personally, He was referring to Abraham being truly a blessed man and inheriting a great name. Abraham was truly a blessed man, and Abraham's name is great in almost every major religion let alone being the father of a multitude of literal nations. There are personal, national, and universal blessings promised in the Abrahamic covenant. None of these promises is anything less than completely literal.

When God made a covenant with David, it is clear He meant a literal throne and kingdom that David would understand. God meant exactly what He said and His own holiness is at stake over these promises made to David (Ps. 89:34–35). David certainly did understand this as an earthly throne and kingdom, the place of rule biblically covenanted in Israel over the Jews, never something in the heavenlies or in the third heaven or some church. This interpretation would be totally ludicrous and impossible by God's covenant design and promise with David, his seed, and Israel. How else can the literal kings of Judah, who sat on David's throne over David's kingdom be explained or understood? All the kings of Israel (Judah) ruled from David's throne down to Zedekiah (Jer. 21:1–22:9; note 22:2). How can anyone justly say that all the history of the Jewish nation with its kings and kingdom through the entire Old Testament, the Hebrew Scriptures, is not to be understood as anything but Jewish and literal? To say God has replaced the Jew or Israel, or He has fulfilled all the massive covenant promises and prophecies related to them takes a great deal more than faith.

God has literally carried out certain promises of the biblical covenants to prove without doubt that He intends to complete all that He has promised by oath. If God does not fulfill these covenants exactly and literally as He has declared by oath, then perhaps God is a liar Who never intended to do so. Because thousands of years have gone by, and the biblical covenants remain to be fulfilled, this does not support the idea that God has abandoned any promise with the nation Israel for what is

that to God in eternity, a second, a microsecond? Those who
support such a claim apparently have forgotten that it took
literally thousands of years for the woman's seed to come the
first time from the promise of Genesis 3:15. Moreover, while it
is true He has come, and the bruise on the heel is now history,
the bruising on the serpent's head by the Seed of the woman has
not yet beenfully realized. As expected there are those who say
it has. Scripture contradicts that (2 Cor. 4:4; James 4:7; 1 Peter
5:8), and if many interpreters were honest with the Text
especially the covenants, then fanciful interpretations would not
be necessary.

Summary and Conclusion

The Scriptures cannot be understood properly without a
fundamental biblical theology of the kingdom of God. When
Jesus said in Matthew 25:34 *"inherit the kingdom prepared for
you from the foundation of the world"*[27] or *"But seek first His
kingdom* [28] *and His righteousness; and all these things shall he
added to you"* (Matthew 6:33), or *"Thy kingdom come,"*[29]

[27] *"inherit the kingdom **prepared** for you from the foundation of the world."* It is
essential to notice the words τὴν ἠτοιμασμένην *(hetoimsnsmene)* perfect passive
participle with articulation making this not only restrictive attribution but
emphasizing the completion of something fully planned in eternity past, lit. *'the
prepared kingdom.'*
[28] Literally 'keep seeking first the kingdom of God.' ζητεῖτε *(zeteite* - pres. act.
Imperative). This is interesting in the fact that the object of the one seeking should be
the *Kingdom of God not the King* quoted by the King. There are many implications
through scripture of a thorough understanding of the kingdom being the clue to
proper biblical interpretations.
[29] Literally 'let Your Kingdom come; ἐλθέτω *(eltheto* - aorist active imperative with
the emphasis on the imperative) The crux of the prayer is really a prayer for the
coming biblically covenanted kingdom of Christ on the planet. There is absolutely no
hint of any church-kingdom theory. 'The expression *"Thy Kingdom come"* expresses
faith in the realization of the covenant, and the predictions based upon it. What
kingdom is the proper subject of prayer, if not *the Theocratic-Davidic*? Faith in its
usage, is manifested that God's oath to David will be respected, that it is His
determinate purpose to have it restored, and that God will institute the means and
arrangements for its recovery. The Theocracy is, as we have proven, God's own

(Matthew 6:10), it is clear from the Text that *'the kingdom'* was something completely prepared in eternity past, understood well to be sought after, and to be the center of prayer. The question is: what is the kingdom or what defines the kingdom? The answer to the question lies simply in the biblical covenants. Without detailed knowledge of and complete dependence on these biblical covenants, the divine plan that God has purposed and spelled out for man through the nation Israel to comprehend and understand will be one of biblical and theological frustration and confusion.

God's purpose for man from the very beginning was that man was destined to rule over creation. Man was to be king of the earth. With the fall of man God has been working to restore man as king of the earth. The ultimate form of man's rule over the earth will be Messiah's kingdom. The unconditional covenants of the Old Testament are important and also point to the kingdom as the center or theme of Old Testament theology. In the Abrahamic Covenant (Gen. 12:1–3) God called a man through whom He would provide redemption and blessing. Under the Palestinian Covenant (Deut. 30) Israel, the offspring of Abraham, was promised a land wherein God would bless them. However, that blessing will ultimately come through Messiah, a descendant of both Abraham and King David (2 Sam 7:12–16; Matt. 1:1). Moreover, the blessing will be made possible through regenerated people as promised in the New Covenant (Jer. 31:31–34). These four covenants form the foundation of an Old Testament theology in which God will redeem and bless His people.[30]

Essential in understanding the biblically covenanted throne and kingdom is that this is the rule of Christ (Messiah) on this earth in Jerusalem. This will be Christ's covenanted rule as the son of David who is Heir Apparent to David's throne and kingdom. Christ will rule on this planet literally, and He must

Kingdom; He being the Ruler in it, gives force to the "Thy." - Peters, *The Theocratic Kingdom,* 1:690.
[30]Paul Enns, *The Moody Handbook of Theology,* 33–35.

rule by God's covenanted design, plan, and purpose. For this He died as *'King of the Jews.'* This is His truly exalted position as the Son of man.

What man did not do in Adam, Christ will do from David's throne. Redemption for Israel and all mankind, the rule of Christ in His covenanted kingdom, freedom from the curse, is what all the biblical covenants are about. This rule will be from the restored and identical throne and kingdom of David as defined by the biblical covenants. Jesus as the Messiah is the direct Heir to this covenanted throne. This rule from David's literal covenanted throne and kingdom is what must be restored. This is not a rule from heaven of David's son from a heavenly throne of which there is absolutely nothing spoken of in Scripture and means absolutely nothing as far as the covenanted throne and kingdom of David are concerned. Christ must reign from the earthly, literal throne of David over Israel, *the Jews.*

"So when they had come together, they were asking Him, saying, "Lord, is it at this time **You are restoring the kingdom to Israel?"** (Acts 1:6). This question can only be answered by understanding all aspects of the biblical covenants made with Israel.

Appendix II

The Heart of Dispensationalism

(Article from Conservative Theological Journal 8:25, December 2004; copied with permission)

"But speaking the truth in love, we are to grow up
in all aspects into Him who is the head, even
Christ" (Ephesians 4:15)

No system of theology is immune to criticism or disapproval and in that arena, dispensationalism is no different from any other major biblical teaching which certainly has its many critics and opponents. What is perhaps different with dispensationalism today as a system of theology is the marked and noticeable departure from dispensationalism by many bible colleges and seminaries that were once highly or completely dispensational. This is not surprising especially when there are continued warnings given in Scripture concerning departure from biblical truth (1 Tim. 4:1; 2 Tim. 3:1–3; 4:3–4). While there has always been departure from great biblical teachings and fact, the major issue here concerns the absolute certainty and truth of dispensationalism as a system of theology.

What truly defines a dispensationalist or dispensationalism? What are the basic and most fundamental teachings of dispensationalism? What are the primary issues that have arisen in the past 20 or so years especially with institutions that were dispensational? All this can be understood quite simply by answering the question: "what is the very *heart of dispensationalism?*"

What is a Dispensation? What is Dispensationalism?

Through the centuries, theologians and theologies have recognized various dispensations in Scripture.[1] Dispensationalism as a system is built upon both biblical distinctions and definitions. The Scofield Reference Bible defines a dispensation as "a period of time during which man is tested in respect of obedience to some specific revelation of the will of God."[2] Charles Ryrie defines a dispensation as a "distinguishable economy in the outworking of God's purpose."[3] Article V of the doctrinal position of Dallas Theological Seminary states specifically, "We believe that the dispensations are stewardships by which God administers His purpose on the earth through man under varying responsibilities ... We believe that three of these dispensations or rules of life are the subject of extended revelation in the Scriptures, *viz.,* the dispensation of the Mosaic Law, the present dispensation of grace, and the future dispensation of the millennial kingdom. We believe that these are distinct and are not to be intermingled or confused, as they are chronologically successive."[4] Dr. Lewis Sperry Chafer, a true giant in systematizing dispensationalism and one of the great and true legends of Dallas Theological Seminary, defines a dispensation as a "period of time which is

---

[1]"Clement of Alexandria (AD 150–220) recognized four dispensations of God's rule. Augustine (AD 354–430) noted the fact God employed several distinct ways of working in the world as He executes His plan for history. Augustine used the term *dispensation* when referring to these different ways" Renald E. Showers, *There Really is a Difference* (Bellmawr: The Friends of Israel Gospel Ministry, Inc., 1990), 27. "The question arises, whether we ought to distinguish two or three, or with the modern Dispensationahsts, seven or even more dispensations" Louis Berkhof, *Systematic Theology* (Grand Rapids: Wm. B. Eerdmans Publishing, 1941), 290.
[2]Charles Ryrie, *Dispensationalism Today* (Chicago: Moody Press, 1965), 22.
[3]Ibid., 29.
[4]WE BELIEVE The Doctrinal Statement of Dallas Theological Seminary; also on page 154 of the 2004–2005 Dallas Seminary catalog.

identified by its relation to some particular purpose of God."[5]
Again, while there may be slight variations, these definitions are
about the same for many dispensationalists. As there are those
who recognize various dispensations in Scripture, this does not
make one a dispensationalist holding to a dispensational
theology. The essential foundation of dispensationalism is very
clear and absolutely supported by Scripture and very easy to
prove.

The larger picture is defining dispensationalism as a system
of theology presenting a systemized interpretation of the
Scriptures. No system of theology can operate without basic and
fundamental definition and distinctions. Two major systems of
theology are covenant and dispensational theology.

Covenant theology is essentially defined by two or three
covenants. These are the covenants of works, grace, and
redemption.[6] Yet covenant theology itself was not systematized
until the 16th and 17th centuries, and even Berkhof admits, "in
the early church fathers the covenant idea is seldom found at
all."[7] While not one of these covenants even exists or is even
addressed in the Scriptures, the covenant theologian insists
upon their validity.

There are various definitions of dispensationalism.
Webster's definition is "the interpreting of history as a series of
divine dispensations."[8] Paul Enns writes, "Dispensationalism
views the world as a household run by God. In this divine
household God gives man certain responsibilities as
administrator. If man obeys God within that economy
(dispensation), God promises blessing; if man disobeys God, He
promises judgment. Thus there are three aspects normally seen

[5]Lewis Sperry Chafer, *Systematic Theology* 8 vols. (Dallas: Dallas Seminary Press, 1948), 1:40.
[6]Covenant Theology can be defined very simply as a system of theology which attempts to develop the Bible's philosophy of history on the basis of two or three covenants. It represents the whole of Scripture and history as being covered by two or three covenants." Showers, 7.
[7]Berkhof, 211.
[8]*Webster's Encyclopedic Dictionary* (New York: Portland House, 1985), 414.

in a dispensation: (1) testing; (2) failure; (3) judgment. In each dispensation God has put man under a test, man fails, and there is judgment."[9] Dispensational theology is defined by the *Dictionary of Premillennial Theology* as "a system that embodies two essential concepts: (1) The church is distinct from Israel, and (2) God's overall purpose is to bring glory to Himself (Eph. 1:6, 12, 14)."[10] Robert Lightner defines dispensationalism as "that system of theology which sees (understands) the Bible as the developing (unfolding) of the distinguishable economies in the outworking of God's purpose and which sees (understands) His program with Israel as separate (distinct) from (with) His program for the Church."[11] Both parts of this definition must be considered very carefully, especially the *distinction* of Israel and the Church.

The sine qua non of Dispensationalism

The *sine qua non* (the most basic, the minimal things) of dispensationalism, or that which distinguishes one as a dispensationalist, is defined very precisely by Charles Ryrie in *Dispensationalism Today* [12] as one who:

1) keeps Israel and the Church distinct
2) uses a consistently literal interpretation (this would mean a *normal or plain* use of the language)
3) understands God's purpose in the world is for His glory (differing with covenant theology's view as soteriological)

[9]Paul Enns, *The Moody Handbook of Theology* (Chicago: Moody Press, 1989), 519.
[10] *Dictionary of Premillennial Theology* by Mal Couch (Grand Rapids: Kregel, 1996), 94.
[11]Robert Lightner, Lectures AST-403, Tape 1.
[12]Ryrie, 43–47.

166 The Greatness of His Blood

One who calls himself a dispensationalist in any sense certainly would basically agree with the above, and this is essential to this discussion. What must be very carefully observed is keeping Israel and the Church distinct. What might be added, but is already implied to the *sine qua non,* is that of *discontinuity.* Older dispensationalists stressed contrasts of Israel and the Church. They stressed discontinuity but this does not mean the issue is totally avoided. What is important are the *discontinuities.* Continuity stresses the similarities, relationship of Israel and the Church (this is stressed too much today). While there may be similarities between Israel and the Church, they are both fundamentally independent with independent programs. This is the very heart of the matter for "the essence of dispensationalism, then, is the distinction between Israel and the Church."[14]

This is the number one issue in the *sine qua non* of classical or traditional dispensationalism. This distinction must be consistently recognized throughout all Scripture. It is much more than just recognizing Israel as a nation and the Church as the body of Christ. It fully understands from the Text that God has two separate programs. He has one distinct and separate program for Israel and one distinct and separate program for the Church. This does not mean the Church is totally divorced from Israel. What is most important in all this debate is to define Israel biblically and the Church biblically. What are they? When did they start? Does either or both have a definitive beginning or end given in Scripture? Did one ever take the place of the other? "Whatever differences there may be within traditional dispensationalism, the one area of uniform agreement is the consistent distinction between Israel and the Church."[15] It is necessary to demonstrate that such a distinction is the essential conclusion from biblical evidence.

[14]Ibid., 46-47.
[15]Wesley R. Willis, John R. Master, *Issues in Dispensationalism* (Chicago: Moody Press, 1994), 113.

Israel

"The term Israel is viewed theologically as referring to all descendants of Abraham, Isaac, and Jacob, also known as the Jews, the Jewish people, Israelites, Hebrews, *etc.* The term is not limited to the present political and national state in the Middle East, which is merely a part of the whole; nor is it limited to those who adhere to the religion of Judaism only."[16] The term Israel is used seventy-three times[17] in the New Testament and it is only used of Israel as a nation, the Jewish nation of Israel. There is really no debate, except by those unwilling to accept the biblical evidence that Israel is always Israel, *the elect Jewish nation.* The key to comprehending God's entire covenanted program with all humanity is the nation Israel, for without the continued existence of the nation Israel, God could not carry out His covenanted program. This is not true of any other people or nation, and it is certainly not true of the Church. To make this very clear, God is not dependent on the continued existence of the Church to fulfill His covenanted program.

Supersessionism or any form of replacement theology wants to make the Church somehow present day Israel based on one or two verses,[18] or that the Church is able to fulfill in any manner

---

[16]*Issues in Dispensationalism,* 113.

[17]The term for Israel is only used for Israel. "Of these seventy-three citations, the vast majority refer to national, ethnic Israel. A few refer specifically to Jewish believers who still are ethnic Jews. Generally, only three of these passages are used by replacement theologians to support their thesis that the church equals Israel On two of these references (Rom. 9:6; 11:26) they are not unanimous, for some replacement theologians also have concluded that these verses speak of national, ethnic, Israel. The key verse for replacement theologians is Galatians 6:16..." *Issues in Dispensationalism,* 120.

[18] 18. Galatians 6:16 is "a passage routinely cited by replacement theologians as evidence that the church is the 'spiritual' Israel." (*Issues in Dispensationalism,* 120). "And those who will walk by this rule, peace and mercy be upon them, and upon the Israel of God" (Gal. 6:16). This one passage by no means proves the Church is Israel or any form of spiritual Israel. S. Lewis Johnson, former professor of Greek and New Testament Exegesis at Dallas Seminary' has this to say "their interpretations demand that καὶ; before the term 'the Israel of God' is an explicative or appositional καὶ; ...

any of Israel's covenants. Nowhere in the Bible is there even a hint of the Church replacing the *elect* Jewish nation of Israel, or excluding Israel as a nation from the program of God. This is not only inconsistent with all biblical teaching, it completely contradicts what God has promised by oath-bound covenants exclusively with the Jews, that is Israel. All the Scriptures are entirely consistent with God's sovereign choice and election of the nation Israel as His covenanted people. No other people, no gentile nation, no gentile people, not even the Church in any sense, can fulfill any biblical covenants other than the Jewish nation Israel, for all the biblical covenants are made with the Jews. The New Testament fully and totally supports this fact and, while there may be some added details to God's program, there are absolutely no changes which can be made concerning God's covenanted promises with Israel. No matter how subtly or cleverly any theology, theologian, or seminary tries to redefine Israel and its oath-bound covenanted land, throne, and kingdom, *etc., Israel* is always His ethnically chosen race and

Johnson rejects this view on three grounds." (Johnson rejects this on grammatical and syntactical grounds; the second ground for rejecting the view is exegetical; the third ground is theological; *Issues in Dispensationalism,* pp. 122–126). Certain non-dispensationalists are trying to defend their position by claiming this κcυ is appositional. Moreover, this would somehow, in their opinion, equate the Church being equal to Israel. What some lengths men will go to defend something in their own theology certainly contrary to the biblical text. There is something even more important in this passage grammatically, and that is there are two prepositions εἰρήνη ἐπ αὐτου καὶ ἔλεος καὶ ἐπι τον Ἰσραηλ τοῦ θεου before and after the καὶ (ἐπ αὐτους καὶ λεος καὶ ἐπι). This is very significant as the καὶ as in apposition are not that common. The more common use of this καὶ here would have to be a connective with the two prepositions ἐπ αὐτους and ἐπ τον Ἰσραηλ τοθεου displaying two distinct groups not just one. The fact that Israel is articulated is significant as this emphasizes the identity of Israel drawing attention to Israel by Paul to the reader. Even if this κcυ were used in apposition, does not prove the Church is somehow Israel or spiritual Israel. Another verse used to teach the Church is somehow Israel is Romans 2:25–29. "Paul's focus in this passage was the Pharisaic concept that all who were circumcised automatically would become part of God's kingdom. Paul recognized that certain privileges accompanied circumcision. But circumcision did not establish the covenant; it was only the sign of the covenant that was already established." *Issues in Dispensationalism,* 127. Just as water baptism as a sign does not save anyone neither does circumcision. These verses are not proving Gentiles become Israel or Jews. This interpretation is almost absurd to ludicrous.

covenanted people through whom God will fulfill every detail of every covenanted promise He has made with them. To believe in any manner that Israel does not have all the biblical covenants[19] made with this elect nation is simply foreign to all biblical interpretation. Even to hint at the idea that God does not have a very specific plan and purpose for the Jewish nation of Israel is to contradict Scripture completely. No other people or nation is a covenanted elect nation. The Church is not a covenanted single elect nation, for it is comprised of the elect from many nations. The Church is a unity of believers united to the risen Christ. It is very interesting that Israel will always have a remnant of true believers, but the Church is only composed of true believers Spirit baptized united to the risen Messiah. Yet, the history of the Church has been consistent in downplaying the nation Israel as His chosen and elect people through whom He will establish His complete covenanted theocratic redemptive kingdom program. To violate this is to simply redefine and ignore what God has declared by solemn oath-bound covenant promises with Israel (Gen. 50:24; Ps. 89:34–37; Rom. 4:20–22; 9:4–5; 11:28–29).

Israel, the Jews, the Elect Nation

There has been the continual failure throughout the history of the Church to realize and maintain consistently God's election of Israel as the only nation from among the nations of the world through which He would covenant His massive eternal program for all humanity. Israel is distinct and elect from the other nations and has a distinct program. It is impossible to overstate this foundational truth, and it is absolutely biblical and fundamental of *true* dispensationalism. Yet this single truth repeated throughout the Scriptures is consistently set aside as either not that important to the human

---

[19]The biblical covenants referred to here are the Abrahamic, Mosaic, Land, Davidic, and New Covenants.

race or redefined by the theology of man. God has literally decreed exactly what He will do, and how He is going to do it and it is bound up completely with the elect nation of Israel. One's theology often determines interpretations, rather than letting the Scriptures speak precisely as the Word of God and the revealed will of God for man. God has been very clear and precise revealing His determined and decreed program for the nations of the world. However, His covenanted program centers directly and entirely with the nation Israel, *the Jews.* All the peoples of the world including the Church are dependent on God's program for and with Israel (Gen. 12:1–3; Rom. 11:11–32; Eph. 2:11–13). This includes not only eternal redemption, but also His complete kingdom program declared from the foundation of the world (John 4:22; Matt. 25:34). While there is much teaching on election, is it not strange that little or no attention is given to the one and only biblically *elect* nation of Israel? Israel, the Jews are usually submitted to redefinition, and this is most common among any form of replacement theology usually resulting in amillennialism.

Israel is Literally an Elect Nation Defined by God

God makes it abundantly clear to all men and nations that Israel is His elect and chosen nation (Deut. 4:20; 7:6–8; 14:2). The context of Deuteronomy 7:6–8 is exclusively that of only ethnic and national Israel God brought out of Egypt. From this passage, note these obvious and significant observations:

1. For *you* (Israel) are a holy people to the Lord your God.
2. God has *chosen you* (Israel) *to be a people* for His own possession *out of all the peoples* who are on the face of the earth.
3. The Lord did not set *His love* (Israel) *on you* (Israel) *nor choose you* (Israel) because *you* (Israel) were more in number

than any of the peoples, for *you* (Israel) were the fewest of all peoples.

4. The Lord *loved you* (Israel) *and kept the oath which He swore* to your forefathers (oaths only to Israel).

5. The Lord *brought you out* (Israel) *by a mighty hand, and redeemed you* (Israel) from the house of slavery, from the hand of Pharaoh king of Egypt.

God has elected this particular people or nation, His *elect* people, the nation Israel, from all the peoples or nations who were existing on the earth. Did God ever 'unselect or unelect' any people or nation that were or are elect? The fact God Himself brought Israel out of Egypt by His mighty hand with many powerful miracles defines this nation in time and eternity. None of this can be applied to another people or group, for that redefines Israel, and in the Scriptures Israel is always Israel, *the Jews.*

God is the One who has formed and fashioned Israel (Isa. 43:1–4). God has formed and chosen one nation through whom He has covenanted His exclusive redemptive kingdom program.[20] The fact that Israel is chosen[21] as an elect nation

---

[20]The only way this would not be true is if one's own theology does not permit it, and this would have absolutely nothing to do with the Scriptures or biblical definitions and distinctions God has already declared as truth. To do this would be to declare null and void, or simply not believe, what God has declared as His inerrant Word. God will certainly establish this people in their covenanted land with a covenanted kingdom and throne in the land according His oath-bound covenant promises. God will *always* be faithful to His oath-bound covenant promises with His elect nation Israel. The fact that God will carry out His promises to Israel should be one of the greatest blessings for all nations of the world. This should also be great joy to the Church especially since He is being faithful and will be faithful to all He has promised with His elect Jewish nation. For if, God Himself does not fully carry out in minute detail every promise He has made with Israel, then why should He continue to carry out any promise He has made with any man or nation, even the Church, for the covenant promises all rest in Israel. All these covenant promises are unconditional, eternal, and unilateral, that is they are dependent on God's grace and not dependent on the obedience of any man or nation.

[21]"For you are a holy people to the Lord your God; the Lord your God has chosen בָּחַר you to be a people for His own possession out of all the peoples who are on the face of the earth" (Deuteronomy 7:6). The word בָּחַר has the meaning choose 1. with בְּ. a.

from all the nations of the world, means that they are chosen or
elect as such for a *very specific plan.* God has made this
covenanted plan very clear even to the Church with a grave
warning (Rom. 11:18–24; esp. 21–22) especially regarding how
it handles the nation Israel which are *always* the natural
branches. George Peters makes these comments:

> "This election is so plainly stated in Scripture, and
> it is so currently admitted in our theological works,
> that it need no proof. Such passages as Deut. 7:6 and
> 14:2, Rom. 11:28 and 9:11, *etc,* are decisive, that the
> sovereignty of God chose in the descendants of
> Abraham, the Jews, a people through whom should be
> manifested this Divine purpose in the salvation of
> man... When the stock upon which we are grafted is
> thus slightly treated! How largely it affects the
> interpretation of God's Word and Purpose! ...
> Theology, departing from the Primitive Church view,
> has too often grossly misconceived and perverted the
> election of the Jews, because *all* the purposes
> contemplated by that election have *not yet* been made
> manifest. ... Our faith in this national election must be
> like Paul's (Rom. 11), that, cut off from its realization
> for a period, it is still sure, and will be openly shown
> by their being re-engrafted because God's *purposes
> are unchangeable,* and cannot be defeated by man."[22]

What made men such as George Peters, C. I. Scofield, Alva
J. McClain, Lewis Sperry Chafer, John Walvoord, and others

divine choice, of Abraham Ne 9:7; Israel Dt 7:7 Is 44:1 Ez 20:5; to become his
people Dt 7:6; 14:2; ... b. human choice, persons Ex 17:9 Jos 24:15, 22 ... things Gn
13:11 (J) 1 S 17:40 1 K 18:23, 25 Jb 34:4. 4. with ace. and יט, choose, select ... 5. ace.
a. divine choice, temple 2 Ch 7:16; Judah \)/ 78:68; servant Is 41:9; 49:7... *Brown,
Driver, and Briggs Hebrew and English Lexicon of the Old Testament,* (London:
Oxford Press, 1907), 103–104.
[22] George N. H. Peters, *The Theocratic Kingdom,* 3 vols. (Grand Rapids: Kregel
Publications, 1988), 1:207, 213.

like these so mighty and confident in all their eschatological dogma and doctrine, was a very deep understanding of the biblical covenants and what God has promised in these covenants to the elect nation Israel. To say that God does not have a separate plan for the nation Israel, the Jews in relation to the other nations and the Church, is simply naivete and/or willful ignorance. There will be a time when He will fully establish this nation as His very own people in their land with Christ reigning from the biblically covenanted David's throne. This is His promise to this covenanted nation. This will also be a testimony of His love to them and the nations of the world.

The Lord had promised never to destroy Israel (Jer. 30:10–11). In fact, everything depends on the perpetuity of the nation Israel, not the other nations and definitely not the Church. God is well known throughout the Scriptures for punishing disobedience especially with Israel, yet this has nothing to do with any complete rejection by God of this people. Of course, God knew of Israel's disobedience and spoke of it many times in advance. How could God specifically reveal things such as this if He did not know exactly every possible detail of what was going to happen? He revealed the specific discipline He would bring on Israel by other nations of languages or tongues[23] they did not even know (Deut. 28:47–49). The other nations would be used as God's disciplinary agents.

While there are those who believe God has totally rejected Israel as a people, many passages confirm repeatedly God will never reject His covenant people forever. They may be in darkness or spiritual blindness for a season, but that blindness will be lifted (Rom. 11:1–5; 11–32). God will then return to

---

[23]"The Lord will bring a nation against you from afar, from the end of the earth, as the eagle swoops down, a nation whose language you shall not understand" (Deuteronomy 28:49). This passage in the context of Deuteronomy 28:48–49 speaks of the discipline God would bring on the nation Israel from the very beginning. Moses is the one speaking of Israel's failures and discipline that would follow in the future. Paul appears to relate to this judgment of God as to what was happening to *this people* or Israel in the New Testament (1 Corinthians 14:21–22).

complete His oath-bound kingdom program with this chosen and elect nation.

Lewis Sperry Chafer, one of the great founding theologians of Dallas Theological Seminary, was a giant among men in many very specific areas. One of these was his wonderful writings, teachings, and meditations on the grace of God and the precious loving salvation offered to all men. Salvation is God's gracious *free gift* in Christ Jesus, and this free gift is offered by His grace to all men. Chafer also understood great prophetic truths based on his recognition of Israel as God's *elect* nation. He makes these comments about anyone, even the nations, who do not have this consistent and covenanted recognition of the elect nation Israel as the basis of their theology.

Inability on the part of believers to comprehend the prophetic Scriptures may be traced almost without exception to some misunderstanding of an essential truth or the failure to realize its practical force and value. In this respect, the majority who are unable to follow the great divine predictions are hindered primarily by their negligence in giving to the nation Israel the place and importance which God in His sovereignty has assigned to that nation. This dereliction is the cause of most of the confusion of mind relative to prophetic themes. The sovereign election of the one nation, Israel - sometimes styled "his elect" (cf. Matt. 24:22, 24, 31) is a revealed fact which the Gentile nations seem unable to realize. It is, however, the attitude of Gentile nations toward God's elect nation which forms the basis on which the destiny of nations is determined (Matt. 25:31–46). The election of Israel is continually emphasized throughout the Scriptures.[24]

It must be carefully observed that Chafer is very clear about the theology which does not understand and recognize, through the Scriptures, the continued election of the nation Israel. Notice the statement, "The election of Israel is continually emphasized throughout the Scriptures." Not one tittle in the New Testament

---

[24]Chafer, 4:310.

changes anything; Israel is still His elect people and nation. "This dereliction is the cause of most of the confusion of mind relative to prophetic themes." Again, Israel is the vital key to God's entire covenanted theocratic program. Only they can fulfill the biblical covenants, for God's covenanted program is promised and covenanted with them. It must also be noted that Chafer knew full well it was "the attitude of Gentile nations toward God's elect nation which forms the basis on which the destiny of nations is determined." This includes all people and most definitely carries over to the Church (Rom. 11:17–21; esp. 21).

Israel as an Elect Nation, Not Individually Elect

What is important to understand in the election of Israel as a nation, or national Israel, is that this is an *elect* or chosen nation from the nations of the world. All God has done with the nation or national Israel is based on their covenanted position as an *elect or chosen nation.* This does not mean every one of the seed of the nation Israel is elect, that is unto salvation. In the Scriptures, His choosing or election does not always mean elect unto salvation, and this can be easily observed with the Pharisees and Sadducees. This does not mean there were not those among them who were not His. Paul was definitely His chosen from the chosen nation. He was also a Pharisee. Yet Israel is chosen and protected by God for His eternal purposes as spelled out in the biblical covenants (Jer. 31:35–37). The Church has no such protection, but Israel does. How can anyone even suggest Israel does not have a separate identifiable program? How can any serious student of the Word of God believe God does not have a separate and very identifiable plan with the nation Israel? There can be no complete and consistent comprehension of God's revealed program unless these biblical covenants are fully understood to be exclusively with Israel as His elect nation.

All through Israel's history is the fact that they are His elect nation, and they will be and always are His elect nation. This violates no truth with the doctrine of election. Israel will always be His elect nation from all the nations of the world. There will be the fulfillment of the new covenant (Jer. 31:31–34) when Israel will be regenerated as a nation (Isa. 66:7–8). Only Israel can fulfill any of the biblical covenants especially the new covenant. This does not mean that the new covenant is not in effect with an outworking to the Church. However, the Church cannot in any way fulfill any of the biblical covenants for the covenants are made with Israel as a nation. Within national Israel as His elect nation will always be His remnant. This remnant is His individually elect from the elect nation.

Israel is Completely Distinct from the Church and Other Nations

As other peoples and nations of the world have been identified and defined throughout history, there is so much more concerning the nation Israel. No one can believe or admit with any manner of credibility, trustworthiness, or reliability that *Israel* has not existed as an identifiable people or nation for thousands of years. No one can admit Israel does not exist today as a living identifiable people. Israel is an ethnically defined people not only by men, but most essentially by God's very Word. Israel has continued to exist through most of world history as an identifiable people, and nation.

This is not by any chance, but by God's sovereign choice and design for His covenanted program. No other nation since the creation of this earth, living in and out of their land, has had this continual, perpetual, and prophesied existence traced from its very patriarchs. The predominantly Gentile Church must realize they are dependent upon the eternal, unilateral, unconditional covenants made with Israel, but the Church is not able in any manner to fulfill any of the national promises made with Israel. The nation Israel, *the Jews,* as His ethnically chosen people are the vanguard and total basis of His entire redemptive kingdom program for mankind, including the Church. To miss this fundamental truth and biblical doctrine is nothing less than willful, and it would be hard to believe this is simply ignorance.

The Distinctness of Israel

1. God fashioned and formed Israel from all the nations of the earth (Jer. 31:3). Israel is the only *elect* nation that exists in God's eternal plan, and has divine protection for perpetual existence (Jer. 31:31–34). They are virtually indestructible by divine decree. Nations come and go but most certainly not Israel, *the Jews.*
2. As salvation is of the Jews and God's entire covenanted program is with the Jews, they must be preserved as His completely identifiable people. If this were not so, it would violate all His promises with them and God would ultimately be a liar incapable of carrying out His decreed program. In addition, there would be no observable consistency and unity in God's program with Israel resulting in confusion. As Lewis Sperry Chafer has clearly taught the confusion is from the dereliction of keeping Israel's election of primary importance.
3. Ultimately, all the biblical covenants are with *Israel, the Jews,* and they can only be fulfilled exclusively by Israel as a nation.
4. In the Messianic kingdom, Israel as a regenerated nation will be the predominant nation (Zech. 8:22–23) of the kingdom in her land with Christ reigning from the Davidic throne in Jerusalem as biblically covenanted. The Church will be the bride of Christ in her glorified state.

5. In the eternal state, in the heavenly Jerusalem, there will be a constant reminder that salvation is of the Jews (Rev. 21:12–14).

It has been difficult to identify the Church through its history as to who are true believers. The Church has had an extremely checkered history even from its beginning (Rev. 2:4; 14–15; 20; 3:1;16).

True Dispensationalism Keeps Israel and the Church Distinct

As it can be easily and biblically understood, Israel is completely distinct with its own plan and purpose. Non-dispensational systems such as covenant theology and progressive dispensationalism do not keep the Church and Israel distinct. They do not believe they are distinct with two separate programs. Progressive dispensationalism, which only has the name dispensationalism, as some sort of an add on, because it somehow sees itself as associated "with dispensationalism's traditional interpretation of the prophecies concerning the nation of Israel."[25] It has really nothing whatsoever to do with dispensationalism. Progressives virtually do not accept the Church and Israel as not only distinct, but *completely* distinct as in Article 13 of the doctrinal position of Dallas Seminary. The Church is defined in Article 13 'as the body and bride of Christ, which began at Pentecost and is completely-distinct from Israel.' At least they have Article 13 as some souvenir or *objet d'art* to remind them where they have come from. It is too bad there are not many standing against the tide of popular opinion and admittedly, it is easier to be user friendly. One does not have to believe the Church and Israel are distinct or even completely distinct, *but a dispensationalist does.*

[25]Robert L. Saucy, *The Case for Progressive Dispensationalism* (Grand Rapids: Zondervan, 1993), 9.

Progressives see only one plan of God unified within God's program of historical salvation. Robert Saucy comments, "The historical plan of God, therefore, is one unified plan. Contrary to traditional dispensationalism, it does not entail separate programs for the Church and Israel that are somehow ultimately unified only in the display of God's glory or in eternity. The present age is not a historical parenthesis unrelated to the history that precedes and follows it; rather, it is an integrated phase in the development of the mediatorial kingdom. It is the beginning of the fulfillment of the eschatological promises. Thus the Church today has its place and function in the same mediatorial messianic kingdom program that Israel was called to serve."[26] It is contrary to traditional dispensationalism because it is not dispensational in any sense. They virtually see no problem whatever with God beginning to fulfill the covenanted promises with the Church in this age. However, this does not mean the Church is divorced in any way from Israel, in fact, it is dependent on Israel, but the Church is not the natural branch(es) and virtually incapable of fulfilling any covenant promises which He made with His elect nation of Israel. Again, progressives have really nothing to do with dispensationalism in any sense. Just to say one holds to some dispensations, or some prophecies being fulfilled, partially now or more completely in the future, by Israel is hardly dispensationalism.

Is it not amazing that some great institutions which were literally bastions for dispensationalism, with great dispensationalists as founders, have caved in to such shallow and cavalier exegetical teachings? If what we are seeing today is even a hint at a sneak preview of the covenanted Messianic kingdom, is anyone impressed? Who wants it? Again, one does not have to believe the Church and Israel are distinct or completely distinct, *but a dispensationalist does.* Why call yourself any kind of dispensationalist when you know you are not.

[26]Ibid., 28.

The Heart of Dispensationalism

Israel is the natural branch, the natural heir. The Church and all others are adopted as heirs, but are not the natural heirs. There are six natural heirs and direct recipients to the biblical covenants; these are Abraham, Isaac, Jacob, Israel, David, and Christ Himself as the Heir apparent to the Messianic Davidic throne. The Jews are those "who are Israelites, to whom belongs the adoption as sons, and the glory and the covenants and the giving of the Law and the Temple service and the promises, whose are the fathers, and from whom is the Christ according to the flesh, who is over all, God blessed forever. Amen" (Romans 9:4–5).

> *"Why the Jew?* Because God made a covenant
> with their ancestor, and gave certain promises
> through that covenant *pertaining to that
> ancestor's seed.* If any one says (as, alas, many
> do), perverting the language of Paul applicable to
> another feature, that having the blood of
> Abraham in their veins amounted to nothing
> (which is true, when accompanied by unbelief, as
> Jesus taught), he simply fails to recognize the
> plain fact *that Jews* were called, and *not*
> Gentiles; a covenant was made *with Jews and
> not* with Gentiles; the promises were given *to
> Jews,* and *not* to Gentiles; that salvation *is of the
> Jews,* and *not* of the Gentiles; that this salvation
> is yet to be openly manifested *through the Jews,*
> and *not* through the Gentiles; and that Gentiles
> receive and inherit *with* the natural descendants
> of Abraham only as they are incorporated."[27]

[27]Peters, 1:211–212.

There are no other people or nation that sustains the continued relation to God that the Jewish nation Israel does. These people are both elect as a nation and covenanted as a nation. The Church which began at Pentecost are the true believers united by Spirit baptism to the risen and ascended Messiah. All this and much more are for His purpose, and His kingdom, and His glory. Everything will be done for His glory. "But as for you, speak the things which are fitting for sound doctrine" (Titus 2:1).

Block Diagrams of Selected Verses

Mat. 26:27-28

"And when He had taken a cup and given thanks, He gave *it* to them, saying, "Drink from it, all of you; [28] for this is My blood of the covenant, which is poured out for many for forgiveness of sins" (Mat. 26:27-28).

Mat. 26:27 καὶ λαβὼν →**ποτήριον** καὶ εὐχαριστήσας ἔδωκεν αὐτοῖς λέγων·

πίετε ἐξ αὐτοῦ **πάντες,**[198] *(they were all to drink even Judas, and they understood this was 'covenant blood' i.e. His blood of the new covenant)*

[28] τοῦτο γάρ ἐστιν →**τὸ αἷμά μου** *(My blood of the covenant)*

τῆς **διαθήκης** [199] *(the covenant's blood)*

τὸ περὶ **πολλῶν** ἐκχυννόμενον [200] *(the emphasis is on 'many')*

---

[198] ποτήριον=cup, πάντες =all; They were all to drink even Judas, and they understood this was 'covenant blood' i.e. His blood of the covenant.
[199] τὸ αἷμά μου τῆς διαθήκης=my blood of the covenant; This is His blood of the covenant. They were all to drink His blood of the new covenant.
[200] πολλῶν=many; The emphasis is on 'many' more than the whole.

εἰς ἄφεσιν ἁμαρτιῶν [201] *(The*
primary purpose of His blood of the covenant is forgiveness of sins
or eternal redemption. The disciples were to understand His blood
was the blood of the covenant for forgiveness of sins or eternal
redemption for them and for 'many' more than the whole. Christ
Jesus taught unlimited atonement, the greatness of His blood for
forgiveness of sin was for EVERYONE!)

Mark 14:23-24

"And when He had taken a cup, *and* given thanks,
He gave *it* to them; and they all drank from it. [24]
And He said to them, "This is My blood of the
covenant, which is poured out for many" (Mark
14:23-24).

Mark 14:23 καὶ λαβὼν →ποτήριον εὐχαριστήσας
ἔδωκεν αὐτοῖς, καὶ ἔπιον ἐξ αὐτοῦ **πάντες**[202] *(All the*
disciples drank from the cup)

Mk. 14:24 καὶ εἶπεν αὐτοῖς·
τοῦτό ἐστιν→ **τὸ αἷμά μου**

---

[201] εἰς ἄφεσιν ἁμαρτιῶν=for forgiveness of sins; The primary purpose of His
blood of the covenant was/is forgiveness of sins or eternal blood redemption;
the disciples were to understand this/His blood was His blood of the
covenant for forgiveness of sins or eternal redemption for them and for
'many' more than the whole. Christ Jesus taught unlimited atonement, His
blood for forgiveness of sin was for ALL even Judas!
[202] πάντες =all; All the disciples drank from the cup.

τῆς διαθήκης [203] *(The disciples were told by Christ Himself they were drinking His blood of the covenant)*

τὸ ἐκχυννόμενον ὑπὲρ πολλῶν [204] *(His blood of the covenant was being poured out for 'many' i.e. more than the whole i.e. for everyone, unlimited atonement)*

Luke 22:20

"And in the same way *He took* the cup after they had eaten, saying, "This cup which is poured out for you is the new covenant in My blood" (Luke 22:20).

[Lu22:20] καὶ τὸ ποτήριον ὡσαύτως μετὰ τὸ δειπνῆσαι, λέγων·

(Note the cup itself represents=the new covenant)
τοῦτο τὸ ποτήριον = ἡ καινὴ διαθήκη [205]

ἐν τῷ αἵματί μου [206] *(by means of My blood)*

[203]τὸ αἷμά μου τῆς διαθήκης=my blood of the covenant; The disciples were told by Christ Himself they were drinking His blood of the covenant.

[204]ὑπὲρ πολλῶν=for many; His blood of the covenant was being poured out for 'many' more than the whole i.e. for everyone, unlimited atonement. This is not just blood, it is covenant blood by definition. The modifier 'of the covenant' cannot be separated from the blood.

[205]τοῦτο τὸ ποτήριον = ἡ καινὴ διαθήκη, this cup=the new covenant; Note the cup itself represents the new covenant.

[206]ἐν τῷ αἵματί μου=in or by my blood; By means of His blood this covenant would be fully in effect i.e. fully operational especially for eternal redemption.

(By means of His blood, this covenant went into full operation providing eternal redemption not only for His disciples (for you) but for 'the many')[207]

for you)

τὸ ὑπὲρ ὑμῶν ἐκχυννόμενον[208] (*note:*

"But behold, the hand of the one betraying Me is with Me on the table" (Luke 22:21).[209]

1 Cor. 11:23

"For I received from the Lord that which I also delivered to you, that the Lord Jesus in the night in which He was betrayed took bread" (1 Cor. 11:23).

23 Ἐγὼ γὰρ παρέλαβον ἀπὸ τοῦ κυρίου *(revelation received from the Lord)*
ὃ καὶ παρέδωκα →ὑμῖν[210] *(you here refers to the Corinthians)*

---

[207] *"And when He had taken a cup and given thanks, He gave it to them, saying, "Drink from it, all of you;* [28] *for this is My blood of the covenant, which is poured out for many for forgiveness of sins"* (Mat. 26:27-28).
[208]ὑπὲρ ὑμῶν=for you; His blood of the new covenant would be fully applicable for His disciples and the forgiveness of sins i.e. eternal redemption promised in the new covenant.
[209] Judas was there at this last supper. Jesus taught His blood of the new covenant was even poured out for Judas. Christ Jesus taught unlimited atonement. This was the greatness of His blood for the forgiveness of sins for everyone, even for Judas.

[210]ὑμῖν=to you; To 'you' here referring to the Corinthians. Paul received this directly from the Lord. Paul was now giving this directly to the church at Corinth.

→ὅτι ὁ κύριος Ἰησοῦς ἐν τῇ νυκτὶ
ᾗ παρεδίδετο ἔλαβεν →ἄρτον

1 Cor. 11:24

"And when He had given thanks, He broke it, and said, "This is My body, which is for you; do this in remembrance of Me" (1 Cor. 11:24).

24 καὶ εὐχαριστήσας ἔκλασεν (→ἄρτον)

(note the position of the ἐστιν w/r/t the ἐστιν with the blood 'in by my blood' vs. 25)
καὶ εἶπεν· → τοῦτό μού **ἐστιν**[211] τὸ σῶμα τὸ ὑπὲρ **ὑμῶν**· *(you=disciples)*

(note the identical expression/s with the blood 'do this')
τοῦτο← **ποιεῖτε**[212] εἰς τὴν ἐμὴν ἀνάμνησιν

1 Cor. 11:25

"In the same way *He took* the cup also, after supper, saying, "This cup is the new covenant in My blood; do this, as often as you drink *it*, in remembrance of Me" (1Cor. 11:25).

25 ὡσαύτως
(ἔλαβεν) καὶ τὸ ποτήριον μετὰ τὸ δειπνῆσαι

---

[211]ἐστιν=is; Note the position of this ἐστιν with respect to the ἐστιν with the blood 'in/by my blood' vs. 25)
[212]ποιεῖτε=be doing this or do this; Note the identical expression/s with the blood vs. 25 'do this'

(appositional construction, the cup=the new covenant)
(note this ἐστὶν)
λέγων· **τοῦτο   τὸ ποτήριον =ἡ καινὴ διαθήκη**[213]
ἐστὶν[214]
(His blood became efficacious at His death.   This is the blood
atonement, blood redemption of the new covenant.   The
church celebrates His body and His blood of the new
covenant)
→ **ἐν**[215] τῷ ἐμῷ αἵματι[216]

(Note the identical expression/s with the bread 'do this')
τοῦτο← **ποιεῖτε**[217]
ὁσάκις ἐὰν πίνητε, εἰς τὴν ἐμὴν
ἀνάμνησιν

1 Cor. 11:26

"For as often as you eat this bread and drink the
cup, you proclaim the Lord's death until He comes"
(1 Cor. 11:26).

26 ὁσάκις γὰρ   *(**note the chiastic construction for emphasis**)*

---

[213] τοῦτο τὸ ποτήριον =ἡ καινὴ διαθήκη, this cup=the new covenant. Note
the appositional construction, the cup represents=new covenant. At Passover
each cup represents something. The four cups might be identified as the
cups of sanctification, of judgment or deliverance, of redemption, and the
cup of praise or restoration.
[214]ἐστὶν=is; Note this ἐστὶν and its position.
[215] ἐν=in; in or by means of my blood
[216] His blood became efficacious at His death. This is the blood atonement,
blood redemption of the new covenant. The church celebrates His body (the
bread) and (the cup) His blood of the new covenant.
[217]Note the identical expression/s with the bread vs. 24 'do this'

ἐὰν ἐσθίητε➔ τὸν ἄρτον τοῦτον²¹⁸ *(this bread=His body)*
καὶ
(the cup=the new covenant) τὸ ποτήριον²¹⁹ ←πίνητε,

If the church does the above appropriately, then the death of the Lord is continually proclaimed by the church until He comes)

τὸν θάνατον²²⁰←καταγγέλλετε ἄχρι οὗ ἔλθῃ.
τοῦ κυρίου

2 Corinthians 3:6

"Who also made us adequate *as* servants of a new covenant, not of the letter, but of the Spirit; for the letter kills, but the Spirit gives life" (2 Cor. 3:6).

(They ministered the new covenant)

---

²¹⁸ τὸν ἄρτον τοῦτον= this bread; 'This bread' represents His body. Note the chiastic construction for emphasis.

²¹⁹ τὸ ποτήριον=the cup; The cup represents the new covenant. The bread=His body; the cup=the new covenant. The blood is His blood of the new covenant. By eating the bread, one partakes of His body representing substitutionary atonement. By drinking the cup, one is partaking of forgiveness of sins of the new covenant.

²²⁰ τὸν θάνατον=the death; When eating the bread and then drinking the cup of the new covenant, then the death of the Lord is continually heralded or proclaimed by the church until He comes.

Ὃς καὶ ἱκάνωσεν **ἡμᾶς = διακόνους²²¹**
(new covenant) **καινῆς διαθήκης**
οὐ
(of letter) **γράμματος²²²**
(Strongest contrast) ἀλλὰ
(of the Spirit) **πνεύματος·**

<u>**τὸ γὰρ γράμμα**</u> ἀποκτέννει²²³ *(for the letter/law kills)*

---

²²¹ ἡμᾶς = διακόνους, us=ministers; They were ministers of a/the new covenant. The new covenant promised complete and total forgiveness of sin/s.

²²² They were not 'new covenant type' ministers for the three 'nouns' in sequence would make no sense i.e. 'new covenant type ministers' not of the 'letter type ministers or law type ministers' but 'Spirit type ministers?' Best to keep these as nouns, for the following explains the 'nouns.' The letter kills=τὸ γὰρ γράμμα ἀποκτέννει; this refers to the law itself. The Spirit makes alive or gives life=τὸ δὲ πνεῦμα ζῳοποιεῖ. God the Holy Spirit gives life. They were in the ministry of God the Holy Spirit Who gives life. This life begins with the complete forgiveness of sins promised in the new covenant: "For I will forgive their iniquity, and their sin I will remember no more" (Jer. 31:34); "And their sins and their lawless deeds I will remember no more." ¹⁸ Now where there is forgiveness of these things, there is no longer *any* offering for sin" (Heb 10:17-18). They were not ministering the law which continually kills, but the Spirit Who gives eternal life.

²²³ τὸ γὰρ γράμμα ἀποκτέννει=for the letter kills; The law even every letter of the law kills i.e. a ministry of death. Paul was not ministering death or the law in any sense. One cannot go back to the law which is death.

τὸ δὲ πνεῦμα   ζῳοποιεῖ.[224]

(but, to the contrary the Spirit gives life)

Hebrews 7:12

"For when the priesthood is changed, of necessity there takes place a change of law also" (Hebrews 7:12)

μετατιθεμένης[225] γὰρ τῆς ἱερωσύνης

[224] τὸ δὲ πνεῦμα ζῳοποιεῖ=The Spirit (God the Holy Spirit) gives life; Note the δὲ for post positive emphasis. They were ministers of life, eternal life promised in the new covenant.

[225] **μετατίθημι** remove, take back; take up (of Enoch); change (of priesthood); literally, as causing a change from one place to another, transfer, etc. There are various meanings but causing a change from one thing, place, etc. to another seems to hold well. Acts 7:16 "And *from there* they were **removed** to Shechem, and laid in the tomb which Abraham had purchased for a sum of money from the sons of Hamor in Shechem." Galatians 1:6 "I am amazed that you are so quickly **deserting** Him who called you by the grace of Christ, for a different gospel." Hebrews 7:12 "For when the priesthood is **changed**, of necessity there takes place a change of law also." Hebrews 11:5 "By faith Enoch was **taken up** so that he should not see death; and he was not found because God took him up; for he obtained the witness that before his being taken up he was pleasing to God." Jude 1:4 "For certain persons have crept in unnoticed, those who were long beforehand marked out for this condemnation, ungodly persons **who turn the grace** of our God into licentiousness and deny our only Master and Lord, Jesus Christ." The best meaning seems to be the change from one priesthood to another as well as from one law or the Law to another which was the new covenant. As the Melchizedek priesthood replaced the Mosaic priesthood, the new covenant replaced 'the Mosaic law.' The writer of Hebrews was making this exact point so to go back to the law was not an option for the believer.

226

ἐξ ἀνάγκης *(change of priesthood __necessitates__
a change of law)*

καὶ

νόμου μετάθεσις *(a change of law)*

γίνεται.

Hebrews 8:6

"But now He has obtained a more excellent ministry,
by as much as He is also the mediator of a better
covenant, which has been enacted on better promises"
(Heb. 8:6).

226 μετατιθεμένης γὰρ τῆς ἱερωσύνης=when the priesthood is changed;
There was a necessity of the law being changed when the priesthood was
changed. This was not futuristic. The changes were in two areas i.e. the
priesthood and the law. This was a very present situation not futuristic. The
new covenant replaced the law. The new covenant went into effect
immediately at the death of Christ the Testator of His own will.

νυν[ὶ] δὲ *(but now-strong transition)*

διαφορωτέρας

τέτυχεν[227] → λειτουργίας, *(He has already obtained)*

ὅσῳ καὶ
κρείττονός
ἐστιν[228] διαθήκης *(He is now mediator of a better covenant)*
μεσίτης,

ἥτις
νενομοθέτηται[229]
ἐπὶ κρείττοσιν ἐπαγγελίαις[230]

[227] τέτυχεν=obtained, received, attained; perfect indicative active 3rd person singular from τυγχάνω. This is not futuristic. He has attained this ministry already (something in the past but continues into the future).

[228] ἐστιν=He is; He is now mediator and has obtained this ministry. He is doing this now as His ministry in the better tabernacle, the true tabernacle, the heavenly tabernacle.

[229] νενομοθέτηται=enacted or established; indicative perfect passive 3rd person singular from νομοθετέω. On the basis of it, i.e. the Levitical priesthood, the people were given the law He 7.11); be based on (He 8.6)(UBS).

[230] The better promises are eternal. This includes eternal life. The law only offered death. He is ministering the better promises as the Mediator of a better covenant in the true/heavenly tabernacle.

Hebrews 9:16-17

"For where a covenant is, there must of necessity be the death of the one who made it. [17]For a covenant is valid *only* when men are dead, for it is never in force while the one who made it lives" (Heb. 9:16-17).

(ἐστιν) Ὅπου γὰρ **διαθήκη**[231] *(Where a covenant or will is)*

θάνατον ἀνάγκη *(there is of necessity the death)*
φέρεσθαι τοῦ διαθεμένου *(to be carried out of the one who made it)*

[17] (ἐστιν) διαθήκη γὰρ ἐπὶ νεκροῖς βεβαία *(will effective when men die)*

ἐπεὶ μήποτε *(never)*

---

[231]διαθήκη=covenant; or simply covenant; will, testament (Gal. 3.15); both covenant and will (Heb. 9.16, 17; Gal. 3.17)(UBS).   The word can be easily interchanged between covenant and will.   Christ has assumed the new covenant as His own will. His death puts this will into effect as any will is normally put into effect or operation. He is also the Testator of His own will. As Testator He is the Mediator and mediating His own will or covenant.

ἰσχύει²³² *(is in force, operational, valid)*

ὅτε *(when)*

ζῇ   ὁ διαθέμενος²³³ *(the one who made the will is living)*

Hebrews 10:29

"How much severer punishment do you think he
will deserve who has trampled under foot the Son of
God, and has regarded as unclean the blood of the
covenant by which he was sanctified, and has
insulted the Spirit of grace?" (Hebrews 10:29).

πόσῳ
δοκεῖτε
    χείρονος
ἀξιωθήσεται τιμωρίας

---

²³² ἰσχύει=be able, can, have resources as a legal technical term, of law and
institutions *have meaning, be valid, be in force* (HE 9.17)(UBS, FRI); *to be
strong, mighty, powerful, prevail (LS)*.
²³³ ζῇ=is alive or living; ὁ διαθέμενος= make (of covenants or wills), literally
the one who makes a will (Heb. 9.16f).

ὁ →τὸν υἱὸν
τοῦ θεοῦ   ←καταπατήσας

καὶ

→τὸ αἷμα *(the blood)*[234]   *(has regarded)*
τῆς διαθήκης[235] κοινὸν[236] ←ἡγησάμενος
(of the covenant)   *(unclean)*

ἐν ᾧ *(by which)*
ἡγιάσθη[237] *(he was sanctified)*

→καὶ τὸ πνεῦμα
τῆς χάριτος   ←ἐνυβρίσας;

---

[234] The writer is emphasizing not just His blood but 'the blood of the covenant.' The modifier is very important to the exegesis. As the old covenant or Mosaic covenant 'blood' (the blood of animals or what was required by Law) sanctified, the reference here is to 'new covenant' blood.
[235] The covenant is a reference to the new covenant. It is new covenant blood which is being emphasized.
[236] κοινός, ή, όν common, in common; common, profane; defiled, unclean, *defiled, (ceremonially) unacceptable...*
[237] The book of Hebrews speaks much of sanctification. This might even be called a book of sanctification. For a Jew to go back to the old covenant types and sacrifices (sacrificial system primarily of animal blood) was to treat as

Hebrews 12:24

"And to Jesus, **the mediator of a new covenant**,
and to the sprinkled blood, which speaks better than
the blood of Abel" (Hebrews 12:24).

(emphasis is on new covenant)
καὶ **διαθήκης νέας**[238] *(of new covenant)*
(mediator) **μεσίτῃ** Ἰησοῦ[239]

(to the sprinkled blood)
καὶ αἵματι ῥαντισμοῦ[240]

[238] νέος, α, ον new, fresh; young; νεώτερος young, younger, youngest; new
of time, as existing only recently *new, fresh*, synonymous with καινός ... of
what is superior in nature to the former *new*; (UBS)(FRI)
[239] "**But you have come to** Mount Zion and to the city of the living God, the
heavenly Jerusalem, and to myriads of angels, [23] **to the general assembly**
and church of the first-born who are enrolled in heaven, and to God, the
Judge of all, **and to the spirits of righteous men made perfect**, [24] *and to
Jesus, the mediator of a new covenant*, and **to the sprinkled blood**, which
speaks better than *the blood* of Abel" (Heb 12:22-24). They have come to
the new covenant's Mediator. The emphasis is on the 'new covenant.' The
stress is that they have to this place where the new covenant is being
mediated. This is not a futuristic mediator but a now 'mediator Who is
mediating the new covenant.'
[240] The new covenant is unconditional, eternal, and unilateral. This covenant
does not depend on anybody doing anything. What put this unconditional
covenant into full operation was/is the literal blood of Christ. These Hebrew
believers are reminded to what they have come. They have come to the new

κρεῖττον λαλοῦντι παρὰ τὸν Ἄβελ²⁴¹

Hebrews 13:20

"Now the God of peace, who brought up from the
dead the great Shepherd of the sheep through the
blood of the **eternal covenant**, *even* Jesus our
Lord" (Hebrews 13:20).

Ὁ δὲ θεὸς τῆς εἰρήνης,
ὁ ἀναγαγὼν
    ἐκ νεκρῶν →τὸν ποιμένα
    τῶν προβάτων τὸν μέγαν

ἐν²⁴² αἵματι²⁴³ *(with blood)*

covenant's Mediator and the sprinkling of blood, literally His blood of the
new covenant. The greatness of His blood speaks of eternal redemption. He
is Mediator and Testator of His own covenant or will.
²⁴¹The blood of Abel speaks of judgment. Christ's blood of the new
covenant speaks not only of eternal redemption but of an eternal inheritance
to be with and in Him. There are also future promises that will be fulfilled in
His millennial reign.
²⁴² ἐν prep. with dat. in, on, at; near, by, before; among, within; by, with; into
(= εἰς); to, for (rarely); ἐν τῷ with inf. during, while, as; ἐν ὀνόματι ὅτι
because (Mk 9.41)(UBS).
²⁴³ With or by His blood seems better.

διαθήκης αἰωνίου²⁴⁴ *(of an/the eternal*

*covenant)*²⁴⁵

→τὸν κύριον ἡμῶν Ἰησοῦν,

---

²⁴⁴ **With the blood of the eternal covenant** (ἐν αἵματι διαθηκης αἰωνιου [*en haimati diathēkēs aiōniou*]). This language is from Zech. 9:11. The language reminds us of Christ's own words in Mark 14:24 (=Matt. 26:28=Luke 22:20=I Cor. 11:25) about "my blood of the covenant." Robertson, A. (1933). *Word Pictures in the New Testament* (Heb 13:20). Nashville, TN: Broadman Press. "For this is My blood of the covenant, which is poured out for many for forgiveness of sins" (Mat 26:28). "And He said to them, "This is My blood of the covenant, which is poured out for many" (Mark 14:24) "And in the same way *He took* the cup after they had eaten, saying, "This cup which is poured out for you is the new covenant in My blood" (Luke 22:20).

²⁴⁵ The only eternal covenant associated with Christ and His precious blood is the eternal new covenant. This is both emphasis and warnings to the Jewish believers not to go back to the non operative Mosaic covenant. What has replaced this bilateral, temporal, conditional covenant is the eternal new covenant. This covenant was fully functional at the death of Christ and literally replaced the Law. The Jewish believers were continually reminded of the greatness of His blood of the eternal new covenant.

Made in the USA
San Bernardino, CA
27 October 2016